ArtScroll Series®

Rabbi Nosson Scherman / Rabbi Meir Zlotowitz

General Editors

by
Yair Weinstock

translated by
Libby Lazewnik

Published by
Mesorah Publications, ltd

for the Soul 3

A famous novelist retells classic stories with passion and spirit

FIRST EDITION
First Impression … November 2001

Published and Distributed by
MESORAH PUBLICATIONS, LTD.
4401 Second Avenue / Brooklyn, N.Y 11232

Distributed in Europe by
LEHMANNS
Unit E, Viking Industrial Park
Rolling Mill Road
Jarow, Tyne & Wear, NE32 3DP
England

Distributed in Australia and New Zealand by
GOLDS WORLDS OF JUDAICA
3-13 William Street
Balaclava, Melbourne 3183
Victoria, Australia

Distributed in Israel by
SIFRIATI / A. GITLER — BOOKS
6 Hayarkon Street
Bnei Brak 51127

Distributed in South Africa by
KOLLEL BOOKSHOP
Shop 8A Norwood Hypermarket
Norwood 2196, Johannesburg, South Africa

ARTSCROLL SERIES®
TALES FOR THE SOUL 3
© *Copyright 2001, by* MESORAH PUBLICATIONS, Ltd.
4401 Second Avenue / Brooklyn, N.Y. 11232 / (718) 921-9000

Typography by CompuScribe at ArtScroll Studios, Ltd.
Printed in the United States of America by Noble Book Press Corp.
Bound by Sefercraft, Quality Bookbinders, Ltd., Brooklyn N.Y. 11232

Table of Contents

Tales for the Soul 3

THE MASTER MATCHMAKER

THE FIRST LEG OF THE VILNA GAON'S PLANNED MOVE TO *Eretz Yisrael* took him to Amsterdam. From there, he planned to sail by boat to the Holy Land. But his plan came to naught in the end. When one of his sons later asked the reason why the Gaon had not continued his journey, this was the answer he received: "I do not have Heaven's permission" (from the *Gra's* sons' Introduction to the *Shulchan Aruch, Orach Chaim*).

The long trip had left the Vilna Gaon feeling extremely weak. Coming upon a small village near Amsterdam, he decided to rest there a while. A rich local Jew invited him to stay as a guest in his home. The man did not recognize the Gaon, as the latter chose to travel incognito. But his holy countenance was a better testimonial than a hundred character witnesses. The Vilna Gaon accepted the man's invitation for the next three weeks.

The wealthy Jew's spacious and elegant home served as a meeting place for the local Jews. Morning, noon, and night, men gathered there to *daven* in one of the rooms. This *"shul"* contained a large library, which drew *talmidei chachamim* like a magnet in an era when no single individual owned an entire set of *Shas*, only isolated tractates. The *shul* library in the rich man's home boasted a complete *Shas*, along with numerous *sefarim* bearing the commentaries of the *Rishonim*. Here, the *Gra* found everything he needed. His meals were brought to him at specific times, and he was able to immerse himself in Torah study day and night in the *shul*. His host provided him with the best room in the house, opposite his own bedroom — but his guest spent little time there.

When he had regained a little of his strength, the Gaon desired to continue his journey. He announced his intention of paying his host for all his hospitality, but the man refused to take a penny from him. *"Baruch Hashem,* Who gives me the merit of welcoming guests to my home. Shall I take a reward for this? Never!"

"Then I will say farewell," conceded the Gaon.

"You have not told me your name," his host said, "but I understand that Your Honor is a great leader in Israel. I have seen the way you do not desist from learning Torah day and night. During the three weeks you have been under my roof, you have learned all of *Shas* with the *Rishonim*, all four sections of the *Shulchan Aruch*, and other works.

"In that case," he continued, "please tell me: Have you noticed anything that is out of order in my home? Anything improper, either halachically or ethically? Do not conceal a thing from me, and do not be afraid to rebuke me. I love rebuke and I wish to improve my ways in this world so that I do not stand ashamed in the World to Come."

"Everything I've seen about your lifestyle is as it should be," the Gaon replied. "I only noticed one thing that is contrary to the *Gemara*."

Aghast, his host begged him to reveal what that thing was.

"The *Gemara* (*Yevamos* 62) states that a man must love his wife as his own body and honor her more than his own body. Of such a man, it says, 'And you shall know that peace will reign in your tent.' But here, in your home, I have seen something new. I have seen a man who loves his wife more than his own body. Every morning, you bring your wife a bowl, water, and a towel so that she can wash *netilas yadayim*, and then you bring her a cup of coffee to drink. But you yourself do not drink coffee (before *davening*). That is what I mean by 'more than his body.'"

Hearing this "rebuke," the host smiled. "I'd like to tell Your Honor the reason for this strange behavior."

Here is the tale he told.

I grew up far from Holland (the man began), in a certain city in Poland. My father was a well-known *talmid chacham* who pored over the Torah night and day and who knew the Talmud to its depths. Our home was a poor one. We ate meager bread and drank water — but the Divine Presence rested in our home, bringing light and contentment to our house and our hearts.

I was only 9 years old when I became engaged to be married. A certain wealthy man who lived near our town — a good and pious man — desired me as husband for his daughter, who was my own age.

From the time of my engagement, my *kallah's* father cared for me as if I were his own son. I was wearing threadbare clothing and shoes that were falling off my feet. Seeing this, my future father-in-law told my father, "I do not want my son-in-law to dress like a beggar." He bought me nice clothes and fine leather shoes. To make sure I would grow to become a *talmid chacham*, he hired a fine tutor at his own expense, and the tutor taught me Torah for six years, until I was a youth of 15.

The wedding date had already been set when the wheel of fortune turned, leaving my future father-in-law destitute.

My father, however, knew nothing of this. He traveled to my future father-in-law's house to finalize the dowry arrangements — and found only a degraded beggar, living in a hovel. In the yard, a girl dressed in rags was tossing feed to some ducks. My father had a hard time recognizing the girl his son was about to wed!

Ashen-faced, my father entered the hovel and collapsed onto a bench. The shock had robbed him of his strength, and he felt on the point of fainting.

The unfortunate beggar gazed mutely at my father, then burst into bitter tears. "You have come to receive the dowry for the wedding — but I do not have anything but the shirt on my back!"

My father felt deeply sorry for the man, but could find no words. At last, he asked, "What shall I do?"

The poor man drew a deep breath. "I release you from the bond of marriage. If you break the *shidduch*, I will bear no grudge against you."

The girl was summoned and asked her mind. She assured them that she completely forgave her *chasan* and his family for breaking off the match, and bore not even a shred of ill-will against them. My father took out the *tenaim* contract and tore it up. The *shidduch* was off.

I was grief-stricken. In one fell swoop, I had fallen from the pinnacle of happiness to the depths of despair. At first, I could hardly believe my father. I thought he was joking. But when he showed me the ripped *tenaim*, my eyes filled with tears. Only then did I grasp the enormity of my bad luck.

My father scolded me for walking around brokenhearted. That same week, he sent word to a certain prosperous Jew in our town, letting him know that his son's *shidduch* had been broken. If the man wished to arrange a match between his own daughter and me, they could talk.

The rich man agreed with alacrity. I had a good reputation. I was a learned boy, tall and handsome. The match was quickly agreed to. At my engagement party I gave a *derashah* that astounded everyone who heard it. For everyone else, the memory of my first *kallah* was erased as though it had never existed. But my own heart was bitter. I could not forget that unfortunate girl for a minute. To tell the truth, I was prepared to give up all the good things I was being offered, in order to avoid embarrassing a fine Jewish girl. But it was no use. No one asked my opinion.

Four months passed between my engagement and the wedding. In my emotional state as my wedding date approached, the memory of my first *kallah* and her ill fortune began to fade. I married the rich man's daughter in a splendid wedding, amid great joy. Dancing and celebrating, I completely forgot the "first round." I was the happiest of men.

But not for long...

The week-long *Sheva Berachos* period came and went. On the following morning, I woke up aching all over. I could not get out of bed. Thinking that I had caught a cold, I remained in bed all that day, and the next. But not only did I not get any better, I began to feel even worse.

Seeing this, my father-in-law spared no expense to bring the best doctors to my bedside. They drew blood, prescribed medicines, mixed potions, and fed me concoctions. Nothing helped. Each day, the doctors examined me anew, but they could not diagnose my illness. My entire body was covered with ugly sores; from head to toe I had no relief. And as if this were not enough, I was suddenly afflicted with painful boils all over. My family found my treatment — and their disgust at the sores and the boils — too much for them to handle. They had me transferred to the city's *hekdesh*, which served as both hospital and guest house for local paupers and itinerant beggars.

In the *hekdesh* my condition worsened, until I nearly reached the state of Nachum Ish Gamzu. My arms and legs did not actually wither away, but they were filled with painful and unsightly sores and boils that were difficult to bear. My eyes were puffy and swollen and a foul odor was on my breath. My wife's family began to whisper. At last, my father-in-law came to me and demanded that I give his daughter a divorce, and I agreed.

I had been punished, measure for measure. Like Nachum Ish Gamzu, I blamed myself for my condition (*Taanis* 21). I understood that Heaven was punishing me with this illness.

I remained in the *hekdesh* for several months before there began to be some improvement in my condition. I could now get out of bed for short intervals, and the sores and boils on my arms and legs grew smaller. My appearance became a little less revolting.

I did not waste my time. Lying in my bed, I busied myself learning *Gemara* and *Shulchan Aruch*. One of the other guests at the *hekdesh* — a bright and witty young fellow — noticed what I was doing. He said, "Why do you lie around in bed? You'll starve!"

"I'm a broken vessel. I won't succeed at anything," I answered.

With a sharp glance, the other man said, "I have a good idea for you. I will rent a good wagon and line the seat with comfortable cushions. Let us travel together from village to village and from town to town. We'll go door to door, and I'll introduce you as a learned man whose fate has turned bitter — and I'll ask for charity for you. Your appearance will arouse compassion wherever we go. I'm sure that the Jews — merciful men and the children of merciful men — will take pity on you and give you twice as much as they'd give any other poor man."

I agreed to this plan.

The young man put his scheme into prompt action. He rented a wagon and a strong horse, deposited me on the cushioned seat, and off we went. We wandered among the towns and villages, and all came to pass just as he had predicted. In every place, he brought me to the local *shul* and described the extent of my learning, my bad luck, and difficult illness. Jews all over, compassionate people and lovers of Torah and its scholars, saw that I was no common pauper, but one who knew how to learn a *sugya*. At once, they came to me with questions on the *Gemara*, bringing me difficult sections of a *Tosafos* or a *Maharsha* from various tractates. I would explain and elucidate to the best of my ability.

I became a valuable commodity — a kind of pearl covered in dust, but a pearl nevertheless.

"Do not look at the bottle, but at what lies within," people would tell me. At first, I cringed. After a while, though, I grew accustomed to my new identity. I was a cripple, one of life's deformed.

I was not alone. Many sick people went around collecting charity, but it seemed to me that none of them was as ill and deformed as I was. One day, we came to a Polish town. In the yard of the town's *hekdesh* we saw a wagon. At the reins sat a man whose pinched and lined face testified to the difficult life he had led. Inside the wagon, in a nest of pillows and faded blankets, lay his daughter. She was sallow-faced, and appeared even more ill than I. We began to talk, the father and I, and eventually reached an agreement: From now on, we would travel together to collect money as partners.

I told my companion that I needed neither him nor his horse and wagon any longer. We agreed to part ways. He had long been growing tired of traveling and had already amassed a decent sum of money from our efforts.

For several weeks my new companion and I traveled together. We became friendly. One day, he suggested that I marry his daughter. I revealed to him that I had been divorced, but that did not deter him. We signed *tenaim*, ate some *lekach* that a kind homeowner had given us, and shared a *l'chaim* from a small bottle of whiskey. A wedding was planned.

About a month later, we stopped at a town. In the courtyard of the *hekdesh* a wedding canopy was erected. In the presence of ten local Jews, the man's daughter and I were married — in a paupers' ceremony, with a bride and groom who certainly suited one another — both sickly and weak, dressed in rags and tatters. A handful of Jews participated in our wedding feast, which consisted of seeded bread and some onions that the guests had brought along in their pockets.

After the *chuppah*, my *kallah* and I were alone together for the first time. The *yichud* room was a cramped chamber at one side of the *hekdesh*, whose tenant had agreed to let us have it for a short time. Despite the poverty-stricken circumstances, I was filled with great happiness.

Not so my bride. No sooner had the door been closed behind us, than she sat down and gave way to a storm of weeping.

"Why are you crying?" I asked in astonishment. "There is a time for rejoicing and a time for weeping, as the wise one said. And this is the time to rejoice!"

"How can I not cry?" she countered. "I remember how I once used to be. My father was a rich man, and when I was a girl of 9, I became engaged to a boy my own age, an outstanding scholar of fine lineage who learned diligently day and night. My father clothed him and took care of his every need. Then, just before our wedding day, my father lost his fortune, and the *tenaim* were torn up. My *chasan* left me, and I remained alone and humiliated. And then, as if that were not enough, I fell so ill that I could not get out of bed. For several years I have wandered with my father, collecting charity handouts to prevent us from starving.

"How can I not cry, when today I have married a sickly *chasan*, as unfortunate as I am, poor and destitute. I do not know who he is or what his family lineage might be."

I stared at her in amazement. The story was a very familiar one to me.

"Is your father called So-and-so?" I asked.

"Yes."

"Did you live in such-and-such a village, and was your house behind the large haystack?"

"Yes. But how do you know that?"

"Look at me!" I shouted emotionally. "I am your former *chasan*!"

Now it was her turn to stare incredulously. She asked me a number of questions, to test if I was indeed the man I purported to be. Then, all at once, she recognized me.

Both of us began to cry then. For a long time we sat and wept together in that *yichud* room. We sensed with powerful clarity the guiding hand of Providence that brings people together and unites sundered hearts. When we left the room to go to the meal, we let the others in on the story. We wanted them all to see how *Hashem Yisbarach*, in His eminent compassion and lovingkindness, establishes homes in Israel. Even if a couple is parted against their will, He will seize them by the hair and bring them back to one another.

And then a wonderful thing happened. Immediately after the wedding, both of us began to recover, my wife and I. We returned to health, as though we had never been sick a day in our lives. We settled here in this small village near Amsterdam, and Hashem blessed us with wealth and honor, and wonderful sons and daughters.

"And now, I ask Your Honor," the host said as he finished his moving tale, "after I caused my wife so much pain and distress for so many years, am I not obligated to appease her with all sorts of gestures, over and above the strict letter of the law? Do you understand why I accord my wife all this honor?"

The Vilna Gaon, hearing this amazing story, changed his mind and decided to remain two more days at the house. Before he left, he blessed his host and the whole family with great blessings.

On his return to Vilna, stymied by Heaven from fulfilling his dream of moving to *Eretz Yisrael*, he related the whole tale to his student, R' Chaim of Volozhin, who then transmitted it to his foremost student, R' Meir *HaKohen* Karelitz, who told it in turn to his own students. One of them set the story down in a volume of *"Chiddushei HaRashba al Sheva Shitos,"* and it was copied from there by researcher and biographer Yeshayahu Winograd.

HE KNEW HOW TO CRY

THE JEWISH COMMUNITY OF OSTROVA WAS IN AN UPROAR. A terrible, sweeping epidemic had broken out in the city, taking its daily tragic toll of victims. Perfectly healthy people — relatives, neighbors, and friends — were suddenly struck down, like stalks of wheat before a deadly scythe.

Ostrova's Jews might have shrugged their shoulders and murmured fatalistically, "A contagious disease of epidemic proportions. It happens... But faithful Jews know that Heaven does not decree such devastation without cause. What made the situation even more striking was the way the disease swept through the Jewish community while leaving the city's non-Jewish population completely unscathed.

The Chief Rabbi of the city and his *beis din* declared a public fast — a full day of prayer and repentance. Their fervent hope was that this mass outcry would succeed in eliciting Heaven's much-needed compassion.

Along with instructions about fasting and praying, the *beis din* added another urgent message:

"Anyone aware of some wrong in this city — of any suspect behavior not in accordance with Jewish law, whether in an individual or a group, creating a break in the city's wall of faith — must step forward and inform the *beis din* at once, so that we may know who is responsible for this great evil!"

The very next day, two men did indeed come forward with their suspicions. They were Efraim Feigel and Paltiel Beinish. And the story they told was dreadful.

They had noticed for some time that their neighbor, Yonah the fish man, had been acting strangely. He never came to the local *shul* to pray with his neighbors anymore. Until now, they had innocently believed that Yonah had simply opted for a different synagogue. After reading the *beis din's* announcement, however, they became alert to possible danger. The two men decided to follow their neighbor's behavior more closely. And what did they discover?

"During the day there was no change at all," the witnesses related. "Yonah continued to buy fish from the non-Jewish fishermen, to clean them and then sell the fish in his store."

But Efraim and Paltiel continued watching. The hours passed. It was only as the clock struck midnight that their long vigil at last bore fruit. A candle was lit in Yonah's house.

"Yonah left his house, dressed in dark clothing. He quietly closed the door behind him and slipped out of the city. We followed close behind," the witnesses said breathlessly. "We were very careful not to give ourselves away. At last, he entered the dense forest — and we lost him.

"Now, we ask you, honorable judges and rabbis: What would a Jew be doing in the forest in the middle of the night — a place so fearsome that no one dares enter it even in the light of day? What other reason could there be, but that Yonah belongs to the gang of thieves and murderers that has been preying on our city?"

The Rabbi listened closely to the witnesses' account. Then he said in a calm voice, "You did not actually see what Yonah the fish man did in the forest, and a person cannot be judged except on an eyewitness account. Therefore, we may not punish him — despite the fact that I, too, am very suspicious of his secret activities.

"But here is something you can do," the Rabbi continued. "Follow Yonah again tonight. This time, if he enters the forest, follow him! Do not be afraid. In this way, you will be able to see for yourselves just what he's up to in there."

The witnesses were beside themselves. "Go into the forest? But — but we'll be taking our lives into our hands!"

"Do not be afraid," the Rabbi repeated. "The well-being of an entire city hangs in the balance. I am sure that Heaven will protect you tonight."

As the two men considered this anxiously, the Rabbi added, "If you see his candle light up at midnight, one of you must run to let me know at once. I will join you in following him."

This calmed the witnesses more than anything else. If their venerable Rabbi was willing to accompany them into the forest, they would fear neither armed robbers nor dangerous murderers. The Rabbi's merit would surely protect them!

Absolute darkness and silence reigned. Paltiel and Efraim tiptoed over to their neighbor's house and peeked cautiously through the window.

"Efraim, look — the candle is lit!" Paltiel whispered excitedly. "Run to the Rav's house. I'll stay here and keep an eye on Yonah. We don't want him to slip away from us again."

Efraim darted away and raced like the wind to the Rabbi's home. He was hesitant about rousing the Rav from his sleep — but soon saw that this would not be necessary. In the Rabbi's window, too, a candle flickered.

The Rabbi was sitting and waiting, fully dressed, with his walking-stick ready at his side.

"Well?" he asked softly. "Do we go?"

"We go," Efraim answered tersely. "We'll catch that crook in the act — and put an end to the epidemic!"

Walking as silently as they could manage, the three men followed Yonah along a circuitous route that took them out of the city and to the very edge of the forest. Gazing up at the dark, looming trees, Paltiel and Efraim trembled with fright.

"What are you afraid of?" the Rabbi asked in a whisper.

"Th-this is not easy," Efraim Feigel stammered. "The forest is pitch dark, and it's swarming with murderers. I have a wife and children at home."

"M-me, too," Paltiel muttered fearfully.

"Is that it?" the Rabbi asked sternly. "You fear for your own lives and those of your families — but what about the lives of all your fellow townspeople? Should the epidemic rage on unchecked?"

Abashed, the two hung their heads. Without another word, they continued on Yonah's trail, plunging headlong into the dark heart of the forest.

Ahead of them, Yonah walked confidently, as though the forest path were as smooth as a paved road. Finally, he reached a certain large tree and hung up his pack.

From the shadows, three pairs of eyes followed his every move. The three men hardly breathed.

What they saw next left them literally stunned. They saw Yonah the fish man take a *siddur* out of his pack, light his candle, and sit down on the ground to recite *Tikkun Chatzos* with bitter tears streaming down his cheeks. The tears, and the heartfelt prayers that went along with them, melted the watchers' hearts. Those three hearts felt acute pain at having suspected an innocent man. And not only innocent, but actually a hidden *tzaddik,* who conducted a moving *Tikkun Chatzos* night after night in this remote and dangerous location.

But the story did not end there.

Suddenly, Yonah's voice was joined by another's. The Rabbi and his companions thought it an echo at first, nothing but Yonah's own words bouncing back through the trees. Gradually, however, they realized that the second voice was no echo. There was someone else present — someone they could neither see nor identify — standing in this impenetrable forest and weeping along with Yonah.

"Whose voice is that?" the Rabbi whispered in wonder. "Do either of you recognize it?"

The others listened carefully. It seemed to them that the voice was an enchanted thing, something not of this world. They had never heard such weeping, purer and more innocent even than an infant's. It was the weeping of an angel that buries itself deep in a man's soul and lifts him up to the stars.

"Let us wait until Yonah finishes," the Rabbi said, awed. "Yonah is no thief or murderer, as you believed. This much we know for certain. When we leave the forest we'll surprise him. We'll tell him we know his secret and ask him to tell us the name of the man with that wonderful voice — the second person in the forest with him."

The plan was not difficult to carry out. The three men waited for Yonah to finish his prayers, then followed him silently out of the forest. In short order they took him by surprise, surrounding him.

"Your secret has been exposed to us tonight," the Rabbi told the startled fish man. "Please forgive us for suspecting a person like you. We had no choice — we must try to stop the epidemic in its tracks."

It was clear from Yonah's expression that he was deeply downcast. He had wished to serve his Creator privately, without any other living thing being the wiser. Now his secret had been found out. He was shocked and distressed.

But the Rav was not about to let him go. "Who was the second man, the one we heard crying along with you in the woods?" he demanded.

Uneasily, Yonah tried to evade the question. The Rabbi asked again, and again Yonah avoided a direct answer. At last, the Rabbi thundered, "I am the *mara d'asra* of the holy community of Ostrova. I order you on the strength of my rabbinic authority to tell me at once who the other man was!"

Yonah sighed. There was no way out. He could not avoid answering now.

In a low voice, he said, "It's been a long time since I began leaving the city to mourn the destruction of the *Beis HaMikdash* in the heart of the forest. It seems that my weeping created such pleasure in Heaven that it was decided to give me a precious gift. Each night, they send down Yirmiyahu *HaNavi,* who personally witnessed our holy Temple go up in flames. Yirmiyahu *HaNavi* comes to say the *Tikkun Chatzos* with me each night. He knows how to cry... because his eyes actually saw the *Shechinah's* dwelling place consumed in the inferno.

"That," ended Yonah the fish man, "was the second voice you heard."

The Rabbi was speechless. When at last he found his tongue he said, "In that case, I have a big question for you. It is actually a question in two parts.

"First, if you are a man on such a high spiritual plane, why can't you have the decree against Ostrova's Jews annulled — or, at the very least, ask Yirmiyahu *HaNavi,* whom you merit seeing every night, to tell you why we have been punished so severely.

"And, second," the Rav continued, "why don't you *daven* in public? Why are you never seen in *shul?*"

Placidly caressing his *siddur*, Yonah replied, "Tomorrow, I will come to *daven Shacharis* in *shul*, together with the rest of you. At that time, all your questions will be answered, and all your complaints against me will vanish."

That night, Efraim Feigel and Paltiel Beinish went from house to house, waking all of Ostrova's Jews to tell them the exciting news: "Yonah the fish man is actually a hidden *tzaddik*. Every night, he merits seeing Yirmiyahu *HaNavi*! He'll be coming to *Shacharis* at the *shul* tomorrow morning!"

Every Jew in the city flocked to *shul* the next morning.

The time for *Shacharis* arrived, but Yonah — the newly-revealed secret *tzaddik* — was late. The Rabbi issued instructions to wait a little while. But when several more minutes had passed with no sign of Yonah, the vast congregation began to *daven*.

It was then, as the others were reciting the *Pesukei D'Zimrah*, that Yonah the fish man appeared. Wrapped in his *tallis* and *tefillin*, he entered the *shul*.

A sudden awed terror descended upon the worshipers. Their voices rose in a confused crescendo. The panic reached the point where several men fell to the ground in a faint.

When they were revived, the *davening* resumed — and what a *davening*! The townspeople could not recall another time when they had prayed with such fervor, such heartfelt enthusiasm. They felt certain that Heaven's gates stood open to receive their prayers. And when they had finished, they turned as one to gaze at the modest countenance of Yonah, the hidden *tzaddik*. Breathlessly, they waited for him to speak.

But it was the Rabbi who spoke first.

"Not only have the two questions I asked yesterday not yet been answered — but I now have a third! What is the meaning of the tremendous awe and fear that fell over this holy congregation the moment you set foot in *shul*?"

Not a breath stirred in the packed room, as every man present waited for Yonah's answer.

"It is quite simple," Yonah explained. "It says in the *pasuk* (*Devarim* 28:10): 'Then all the peoples of the earth will see that the Name of Hashem is proclaimed over you, and they will revere you.' Our Sages have said (*Berachos* 6:1) that this refers to the *tefillin* that is worn on the head.

"*Tefillin,* you see, has the power to incur fear and awe in others. It was not I who aroused those emotions — but my *tefillin!*"

The Rabbi stared. "That is your explanation? Yet look around you. Do you see a sea of heads bare of *tefillin*? What you are saying is no news to us. We, too, wear *tefillin,* praise be to Hashem — but we have never experienced such fear!"

"Yes, you all wear *tefillin,*" agreed the hidden *tzaddik,* "but you do not care for them properly. In all my life, I have never spoken one mundane word while wearing my *tefillin*. I wear them always solemnly and with humility. And so, my *tefillin* never lost the Heavenly holiness that rests upon them."

The "fish man" looked around at the assembled crowd. "Here is something you should know," he said. "Every pair of *tefillin* — every single pair — possesses the power to arouse an awesome fear, even to the point of making the common man lose consciousness. But if you treat them lightly and frivolously, they lose this special power with which the Creator originally imbued them.

"And that," continued Yonah, in a ringing tone, "is why I have not been coming to *shul*. I cannot bear your lack of proper care. You speak of mundane matters inside the walls of our holy *shul*! Afraid that I, too, would be dragged into such behavior, I chose instead to *daven* alone."

Then the *tzaddik* reached the topic uppermost in everyone's mind. "That is why the epidemic has broken out in our city!" he cried. "It is because you speak this way in *shul* during *davening*, especially while wearing your *tefillin*. You have desecrated the Name of Heaven and have been sentenced to death! This is the reason behind the deadly disease that has spread everywhere.

"If you will undertake, here and now, to revere your *tefillin* and treat them as they must be treated — if you will not profane your prayers with mundane speech — the epidemic will disappear!"

With these words, Yonah spun around and left the *shul*. From that day forward, he was never seen in the city again.

On the spot, the Rabbi gave a rousing sermon to the huge assembly, reminding his people of the severity of speaking of mundane and trivial things during *tefillah* — and especially while wearing their holy *tefillin*. And the Jews of Ostrova undertook, for themselves and for their children after them, to refrain from this kind of talk in *shul*.

The resolution was engraved in illuminated letters on a marble tablet that was erected in the *shul* … and, even more importantly, on the tablets of their own hearts.

And the epidemic ended.

R' HILLEL SAVES A LIFE

THE HOLY *GAON*, R' HILLEL OF PARITCH, WAS A FOREMOST disciple of the "Middle Rebbe," R' Dov Ber of Chabad. R' Hillel was an outstanding member of the Rebbe's inner circle, held in great esteem by his friends and by his Rebbe. But because he concealed his talents and behaved as humbly as a doormat — and because man sees only with his eyes but Hashem sees into men's hearts — even those closest to him did not know the true extent of the heights which R' Hillel had attained.

Then something happened that exposed his true greatness to his friends, once and for all.

It was the afternoon of *erev Yom Kippur*. Throughout the city, Jews prepared to greet the awesome and holy day; some had already washed their hands for the final meal before the fast, the *seudah hamafsekes*. In R' Dov Ber's *beis midrash*, his students, too, had gathered at a table laid with *challos* and bowls of soup. The quicker among them had already recited the blessing over bread and swallowed their first bites of *challah,* while others were still filling the washing cups with water. Suddenly, the *beis midrash* door was violently flung open. In burst a woman, her face contorted in anguish.

"Compassionate Jews, help me!" she screamed.

The *beis midrash* was thrown into turmoil. The group of students tried to find out what was troubling the woman, but she could hardly speak for crying. Her voice kept drowning in her tears. At last, someone offered her a glass of water, which calmed the woman to the point where she could tell her story.

"My husband, may he live and be well, leased a parcel of land from the cruel *poritz* (landowner). We've had a hard year, and my husband has no money with which to pay the rent. The *poritz* has thrown him into his dungeon. He has been sending messengers to me from time to time. Today, the final warning came: If I do not pay him the rental fee of 300 silver rubles today, he will take my husband out and kill him this evening, after dark!"

Once again, the woman broke down in bitter tears. Beating her head with her fists, she raised her voice in an awful wail. "Merciful Jews! I beg you to listen! I have six little ones at home. The youngest is but an infant of three months. Have pity on me and on my unfortunate children, that they may not be orphaned of their father!"

For a moment, the disciples stood helpless. Then they gathered their wits and began searching through their pockets for the few meager coins they possessed.

On the spot, the group managed to collect four silver rubles. After another student came to join their meal — a man slightly better off than the others — the grand total came to six silver rubles.

The woman took the coins, thanked the men, and prepared to leave the *beis midrash.*

"Wait a moment," someone called. It was R' Hillel.

The woman paused on the threshold.

"What will you do with six rubles?" R' Hillel asked. "How will six rubles save your husband, in the face of the 294 that are still missing?"

At these words, the woman burst into a fresh bout of tears. Her bitter wails shook the walls. R' Hillel stood up, tied his *gartel,* and put on his overcoat. "Go on with your meal," he told his friends. "Don't wait for me. This is a matter of *pikuach nefesh* — a life in danger. I will search in the marketplace and on the city streets. Perhaps I will manage to collect the rest of the money."

Only one hour remained until sunset. R' Hillel did not begrudge the loss of his meal and did not waste a thought on the long fast ahead of him. He did not dwell on the nearly nonexistent chances of collecting such a large amount of money in so short — and difficult — a time, when everyone was sitting around their tables concentrating on eating quickly before the onset of Yom Kippur. A single goal burned constantly before him: to save a Jewish life! And this goal obliterated any other consideration.

"How will I find 294 rubles before dark?" R' Hillel mused, as he set out for the marketplace. The wicked *poritz* knew that once the stars were twinkling in the sky that night, all the town's Jews would be immersed in prayer to the exclusion of all else. The *poritz* would have a free hand to do as he pleased. The money had to be found, and found soon. But how?

R' Hillel did not let the troublesome question destroy his calm. He prayed to his Creator to grant him a measure of tranquility, so that he might not be thrown into confusion by the task ahead of him.

His prayers bore fruit. R' Hillel's spirit remained peaceful and his mind became crystal clear. Coldly, he calculated: If he went from door to door to collect the money, he would lose valuable time that could not be restored. No, he would take a different approach. He would go straight to the city's largest tavern!

Just what he would do once he got there he did not yet know. But he directed his steps there — long, purposeful strides to hasten him to his destination.

A pious and G-d-fearing Jew did not normally cross the threshold of the large, public tavern from one end of the year to the other, let alone on *erev Yom Kippur*. It was with wonder and astonishment, therefore, that the patrons stared at R' Hillel upon his entrance.

"Jew, what is your business here?" they asked.

"I am seeking my brothers," R' Hillel replied. "Are there any Jews here?"

"Jews?" the men were convulsed with drunken laughter. "There are no Jews like yourself in this place. Only Jews like us, who know how to drink and how to dance!"

"Where are they?" R' Hillel asked calmly.

The others pointed at a distant table, where a few Jewish men sat together, drinking and playing cards. At their elbows stood large piles of money, ready for further play. From time to time, one of them would lift a bottle of whiskey to his mouth and take a long swig.

With measured steps, R' Hillel approached the table.

The card-players stopped their game. They stared with wonder at the glowing face of the Jew who stood by their table, until one of them ventured, "Reb Yid, what do you want?"

R' Hillel had been waiting for this moment, and this question.

"Do you want to buy yourselves the World to Come without any effort at all? It is very simple. Just do one little thing, and you will be assured a place in *Gan Eden!*"

"What 'little thing' is the Rabbi referring to?" they asked cautiously.

R' Hillel told them about the unfortunate Jew imprisoned in the *poritz's* cellar, tortured and suffering for many long days, and of the decree of execution that hung over his head that very night. He tried to arouse the men's compassion with a vivid description of the family's pain and fear. He related how his friends had donated their last coins, but had managed to collect only six rubles altogether. By the time he had finished his tale, R' Hillel was certain that the gamblers would pick up their piles of money and donate it all to this worthy cause.

But they were obstinate men, men whose hearts did not easily melt at tales of other people's suffering. After a whispered consultation, they told him, "Listen, we are compassionate men. We are prepared to give you 100 rubles — if you'll drink this full bottle of whiskey!"

R' Hillel searched their eyes beseechingly, but there was no trace of pity there. The gamblers were determined to have their fun. Imagine the amusement, to see this eminently respectable Jew imbibing a full bottle of *schnapps* on the brink of Yom Kippur!

Slowly, R' Hillel picked up the bottle, poured himself a large glassful, and recited the blessing, *Shehakol*. The fiery drink burned his throat and scorched his insides. But R' Hillel knew that every sip was worth several rubles. Glass after glass, with determination and courage, he drank down the whiskey to its very dregs.

His eyes watered and his stomach rebelled — but what did any of that matter if these gamblers would hand over 100 rubles? He was happily placing the money into his pouch when one of the gambling men called out slyly, "Rabbi, a second round?"

Everything inside R' Hillel wanted to shake his head and say, "No!" But the gambler continued, "Another bottle, another 100 rubles!"

"It's a deal," said R' Hillel.

He threw a sad glance out the window at the sinking sun. It had not yet set. There was time!

"Come on, I'll drink it now."

They handed him a second bottle. R' Hillel poured himself a glassful, and began to drink. His insides churned as though consumed in flames. His throat felt raw. But he kept on drinking. He would not give up. Draining the last glass, he gasped, "*Nu,* I've done my share."

And another 100 rubles were counted out into his hand.

But the group were not content to end the game so soon. "A third bottle, and you'll have the entire sum that you need. Three hundred rubles! The leaseholder will be set free, and you'll even have six rubles left over!"

R' Hillel had never been much of a drinker. He was certainly not accustomed to drinking large quantities of liquor. And he surely did not ever drink as the sun was slipping over the horizon, heralding the beginning of the holy day of Yom Kippur. His friends were in *shul* now, having recited the *Bircas HaMazon,* removed their shoes, and donned the white *kittels* that made them resemble angels. Very soon now, everyone would begin reciting the *Kol Nidrei.*

"And you, Hillel, are standing here at this holy moment, and in such company!" R' Hillel thought to himself.

He turned resolutely to the gamblers. "Bring me a third bottle." A fine Yom Kippur he was going to have, with a belly full of whiskey... But the important thing was to save the Jewish leaseholder's life. That was all that counted.

Another bottle was duly brought to the table. "Fine whiskey," one of the men remarked mockingly, placing the bottle in R' Hillel's trembling hands.

Ignoring his screaming insides, ignoring everything but the need to fulfill his mission, R' Hillel poured a glass of the fiery stuff and tossed it down his throat. Everyone he knew was standing near open Arks now... but he drank. He drank with his eyes squeezed shut. He drank with his throat searing, on fire. He drank though his stomach felt close to exploding.

"Any second now, he's going to fall down dead," one of the gambling men whispered to another.

But R' Hillel drank on. He drained the entire third bottle to the last drop — and placed the last 100 rubles into his pouch.

His gait swayed as he tried to walk. The quantities he had drunk threatened to topple him at any moment. But R' Hillel did not lose sight of his goal. As long as he could remain conscious, he would run to the *poritz's* house. Puffing and panting, he arrived at last. Triumphantly, he counted out the grand sum of 306 rubles into the *poritz's* hand; he could not keep back the six extra rubles because they were *muktzeh*.

The leaseholder was free!

The group of disciples were in the midst of *davening Maariv* when R' Hillel walked into the *beis midrash*.

He looked ghastly. His face was beet-red, like that of the most common drunkard. His entire body gave off the smell of strong liquor.

The others exchanged glances of total incomprehension. R' Hillel had left on a mission to save a Jewish life — and had returned reeking of drink! This had not been part of the plan.

R' Hillel tried to pick up a *machzor* and to *daven*. But three full bottles of whiskey are no insignificant thing. The moment he sat down with his *machzor*, his eyes closed. R' Hillel fell instantly into a deep sleep. Presently the *machzor* slipped from his nerveless fingers and fell to the floor — to be followed a moment later by R' Hillel himself. He was dead to the world.

As soon as they had finished *davening*, the other disciples hurried to the Rebbe, to direct his attention to the startling spectacle of his prize student lying on the floor in a drunken sleep.

"Leave him alone. He knows what he's doing," was all the Rebbe said.

Several hours passed. None of the students left the *shul*. They remained there, reciting *Tehillim*, learning *Mishnayos* and *Gemara* and *chassidic* wisdom.

All at once, R' Hillel awoke. In a panic, he stood up and approached the *aron kodesh*, eyes overflowing with tears. His face shone as though illuminated by burning torches.

With one hand he moved the curtain aside, opened the door of the ark, and cried out in a mighty voice, "*Attah hareisa* ... Now you have seen that Hashem is the L-rd! There is none other beside Him!"

His friends were astonished. *Attah hareisa* on Yom Kippur night?

Then the Rebbe, R' Dov Ber, explained.

"The entire month of Elul with its repentance, Rosh Hashanah with its *shofar*, the *Aseres Yemei Teshuvah* with its rectification, Yom Kippur with its atonement, Succos with its *lulav* and *succah* — they are all only a means to reach the level of Simchas Torah, when all the heavens open before man, and he sees with his human eyes that only Hashem is G-d. *Hashem hu haElokim, ein od milvado!*"

And the Rebbe concluded, "With his self-sacrifice, with the awesome *mitzvah* he did this night, R' Hillel has merited reaching that exalted level already. Are you surprised?"

"JUST ONE SLAP"

R'LIPA, RABBI OF SHARIGROD, WAS THE EPITOME OF diligence. His learning knew no boundaries of day or night, place or time. The borders of the outside world grew blurred for him, as through all the chaos of the universe he saw only the holy Torah. He was always either learning *Gemara* or speaking about something he had learned in it. Sharigrod's Jews accorded their Rabbi great respect. When he passed in the street, they would step aside to make way for him, and they treated his wife with similar respect.

If he was supremely diligent in his learning on the weekdays, this was nothing compared to the way he conducted himself on Shabbos, as it says, "He will make Shabbos all Torah" (*Tanna Devei Eliyahu* 1). On Shabbos, he learned double his usual quota.

Immediately after the Shabbos night meal, he would climb into bed, sleep a little, and then rise many hours before dawn. He had a regular regimen of learning that took him through the night hours, in both the revealed and hidden Torah, in *Midrash* and *halachah*, in the weekly *parashah* and its commentaries. The *sefarim* would stand in a pile on his table. He would open one, learn from it for a specified amount of time, close it, open the next *sefer*, and so on.

He owned no watch, and was capable of learning straight through to *motza'ei Shabbos* without sensing the passage of the hours. But when the time approached for *Shacharis* in Sharigrod's big *shul*, Mordechai the *shamash* would come knocking on the Rav's door to summon him to *shul*. This was their regular Shabbos routine.

They were reading *Parashas Shemos* that Shabbos, and Mordechai the *shamash* was preoccupied. One of Sharigrod's wealthiest Jews was about to marry off a son, and the *chasan* was to be called up to the Torah. The *shamash* was busy arranging seats in *shul* for the guests and in-laws, holding whispered conferences with the *gabbai* about which guests were most important and should be treated with the greatest care, and dealing with a myriad of other concerns.

Thus it came about, for the first time in his career, that the *shamash* forgot to go to the Rav's house on Shabbos to summon him to *shul*.

The congregants, caught up in the excitement of the *aufruf*, did not notice the Rabbi's absence until it was almost time to recite *Borchu*. Then, in signs and whispers, the news began to make the rounds of the *shul*: "The Rav is not here!"

Poor Mordechai clapped himself on the side of the head and cried out aloud at his forgetfulness. He raced out of the *shul* like a deer, heading straight for the Rav's house.

Absorbed in his learning, R' Lipa did not sense that the *shamash* had come to call him later than usual. As for Mordechai, he said nothing about the delay. For one thing, he was unable to speak in the middle of his own *davening*; for another, he was too ashamed to even hint at his mistake to the Rabbi. R' Lipa strode beside him energetically. Entering the *shul*, he was surprised to see it packed to the rafters. Then he heard the *chazan* call out, "*Borchu!*" and understood at once that the *shamash* had been negligent about fetching him on time that morning.

R' Lipa was furious. He normally spent a good deal of time over his *davening*. He enjoyed saying every word in a measured fashion, like a man taking pleasure in counting his money, coin by coin. In his anger, he made a mistake. He whirled on the *shamash* and slapped him on the cheek.

The *shamash* accepted the slap without resentment. "Let this humiliation be my atonement," he thought.

The time came for the reading of the Torah portion. R' Lipa was honored with *shelishi*. The *baal korei* had just began to read, when a sudden powerful terror swept the Rav. These were the words that the *baal korei* had just recited: "He said to the wicked one, 'Why do you strike your fellow man?'"

R' Lipa trembled. He understood that Heaven had sent him a hint: He had sinned in humiliating the *shamash* with that slap. He knew what R' Chaninah had commented on this verse: "One who slaps a Jew's cheek is like one who slaps the *Shechinah's* cheek" (*Sanhedrin* 58).

"Woe is me!" The thought was like a silent groan in R' Lipa's heart. "How could I have been so foolish? How could I have let my anger rule me?"

As soon as he stepped down from the *bimah*, R' Lipa stopped beside the *shamash*, intending to apologize. But Mordechai recoiled. "Does the Rav want to hit me again?"

"*Chalilah!*" R' Lipa cried. "The opposite, the opposite..."

And right there, in front of the entire congregation and the numerous guests, R' Lipa begged the *shamash's* forgiveness.

"*V'nahafoch hu* — things are all turned around!" Mordechai protested. "It is I who must beg the Rav's forgiveness. It was my fault that the Rav came late. I forgot to call him to *shul* on time."

"No, no, it is I who sinned," R' Lipa said. "Please forgive me!"

But the *shamash*, in his humility, only reiterated, "I am the one who needs the Rav's forgiveness."

The Rav went home after *davening*, brokenhearted. He understood that Heaven was not allowing the *shamash* to forgive him, because the Rav's sin had been a grievous one, a sin which does not find atonement in a simple, "I'm sorry."

On *motza'ei Shabbos*, R' Lipa turned to his rebbetzin.

"I performed a great sin today. There is no atonement for it except exile. I will wander until I receive a sign from Heaven that my sin has found atonement."

The rebbetzin tried to dissuade him, but R' Lipa was adamant. He felt himself the worst of men. His sin required a harsh punishment before atonement could be his.

Tying a few things up in a bundle, R' Lipa parted from the rebbetzin and slipped secretly out into the night.

His wanderings lasted four full years. R' Lipa went from city to city and from town to town, on foot. His appearance changed completely. Anyone seeing him on the road would never have recognized the venerable Rav of Sharigrod. The old R' Lipa had been a well-fleshed man, dressed in accordance with his stature, and his face had shone like the sun. The wanderer was thin, his face weathered from the sun and pinched with hunger. His clothes were ragged and his beard had grown wild. He looked like one of the poorer class of beggars.

For four years, R' Lipa awaited a Heavenly sign that his sin had been forgiven. But the sign did not come.

One Friday morning, R' Lipa came to the gates of Sharigrod. He cast his eyes over the familiar streets of his beloved city, and a wave of pain washed over him. "When will I be able to return to this place? When will my exile end?"

He dragged his weary feet down the streets of his city. He was like a stranger. No one recognized the Rav they had once held in such honor and esteem. But R' Lipa did not allow this to overly upset him.

In every new suffering he saw another brick in the edifice of atonement he was trying to build.

He went to the *beis midrash* and seated himself among the beggars, behind the stove. After *davening*, the other beggars scattered in search of a crust of bread for breakfast. R' Lipa was left alone. He opened a *Gemara* and began to learn with rapt absorption.

Mordechai the *shamash* approached. He, too, did not recognize the man in rags, but he sensed something special about the beggar.

"Do you have a place to eat on Shabbos?" he asked.

"No," answered R' Lipa.

"I will give you a note for one of our community supporters. He is a rich man, and you'll be able to enjoy a fine meal at his house."

The *shamash* scribbled a few words on a scrap of paper, letting the wealthy Jew know that a beggar of good character was coming to him for the Shabbos meal. He gave the note to R' Lipa.

The wealthy Jew was no ignoramus. During the Friday night meal he began to discuss a certain *sugya* in *Gemara* with his learned son, who lived there together with his young wife. From that topic they soon passed to a second, and then a third. The two dove into the deep waters of the Talmud and came up bearing pearls. Their destitute guest took his share in the discussion. With every word he contributed, he revealed a breadth of knowledge that amazed and excited his host. The discussion continued until it was clear that the guest was a great Torah scholar. At once, the host asked, "Do you have a place to sleep tonight?"

"No," answered R' Lipa.

"In that case," the wealthy Jew said joyfully, "spend the night here!"

Earlier, he had hesitated to extend the invitation. Without knowing his guest's character, he was afraid that the poor man might decide to steal his money. Now, he hesitated no longer.

From the moment that R' Lipa had stepped into his self-imposed exile, he had been like a ball being tossed from hand to hand. He had no mind of his own. Whatever others told him, he agreed to do.

He accepted his host's invitation.

In the middle of the night, as was his custom, R' Lipa got out of his bed and began to learn. The other members of the household, hearing his steps in the dark, were anxious — until the sound of his sweet voice learning Torah reached their ears, and calmed them once again.

In the morning, the family rose quickly to prepare for *shul*. One of the city's most prosperous Jews was making a *Sheva Berachos* celebration that day. All at once, a piercing shriek sounded. It came from the daughter-in-law, the young wife of the host's learned son.

"My pearl necklace is missing!" she screamed. "I left it here under my pillow — and now it's gone!"

In those days, pearls were extremely rare and valuable. Today, we can cultivate pearl-bearing oysters in inhabited areas. Not so then. Pearls were to be found only where they had lain since the beginning of Creation, in the depths of the sea. Divers would descend in large metal bells to gather oysters and their pearls. More than one diver met his death in the deep ocean waters. Doom might come in the shape of a vicious predator fish, or a sharp boulder. Most often, however, it was simply a case of air seeping through a crack in the metal bell, leaving the diver to drown before he could reach the surface.

In light of the danger and the difficulty inherent in fishing for pearls, these divers charged exorbitant prices for them. A string of pearls was worth a fortune.

The household was thrown into turmoil. They employed a gentile maid, but no one suspected her of taking the pearls. In the time she had worked for them, the maid had earned a reputation for honesty and loyalty. She had certainly never taken any of the family's belongings.

The full weight of suspicion, then, fell on the wandering beggar whose footsteps in the dead of night they had heard with their own ears. Now, they saw his learning as something he did only for appearance's sake.

"He took advantage of our generosity and our hospitality," the family members told one another angrily. "In the middle of the night, he sneaked out of his room and stole the precious pearl necklace!"

They seized R' Leib, interrogated him, and threatened him. Of course, R' Leib denied everything. "I am innocent. I have never taken anything that does not belong to me."

But no one believed him.

Walking into the rich man's house, Mordechai the *shamash* was taken aback at the turmoil and commotion. He found the head of the house and complained, "Why haven't you come to *shul*? The *mechutanim* and the whole crowd are waiting."

"And how am I to go?" fumed the other man. "Yesterday you sent me a beggar, telling me that he was a decent man. Now it turns out that he is a thief! He was not above stealing my daughter-in-law's valuable pearl necklace in the middle of the night!"

The *shamash* felt responsible. He approached R' Lipa and scolded him soundly. "For shame! I took the trouble to find you the best lodgings for the night, in this rich man's home — and this is how you return the favor? Return what you stole at once!"

"How shall I return something that I never took?" R' Lipa asked. "I stole nothing."

The *shamash* became enraged against the brazen beggar who was not ashamed to look him in the eye and lie. He lifted his hand and gave the poor man a ringing slap on the face. Not satisfied, he raised his hand to deliver a second slap.

R' Lipa, who had been standing till then with hanging head, suddenly lifted his face. His eyes sparkled with sudden light. He seized the *shamash's* uplifted hand and cried aloud, "Mordechai, enough! I am owed just one slap from you!"

The *shamash* gaped at him, thunderstruck. In a flash, layers of exile fell from the wanderer's countenance, and out gleamed the familiar features of the city's Rabbi, R' Lipa.

"Woe is me!" screamed Mordechai bitterly, eyes rolling around in a frenzy. "Are you not R' Lipa, Rav of our city?"

"Indeed," came the answer.

"Woe is me! R' Lipa! I struck R' Lipa!" He threw himself onto the ground and sobbed like a baby. "Forgive me! Oh, forgive me, holy Rabbi, for I struck unintentionally."

The host had been scrutinizing the beggar's changing face. Suddenly, he, too, cried out, "Woe is me! It is our Rabbi, R' Lipa, who disappeared four years ago! Forgive me, Rabbi, for suspecting a man like you!"

The family stood flabbergasted. The "beggar's" face looked familiar now. It took no more than a small effort to recognize that the man standing before them was indeed none other than their vanished Rabbi, R' Lipa!

They joined the sobbing *shamash* on the floor, adding their wails to his own. "Rabbi, forgive us. We suspected a man like you. We have humiliated you!"

But R' Lipa was as thrilled as a man who has just stumbled upon newfound treasure.

"Do not distress yourselves," he advised, in the manner of Yosef *HaTzaddik* comforting his brothers. "You have not humiliated me. At long last, Heaven has sent me a sign that my great sin has found atonement. Four years ago, I did something I should never have done. I gave way to my anger and slapped dear Mordechai on the face — simply because, completely unintentionally, he forgot to call me to come to *shul* on time.

"I took myself into exile in order to atone for my sin. Now I have received a sign that my atonement is complete. My *shamash*, Mordechai, returned my slap — *middah k'neged middah*, measure for measure, humiliation for humiliation!"

R' Lipa looked at the others with a broad smile. "Your reward is right here," he said. "From this day on, I will never be far from you again. I have returned."

His long exile was ended.

THREE MEN ON A ROOFTOP

"I adjure you, daughters of Jerusalem" (Shir HaShirim 2)
"HaKadosh Baruch Hu adjured Israel not to go up [en masse
as if surrounded] by a wall, and not to hasten the end
of days" (Kesubos 111)
"That they will not force by excessive prayer" (Rashi).

LONG LINE OF MEN, SHOULDERS BOWED, PASSED THROUGH the walls of Jerusalem's Old City and descended the dusty path that winds down to the Yehoshafat Valley on its way to the Mount of Olives.

At the center of the group were several figures with torn clothes, but only the sharp-eyed might discern a difference between the clothing of these mourners and the generally ragged garb of the poverty-stricken crowd. Ten young men gripped wooden poles supporting a simple metal bier that bore a body to its final resting place. Bitter sobs accompanied them along the steep downward slope.

This was 200 years ago. The roads and pathways were very different then than they are today. The most vivid imagination back then could hardly paint a picture of the way things would come to look in our own day. Opposite the mourners stood white stones marking the graves of *Har HaZeisim,* the Mount of Olives. The tombstones stood in clumps, scattered across the hillside.

The man they had come to bury had been one of Jerusalem's foremost *tzaddikim* and Kabbalists. His name was R' Chaim de la Rosa. His disciples, talking quietly before the funeral procession had left their teacher's house, shared facts and images from R' Chaim's life. From their words a clear picture emerged: the picture of a true *tzaddik* who had served his Creator devotedly and indefatigably with Torah and prayer, always striving for the perfection of his soul.

As the mourning students carried the bier down the slope, a large crowd of Arab youths watched them from a vantage point off to the west. Suddenly, without the slightest provocation, the youths began to curse the Jews. All too quickly, they moved from words to actions, raining large stones on the funeral procession. Some of these rocks were hurled into the very heart of the group, which only by a miracle escaped serious injury. R' Chaim's students were thrown into confusion. Desperate to save themselves, they ducked the hail of stones and ran for their lives.

In their haste, they left the bier resting on the ground.

The moment the Jews had dispersed, the Arab youths descended on the bier like a pack of wolves. They pulled the *tallis* off the dead man and began showering violent blows on the immobile body. They lifted the body and hurled it contemptuously to the ground. They did this a second time. Finally, they dragged the corpse along the ground in the most degrading manner, kicking it and slashing at it with thin, sharp branches. R' Chaim's disciples, watching aghast from a safer spot not far away, were shaken to the depths of their being at the spectacle of the wicked violence being perpetrated upon the holy body of their beloved teacher.

After a while, their violence spent, the Arabs departed.

R' Chaim's disciples watched the wild men disappear over the horizon. Weeping grievously, they scrambled back to the body and begged their Rebbe's forgiveness for the degradation he had suffered. They continued their sorrowful procession to the Mount of Olives, where they buried R' Chaim. Then, brokenhearted, they returned to town.

The news ignited a storm in Jerusalem. Some hot-headed Jewish youths declared their desire to invade the Arab section and exact justice from those who had perpetrated the violence. Such an act would have been virtually suicidal. The Jewish community in Old Jerusalem (the newer part of the city did not yet exist) was an island surrounded by a much larger Arab sea, plus small clumps of Armenians, Christians, and other gentiles.

In R' Chaim's *beis midrash*, a student stood up to speak.

"*Rabbosai!*" R' Yaakov Chai-Entebbe cried out in a trembling voice. "We are the ones who are to blame! Before his death, our Rebbe ordered us to inflict the four deaths of *beis din* upon him, and to debase his body by hurling it onto the ground. Out of respect, we did not wish to carry out this order. We have sinned! Instead, his pure body was polluted by the cursed Ishmaelites."

His words found acceptance in the other students' hearts. R' Chaim de la Rosa had indeed issued such an order before his death. The question was — why?

From mouth to mouth, whispers passed through the *beis midrash*. The whispers told of a great and dreadful secret which had involved R' Chaim some decades before. It was because of this that he had wished to suffer such punishment after his death.

In whispers, they told the story.

The year was 5513 (1753). Jerusalem's small Jewish enclave witnessed the realization of the tragic, age-old prophecy: They saw *Har HaBayis* desolate, foxes prowling where once the *Kodesh HaKodashim* had stood in all its glory. The longing for *Mashiach* grew hourly, as Arab religious leaders led nearly non-stop prayers and ceremonials on the very spot where the *Shechinah* had rested during the time of the *Beis HaMikdash*.

The greatest among the Kabbalists in Jerusalem, R' Shalom Mizrachi Didia Sharabi (the *Rashash*), was consumed with a burning desire to raise up the *Shechinah* once again, and to hasten the coming of the *Mashiach*. R' Shalom had many devoted disciples in his Kabbalistic yeshivah, "Beit El." From time to time, Rebbe and students would sign a document sealing the pact between them — senior students such as R' Yom Tov Algazi, R' Chaim Yosef David Azulai (the *Chidah*), R' Chaim de la Rosa, R' Yitzchak Mizrachi, R' Avraham Sangaviniti, and others: twelve remarkable disciples in all, symbolizing the twelve tribes of Israel. The goal of the pact was to bring about total unity amongst the member students, a bond of genuine love stemming from taking mutual responsibility for one another. In this way, they hoped that their prayers would be acceptable to Heaven, and would help make the Jewish People worthy of redemption.

As the year 5513 (1753) began, the *Rashash* chose two top students, the *Chidah* and R' Chaim de la Rosa, for a very special mission. They were to purify themselves to the level of holy angels, in order to be able to perform acts that would hasten the *Mashiach's* coming. The troubles of their Jewish brothers in their scattered communities the world over — not to mention in Jerusalem itself — were growing ever more difficult to bear. Men who interested themselves in hints and portents found an encouraging one in the *gematriya* (numerical value) of that year: 513 was the numerical value of the word *hashachar* — the dawn — hinting at the glorious dawn of the redemption. It was also equal to the value of the word *V'nivnesah* (*ir al tilah,* "And the city shall be built upon its hill").

The *Rashash* and his holy partners began to purify themselves in preparation for the great event that was poised to take place.

That winter was a very cold one, replete with heavy snows. The snowfalls were not measured in inches that year, but in full feet. White stuff covered Jerusalem and its enclosing hills in thick, frigid layers.

On those bitterly cold nights, R' Shalom Sharabi, R' Chaim Yosef David Azulai, and R' Chaim de la Rosa left the city for the barren hills beyond its walls. There, in the broad snow-fields far from human observation, the three rolled in the snow with special Kabbalistic meditations known to few. Though the wind shrieked and howled, wrapping them in frigid tentacles and slowly turning them into human icicles, Rebbe and students were not deterred. Night after night, they continued to leave the city to perform their solemn rite in the snow.

One might think, perhaps, that they armed themselves for the ordeal beforehand with a hearty meal and a generous drink of *schnapps* to warm them in advance of their encounter with the icy air … No! The very opposite was true. For three days before each venture into the snow, the three men fasted day and night, in order to weaken the physical component of their beings. The self-inflicted torture took place when they were at their weakest and most vulnerable.

After several weeks of this harsh regimen — weeks that included fervent prayers, separation from their homes and families, three-day fasts, and rolling in the snow — the three men met on a night appointed by the *Rashash*. In the dark of the night they met in the Beit El *shul* and climbed silently up to the roof.

That night, too, was snowy, as had been all the nights of the preceding week. As they climbed, they could see Jerusalem through the windows, gleaming under its blanket of pure white snow. This was no modern-day city, aglow with electric lights. Jerusalem was small and dark. Its homes were small and crowded together, its narrow streets huddled against an invisible enemy. The wind tore at the Rebbe and students as they stood shivering on the roof, and the cold nearly froze them in their place. But they were not afraid, either of the dark or of the awful cold.

Their faces shone with a holy fire, and they seemed to be enveloped by a heavenly glow. They were preparing themselves to pronounce certain awesome Names which held the power to shake the world. With tears coursing down their cheeks, they began to move their lips, murmuring prayers. The grief-stricken tears were for the *Shechinah*, still in exile and still in mourning — "Woe is Me, for I have destroyed My House and burned My Hall."

A long period was spent in intense introspection, seeking out any sliver of a sin, and scouring their souls to their utmost purity. They trembled lest they lacked the merit to perform this daring deed — one which held the key to "coercing" the *Shechinah* into releasing the *Melech HaMashiach* and forcibly bringing him out of his place of hiding, to redeem Israel and the world.

After a number of prayers, long and short, the three men began to pronounce the lofty Names. Their eyes were closed and their limbs trembled, every inch of their beings focused on the heavenly light — the light of the *Shechinah*. With pounding hearts and unparalleled concentration they began to pronounce the holy Names, known only to a few special individuals in each generation. Higher and higher rose their consciousness, yearning for the Eternal, until only a single small step remained to block their souls from breaking the fragile link with their physical selves.

Suddenly, the three heard a voice emanating from the heavens.

"My dear sons, cease your prayers and end your pleas! Why do you seek to force the End of Days and to hasten the Redemption, when the proper time has not yet come?

"Know this: If you do not desist from your actions, the world will revert to chaos and will be lost!"

The three men threw themselves on the ground in terror. Their faces were pale as death and they were robbed of speech. They understood now that they did not have the power to change the course of the world and to hasten the Redeemer before the proper time.

Shakily, they got to their feet. As they stood mesmerized in their places, the voice added, "Because you have done this thing as a unit of three, one of you must leave this city and this land. For only together, as a threesome, can you conquer the *Mashiach*."

When the voice left, utter silence reigned in its place. It was a silence that felt as though nothing had ever come before it and nothing would ever come after. The heavenly voice rang in the three men's ears for a long time.

At last, they began to discuss the matter. They did not know which one of them should be forced into exile, and so they decided to draw lots. R' Chaim Yosef David Azulai's name was drawn. He accepted his fate lovingly, and was quick to put it into action.

That night, the *Chidah* returned to his home, packed his *tallis* and *tefillin*, his precious manuscripts, and his few belongings. And on the very next morning, on 4 Shevat 5513 (1753), he left Jerusalem with a haste that astounded and bewildered his acquaintances for years to come. (There were those who wrote that the Sages of Chevron had sent the *Chidah* on a mission to Western Europe, but they did not understand what prevented him from returning to Eretz Yisrael.)

The *Chidah* never set foot in Jerusalem again. He traveled first to Livorno, Italy, and continued from there to visit many far-flung Jewish communities the world over. Whenever he found a breach in the ramparts of his faith, he did not rest until he had brought about the necessary repairs. He knocked often at the doors of rich philanthropists, to acquaint them with the lot of Jerusalem's poor and collect money for their aid. Wherever he went, he was eloquent in his praise of *Eretz Yisrael*.

In his last years, the *Chidah* settled in Livorno once more. On four special *Shabbasos* he would deliver a sermon to a vast public in his *beis midrash*, built for him by the wealthy Eliezer Chai Shealtiel Rikanti. R' Yisrael Kushta, one of Livorno's learned men, wrote this about the *Chidah's Shabbos Shuvah* talk:

"Waiting for him from his own door to the door of the *beis midrash* was a vast crowd too numerous to be counted. They stood on either side, and the Rav would pass among them, his appearance like that of an angel of Hashem. As he passed, everyone followed after him. He found favor in all who saw him because of his lofty and wondrous wisdom and his pleasant and beloved words of *mussar* — words of yearning that flowed from the heart and drew others. And his renown spread all through the land, and he was honored among the Jews and the gentiles."

The *Chidah* departed this world in Livorno at a ripe old age, on *Shabbos Kodesh Parashas Zachor,* 11 Adar 5567 (1807) — 54 years after he had left *Eretz Yisrael* by Heaven's decree. More than 150 years later, in the year 5720 (1960), his body was brought up from Italy to *Eretz Yisrael* and buried on Jerusalem's *Har HaMenuchos*.

(According to other sources, the *Chidah* returned to *Eretz Yisrael* after five years in exile, and only left again many years later.)

The two remaining partners continued to *daven* for the *Mashiach* as before, and to bewail the *Shechinah's* exile. But no longer did they perform any action that might forcibly hasten the Redemption. After their experience on that wind-blown rooftop, they were very cautious never again to try to hasten the End of Days, whose date is concealed from every human eye.

R' Shalom Sharabi was careful from that day on never to leave the holy city of Jerusalem. Apparently, he was informed through *ruach hakodesh* that as long as he remained within the walls of that city, her merit would protect him from harm.

For twenty-four years, the *Rashash* did not venture forth from Jerusalem. Then, in the year 5537 (1777), the Jewish settlement was stricken with locusts — which came right on the heels of a terrible drought. The sky was like steel and the ground hard as brass. The sparse vegetation and fruit that had managed to grow during the months of meager rainfall were totally consumed now by locusts, in the millions, swarming over the land.

The people came to the *Rashash,* crying, "We will all die of hunger! The locusts are eating every living tree and every stalk of wheat, leaving nothing behind. Pray for us, *Rabbeinu*, that we may live and the last remnant of Israel not be lost!"

The *Rashash* hesitated. After the *tefillos* prayed in Jerusalem had gone unanswered, a mass rally was planned at the *kever* of Rachel *Imeinu,* in Beis Lechem. R' Shalom Sharabi was afraid that leaving Jerusalem would spell his doom. Still, his compassionate heart could not withstand his brothers' tearful pleas, as they stood before him wasting away from hunger. He consented to join them at *Kever Rachel.*

On the way there, he witnessed the awesome devastation in the fields and orchards, which were solidly coated with locusts as far as the eye could see. R' Shalom Sharabi stood for many long hours at the grave of Rachel *Imeinu,* weeping and pleading for her children, who were starving from lack of rain and from the devouring locusts. So many tears did he let fall that they gathered in a pool around his feet. He was still standing and praying when the sky began to turn dark with clouds. For the first time since the onset of that winter's long drought, a heavy rain began to fall.

Then, suddenly, the sky darkened a second time. A mighty black cloud ascended from the ground skyward, as millions of locusts rose to flee Jerusalem and its environs — indeed, the entire land — as though acting on some secret command. The dread enemy left all together and all at once, disappearing over the horizon just as the *Rashash* was finishing his *tefillos.*

The *Rashash* returned home that day — and immediately fell ill. On *Shabbos Kodesh,* 10 Shevat 5537 (1777), he was gathered to his fathers and rose to join the Heavenly Yeshivah.

Thus ended the lives of these three great men of their generation, who had made the mighty experiment of trying to hasten the Redeemer through the exercise of practical Kabbalah.

And it was in order to atone for this undertaking that R' Chaim de la Rosa had ordered his students to inflict the four deaths of *beis din* upon him.

A SMALL WOODEN CUP

EFRAIM FISHEL WAS NEVER A PARTICULARLY LUCKY MAN, BUT his fortunes had never sunk lower than today. Poor from birth, he found that marriage and children inflated his expenses at an alarming rate, while his income seemed to shrink in inverse proportion.

Another man might have despaired of ever improving his lot, but Efraim Fishel was a Torah-educated young man who lived by the tenets of *Chassidus*. He never stopped praying to Hashem to raise the banner of his lot.

Then all at once, it seemed, there was a chance that this could happen.

Good times had come to Poland, his birthplace. The borders between Poland and Prussia (part of Germany today), which had been sealed shut for many years, were suddenly thrown open with the change in Poland's political climate. The opening of the borders created all sorts of tempting new opportunities for many Polish citizens — among them a good number of Jewish yeshivah men. The sight of these men traveling across the border to Prussia and returning with wagonloads of merchandise became a common one. These new merchants sold their goods at attractive prices in impoverished Poland, and quickly grew rich and prosperous.

Efraim Fishel saw his friends' success, and longed to imitate them. Packing his skimpy bag, he kissed the *mezuzah* at the front door of his ramshackle cottage and parted from his wife and children. He traveled directly to his Rebbe, R' Moshe of Lvov, son of the Lvov dynasty's founder, the *tzaddik* R' Dovid.

Generally, Fishel avoided asking his Rebbe for help with his physical needs. This time, however, circumstances forced him to take an unusual step. Over the course of a long meeting, he poured out to the Rebbe the sorry tale of his poverty and distress. He ended with an enthusiastic description of the Jews who had become rich overnight from the new business.

"I would like to become a successful merchant, like them," Fishel sighed. His imagination painted a rosy picture of his triumphant return from Prussia, driving a wagon filled to the brim with merchandise, and the glorious possibility of wealth…

The Rebbe, however, was unmoved. "Not everything that is good for your friends is good for you," he told an astonished Fishel. "I'd advise you to look elsewhere for your livelihood."

Fishel returned home. He accepted the Rebbe's advice, and tried a different occupation. But the bad luck which had dogged his steps all his life continued to plague him now. His debts grew apace, while his expenses became not a whit smaller. In light of the way the booming cross-border business was helping Poland's economy, the government lightened the tax burden on the new merchants. Business with Prussia became even more popular. Every day, in the *shtiblach*, fresh names were added to the rolls of the newly wealthy.

Fishel felt he couldn't bear it. He returned to his Rebbe and pleaded with him not to close the door to the business world. "I feel that I'll be successful," he said repeatedly.

R' Moshe of Lvov sat lost in thought, eyes closed. Several times, he opened his eyes to gaze into his faithful Fishel's face. He saw the worn clothes enveloping an emaciated body, dual testimony to the poverty in which the *chassid* lived.

"All right. In that case, go become a businessman, too," the Rebbe said suddenly. "So many others are succeeding — so can you!"

Fishel's heart nearly burst with joy. The Rebbe had agreed. The Rebbe had agreed!

R' Moshe pulled open a drawer in his desk and took out a small wooden cup. It was a simple cup, without ornamentation or design. He handed the cup to Fishel, saying, "Take this cup with you when you leave on your business venture. It will bring you protection and success."

Fishel stood frozen in his place. Since when did the Rebbe give out cups for success? And what was the meaning behind the strange words, "*protection* and success"? If the Rebbe was talking about protection, there were apparently things that he, Fishel, must watch out for — things that threatened him from behind the scenes.

On the other hand, the Rebbe had blessed him with success in his endeavor. That was a sign that he would emerge victorious.

The Rebbe did not give him much time to hesitate. With another blessing for success in his new venture, he sent Fishel home in peace.

A wagon moved down a road lined with two rows of thin trees. It carried a man whose heart sang with joy and thanksgiving to the good G-d above. The earlier snows had thawed and the road was dry and easy to travel. When business with Prussia had first blossomed, every trip to that country had been fraught with difficulty because of the frigid winter winds and heavy snows.

Fishel looked forward to filling his wagon with a large load of merchandise. Just now, however, the wagon was empty — and his pockets full. From the moment he returned to town with the Rebbe's blessing, the word had spread: Fishel had turned businessman. Everyone wished him well, and his good friends lent him money to help him take his first steps in the business world.

He had also knocked on the doors of the town's more prosperous Jews, taking out other large loans, until he had amassed a large amount of cash with which to buy a great deal of merchandise. Even the wagon in which he rode had not come for free: Fishel had hired it at a steep price.

All he had left to do now was hope and pray that the trip would go well, and that good luck would beam down on him at last.

The wagon plunged into a deep forest. On every side, tall trees closed in, blocking the sun's light. Driving in the gloom, Fishel began to feel the first stirrings of anxiety. More than one of his friends had told him that these huge forests were swarming with bands of armed robbers who might spring out and surprise him at any moment.

"I must keep my eyes open," Fishel murmured nervously to himself.

Suddenly, as though to confirm his deepest fears, a voice bellowed through the woods: "*Zhid, dyo danagi!* Jew, hand over your money!"

Fishel stopped breathing. Out of the towering trees burst a horrific vision. An enormous gentile, looking like the giant King Og in Polish garb, advanced on the wagon at a sprint. He easily overpowered the tired horse. Then the giant of a man turned on Fishel, a sharp knife pointed directly at the frightened Jew's throat.

"Jew, hand over your money!" shouted the robber again, the knife dancing in his fingers.

Fishel grew pale as a ghost. The money did not belong to him. All his hopes rested on a single plan: to use the money to buy merchandise, then sell it for a good profit, return the principal, and live off the remainder. Such a blow to his dreams had never entered his mind!

All at once, he realized why the Rebbe had not wanted him to go into business. The Rebbe, with his far-seeing eyes, had doubtless foreseen Fishel's melancholy end.

But Fishel's courage did not abandon him even now. "I have no money. I am simply out for a pleasure drive," he told the robber.

The giant burst into raucous laughter. "Jew, do you think me a simpleton? 'Out for a pleasure drive'! Quick, give me your money before my sharp blade visits your insides!"

The large knife seemed entirely superfluous in the enormous man's fist. The robber apparently used it merely to encourage his "customers." His appearance alone — the bulging muscles and huge, balled fists that looked like sledgehammers — were quite enough in themselves to sow terror in his victims.

The robber advanced on Fishel, snorting impatiently. There was almost enough force in the huge man's breath to send poor Fishel flying through the treetops. The last drop of blood drained from his cheeks as he groped in the secret pocket sewn into his coat. With trembling hands he pulled out the bundle of money. The robber watched every move with greedy eyes.

Rude laughter echoed through the forest as he snatched the bundle from Fishel's fingers. "I knew it!" he crowed. "What, did you think that you'd fool Ivan? I'm the greatest robber of them all! It is impossible to pull the wool over Ivan's eyes. Just one look is enough to tell me who has money and who doesn't."

To make sure that Fishel was not holding back any cash, the giant robber thrust his hand into Fishel's coat.

"Won't you leave me alone now?" pleaded Fishel, quailing before the robber's murderous gaze.

Ivan laughed again, and the laughter was not pleasant to hear. "I haven't met such an amusing Jew in a long time. You know what, Jew? I'm going to kill you!"

Fishel's blood froze in his veins. The man, then, did not merely look like a murderer — he *was* one!

"What have I done?" Fishel wept. "You wanted my money and I gave it to you. Have pity on me! I have small children at home. They will ask, 'Where is Papa?'"

But his pleas fell on deaf ears. The robber tested his blade with one sausage-like thumb. Fishel thought miserably that a single blow from that powerful fist would be enough to smash him. Fishel himself was hardly strong enough to pull a radish from the ground. The disparity in their strength spelled bad news for the Jew from the start.

"What do you want from me? I haven't done anything to you," Fishel said, trying to placate the stony heart hidden inside that pile of muscle.

Ivan grinned cruelly. "It's not what you have done, Jew, but what you're about to do," he growled. "If I let you go, you'll run straight to the police. And so — your grave will lie right here, among the trees!"

Fishel resigned himself to his fate. He asked the robber for a few minutes in which to recite the *Vidui*. Ivan graciously gave it to him.

"We Christians also confess before our death," he said, as if to explain his unusual kindness.

Hot tears coursed down Fishel's cheeks as he prepared to return his soul to its Creator. His pale lips murmured the *Vidui* and *Shema*, choking on tears with every word. His heart felt torn to shreds at his bitter lot. After losing all the money, the wicked robber would not even let him escape with his life.

Suddenly, a new thought flashed into Fishel's brain. The Rebbe had given him a cup — for protection, he had said.

"I'll have a look at the cup," Fishel decided. "Maybe Heaven will take pity on me in the holy Rebbe's merit."

Turning to Ivan, he asked in a quavering voice, "You would not refuse the last request of a dying man, would you? I have a flask of whiskey in my bag. Let us drink a glass together before I die!"

This was an offer that Ivan had no desire in the world to refuse. Heartily, he exclaimed, "Certainly, certainly, very good, Jew! Give me something to wet my parched throat."

Fishel took the flask from his bag — and the wooden cup as well. He filled the cup with whiskey. As he did, he whispered a silent prayer, "Holy Rebbe, you blessed me with protection and success. Please, I need protection now, more than ever before."

The Rebbe's shining visage swam before his eyes. Fishel felt as though R' Moshe of Lvov was standing right in front of him, calling down Heaven's blessings. A sense of great serenity enveloped the poor Jew. He knew with absolute certainty that Hashem was with him, that Hashem would never leave him, and would not allow him to fall into the hands of the wicked robber.

The liquor's aroma tickled the robber's nostrils. With a raging thirst he seized the cup from Fishel and tossed it down his throat at a gulp. As Fishel watched, it seemed to him that all the world's wicked cravings were to be found in the robber's crude gulping. Ivan tilted the small wooden cup to get at the last fiery drops. He was totally absorbed in the whiskey gurgling down his throat. For an instant, the rest of the world did not exist.

Fishel knew what to do. Without hesitation, he thrust his palm with all his might against the bottom of that uptilted cup — pushing it deep into Ivan's throat.

Ivan emitted strangled sounds. He coughed, trying to extricate the cup from his throat, where it was obstructing the flow of air to his windpipe. But Fishel kept up a steady pressure on the cup, pressing it ever deeper inside. The robber's thick hands were unable to reach into his throat to extract it. Squealing with terror, he swayed on his thick legs and then toppled to the ground.

For a few minutes Ivan's arms and legs continued to twitch, but that, too, soon ceased. The giant of a man lay lifeless on the ground.

Fishel stared at the sprawling figure disbelievingly. Just a moment ago, the terrible robber had planned to murder him. Now he was lying on the cold earth with no breath of life in him. Fishel filled his own grateful lungs with air. The relief was overwhelming. The threat to his life had disappeared — *baruch Hashem*!

When he had recovered from the shock, Fishel remembered the bundle of money. He began searching through the robber's clothes to retrieve it, when his eyes nearly popped out of their sockets. Not only was his own bundle there, but Ivan's bulging pockets were filled with treasures that he had amassed from all his other unfortunate victims. There were huge sums of money, along with pearls and many pieces of golden jewelry.

"What shall I do?" Fishel wondered. "It would be best for me to run. On the other hand, if I leave his body here, it will be found sooner or later. The police will start investigating his death. Neither the Polish police nor Ivan's cronies will believe that this giant gentile attacked me, a frail Jew, and that I killed him in self-defense."

Moving quickly, he dragged the huge body onto his wagon, covered it with dried grass and wildflowers, and galloped away in a hurry. He made up his mind to travel to the nearest Jewish settlement and tell his fellow Jews the whole story. Together, they would plan a way to get rid of the body.

The wagon traveled all through the night. Fishel was anxious to put as much distance as possible between himself and the place where Ivan had breathed his last. As dawn streaked the sky, he came to the Prussian border. The soldiers patrolling the border had no interest in his wagon, and Fishel soon saw why. They were concentrating completely on the words of a government messenger who had come to make some sort of announcement.

Fishel became curious to hear what was being said. He ventured closer to the speaker, who was surrounded by a crowd.

To Fishel's amazement, the government man was speaking about Ivan!

A terrible robber by that name, said the man, had terrorized the area long enough. He had robbed and murdered scores of travelers — if not hundreds. The Prussian government was making every effort to trap him, and was prepared to offer a handsome reward to anyone who would bring in the robber, dead or alive.

The man held up a picture of Ivan.

Fishel took one look. Then, with every ounce of speed he could muster, he ran back to his wagon. Peeking secretly beneath the dried grass, he studied the dead robber's face. Fishel's eyes glowed. Yes, it was the same man!

The prize sought by the Prussian government lay hidden in his wagon.

Fishel hitched up his horse and drove directly to the nearest police station. He requested an urgent meeting with the chief of police.

At first, the chief did not believe Fishel's story. But his incredulity turned into tremendous excitement when Fishel took him to view the dead body in his wagon — the small wooden cup still lodged firmly in his throat.

It wasn't long before Fishel became a rich man. He received a king's ransom for his role in bringing Ivan in. But the story does not end there.

Government officials heard the incredible tale of the giant robber who had met his end at last at the hands of a simple Jew. They offered another huge sum in exchange for the wooden cup that had brought about Ivan's downfall. They would put it in a museum, they said.

But Fishel refused to sell the cup at any price. Instead, he headed for the markets at Danzig, where he bought large quantities of Prussian merchandise. He paid with his own money and with the money he had won through Ivan.

His purse was still quite full when he started the return trip, his wagon groaning under its load. He drove back to his own town, where good fortune and prosperity never left his side again. R' Moshe of Lvov's blessing for "protection and success" had come true in the very best sense of the word.

As for the famed cup, Fishel left that as an inheritance for his offspring. Many years later, when the Rebbe, R' Shimon of Lvov, left Jerusalem for Poland for a short time, he saw the historic wooden cup. It was then in the possession of a grandson of Fishel — the man to whom the miracle occurred, and the *chassid* who became rich overnight.

IN THIS I TRUST

THE VERY EXISTENCE OF A YESHIVAH SUCH AS THE FAMED Volozhin Yeshivah, under the difficult conditions existing 200 years ago, is one of the wonders of the Torah world. The man responsible for maintaining that yeshivah, the *gaon* R' Chaim of Volozhin, foremost student of the Vilna Gaon, founded what came to be known as the "Mother of Yeshivos" in the year 5563 (1803).

It all began with a few dozen young men who thirsted for Torah, and attached themselves to R' Chaim's cloak. "Teach us Torah!" they pleaded. This coincided very well with R' Chaim's own burning desire to teach Torah. At that point, the concept of housing a yeshivah in an established building was a new one. R' Chaim collected his young students, sat with them in a *beis midrash* in the city, and taught them Torah. Apart from delivering *shiurim*, he bore the responsibility of physically supporting his diligent students, who poured all their interest and energy into learning *Gemara* and knew nothing of the world outside.

Apart from the difficult job of teaching the students, R' Chaim would go from door to door, requesting donations from Volozhin's Jews, who gave their few pennies, or their own crusts of bread, to their beloved yeshivah students. While some townspeople gave money, others provided actual foodstuffs, such as bread, cheese, and onions.

But those days did not last long. As the yeshivah's reputation spread throughout Lithuania, a steady stream of young men began to pour into Volozhin. All of them were eager to learn Torah in an organized and in-depth fashion, and to hear *shiurim* on a daily basis from the great R' Chaim.

R' Chaim could not turn these wonderful youths away. All they wanted was one thing: to grow in Torah! He accepted them into the yeshivah — and immediately faced a new problem: Where could he house all these new students, and how would he feed them? R' Chaim disliked the prevalent practice of sending students to eat at different homes each day. He wanted to put an end to this, by keeping them all in one central location. In this single building they would learn, eat, and sleep.

With a monumental effort, R' Chaim managed to secure a building for his students. Now, however, the problem of finances loomed twice as large. He was responsible for providing bread for some one hundred mouths, apart from preparing the complex *shiurim* he delivered in the yeshivah each day. Volozhin's Jewish community was a poor one, unable to support such an institution. Their love for Torah and its scholars was legendary, and the yeshivah students in their city were beloved to them — but it was simply impossible, in their own poverty, to support a yeshivah of this size.

R' Chaim was forced to travel to nearby communities for funds. Every place he went, the Jews gave what they could. Thus the yeshivah successfully crossed the first difficult hurdle of its existence.

The Volozhin Yeshivah rested on very solid ground: the unshakable faith of its *rosh yeshivah,* R' Chaim. This was the kind of faith of the giants of previous generations. R' Chaim trusted in Hashem with a wondrous trust to provide all the yeshivah's needs at the proper time. In a yeshivah "newsletter," he wrote, "And in the lovingkindness of Hashem, Who has guided and succored me from my youth, I trust in Him and I depend on Him to provide me plentifully with the students' requirements as they become necessary."

Simple words, these, far removed from large, sweeping phrases and bombastic expressions. Behind them, however, lay an entire world. R' Chaim here testified that he had never in his life lacked for anything because he always trusted in Hashem. To him, it was self-evident: If *HaKadosh Baruch Hu* is all powerful, He is fully capable of supporting a single individual — R' Chaim — and his family, as well as providing for the needs of a hundred students or more.

But the full meaning of these simple words is to be found in an incident that happened to R' Chaim during those first difficult years. The story illustrates in the clearest way what R' Chaim meant when he said, "I trust in Him."

The year 1812 will be remembered in Russia as one of the most difficult times in its history. A great war swept the country in that year, instigated by the enemy, Napoleon I, who invaded with his French army and managed to claw his way to the capital city of Moscow. The toll of deaths and casualties was astronomical. And then Napoleon set the city on fire.

The poverty was dreadful. Every able-bodied man in the land was drafted for military service; hundreds of thousands of soldiers and citizens were killed, and as many or double that amount lay wounded in miserable hospitals. Conditions in these houses of healing were terrible. The vast majority of the wounded remained crippled or injured for life, due to a lack of proper medicine or an even minimal medical standard.

At such a difficult and poverty-stricken time, who had a thought to spare for the sufferings of yeshivah students? They were forced to go hungry for a long time.

A horse-driven carriage pulled up in front of the Volozhin Yeshivah gates. A solid, compact figure leaped off hurriedly. In his well-cut clothes, it was possible to identify him at once as a high government official. He entered the yeshivah building with a measured and authoritative gait, his steps falling heavily. He came to the *beis midrash* hall.

He gestured imperiously at some students, summoning them to him. When the students came out, he told them, "I'd like to see R' Chaim."

Apprehensively, the students studied the visitor. His high-ranking demeanor worried them. Did this visit portend, Heaven forbid, some new law that could harm the yeshivah?

R' Chaim was called away from his *Gemara*. He met with the visitor in his private office. "What can I do for you?" he asked as soon as they were alone.

The official said, "I am a Jew. I've heard great things about the honored Rabbi, and I have come to request his help. I hold a senior post — quartermaster for the army, responsible for supplying food to the troops serving at this end of the front."

R' Chaim listened closely. He then asked, "Such a high-ranking officer ... What can you possibly need from a simple Jew like me?"

The officer poured out his heart. "R' Chaim, I have been connected with the military for a long time. For many months, I have had no contact with my family and my home. When I left, I took along a bundle of money — all the money my family had. I was afraid that the family would not look after it properly, and it would be lost. But the burden of keeping watch over this bundle lies very heavily on me.

"My job entails great responsibilities. Every day, I must come up with food for 3,000 soldiers. I travel a great deal. More than once, it has happened that I've had to approach very close to the battlefront, where enemy bullets literally shrieked past my ears.

"Right now, I have been relieved of my post for one year. Someone else is going to take my place. I carry my bundle of money around with me everywhere — 800 silver rubles in cash — and all the time my mind is charged with fear, lest something happen to me. This is wartime, and every road is fraught with danger. What if an enemy bullet finds me and all my money is lost?"

"And what do you want from me?" R' Chaim asked gently. Though he had discerned the officer's motive from the first, he played the innocent and let the other man arrive at his goal in his own way.

From the recesses of his coat, the officer pulled out a large, well-wrapped bundle. "Holy Rabbi, I beg of you to keep this money for me for one year. As long as it lies in your possession, you have my permission to use it for the yeshivah."

R' Chaim rejoiced inwardly. "In one fell swoop, all the yeshivah's problems have been solved!" This sign of Divine Providence did not surprise him. It had been clear to him from the outset that something like this would come along to help him. But trust is no contradiction to happiness, or to heartfelt gratitude at finding salvation.

The officer counted out the money calmly. When he reached the total of 800 rubles, the counting was done. He handed the bundle to R' Chaim, saying, "Rabbi, the money is yours to do with as you will. In one year I will return to ask for it back. If I do not return in that time, you may continue to use the money until I do."

R' Chaim parted warmly from the officer. He was filled with exultation. The yeshivah had been saved for a long period of time from its physical distress. Now the students would be able to devote themselves to their learning in peace — and new students would be welcome to join them.

He marked down the date in his calendar.

The yeshivah enjoyed a long period of peace. While the rest of the country suffered shortages and poverty, the yeshivah students ate their fill and were able to pore over their *Gemaras* without having to fight hunger pangs. For the Volozhin Yeshivah, the officer's money was a true lifesaver.

But before the year was out, the money was gone. Once again, the *rosh yeshivah* was forced to collect funds, as he had done in the past. The job was hard and the incoming money sparse. Accordingly, each day that passed without a visit from the officer was a holiday for the yeshivah administration.

A full year had gone by. R' Chaim awaited the officer's return, but the date passed without any sign of him. Another year went by in the same way.

Only after two and a half years had passed did the officer return at last. He walked directly to the yeshivah office, went to the yeshivah *gabbai*, as the financial administrator was called in those days, and asked for his money back.

The *gabbai* requested that the officer be seated while he consulted with the *rosh yeshivah*. The administrator's face was drawn with worry as he stood before R' Chaim.

"Rebbe, the officer who lent us the money has come, and is asking for it back — 800 silver rubles in cash."

"How much do we have in the yeshivah's fund?" asked R' Chaim.

With a deep sigh, the *gabbai* replied, "Not even 50 rubles."

But R' Chaim refused to be dismayed. "The yeshivah does not have 50 rubles, but the Master of the Universe has millions! Go tell the officer to return tomorrow, at 3 o'clock in the afternoon. With Hashem's help, we will return his money to him, down to the last cent. Eight hundred rubles — not a penny less!"

The *gabbai* knew with whom he was dealing. Without hesitation, he returned to the officer and gave him R' Chaim's message, word for word.

The *gabbai* and R' Chaim had not been alone during the preceding interchange. Also present was R' Itzele Volozhiner, R' Chaim's son, 32 years old and a scholar at the yeshivah. Hearing his father's promise, his heart quailed. He knew that R' Chaim was a tremendous believer, and that if he guaranteed something, that guarantee could be relied upon. At the same time, he knew that Heaven's gates were not about to open up and pour out money the next day. He shared his worries with his father.

"Father, why did you promise to return the money in such a short time? Why not push him off for a few weeks or a month? In that time, you may be able to secure some large loans … But *tomorrow?* Who will give you 800 rubles in one day?"

R' Chaim merely looked at him, and did not say a word.

The next morning, before *Shacharis* and after, R' Itzele kept glancing repeatedly at his father. To the best of his knowledge, the money had still not arrived — not even a portion of it. R' Chaim's pockets were empty. But the *rosh yeshivah's* face was tranquil and trusting. Not the tiniest cloud of worry overshadowed it.

After *davening*, the students joined together for breakfast. R' Chaim then went to deliver his daily *shiur* to them — and still, no sign of anxiety marred his features. He was as calm as if the money lay secure in his pocket and there was nothing to do but wait until 3 o'clock to hand it over to the officer.

More than once, during that long morning, R' Itzele wondered whether the money had not, indeed, fallen out of the sky that night, right into R' Chaim's hands.

Absorbed in his *shiur*, R' Chaim did not hear the rattle of carriage wheels at the yeshivah gates. Outside, however, the city's Jews were hissing and whispering. They recognized the owner of that carriage at once: It was the Polish *poritz*, Josef Tishkivitz, who owned the town of Volozhin and all the surrounding property. They wondered what business the *poritz* might have here, at the yeshivah.

The *poritz* did not make them wonder for long. He strode into the building and demanded to see R' Chaim. In short order, he burst into the *shiur* room.

In front of all the thunderstruck students, the *poritz* whipped ten 100-ruble notes from his pocket. He counted them out — 1,000 rubles in all — and thrust the notes into R' Chaim's hands.

When R' Chaim asked what this was all about, the *poritz* answered frankly, "I don't know! It suddenly occurred to me that I don't want to keep this cash with me. I decided to lend it to the Rabbi, to be used for the yeshivah's expenses, for a period of ten years. You can pay me back 100 rubles a year. Is that acceptable to you?"

"Very acceptable," murmured R' Chaim happily. He thanked the *poritz* for his generosity and saw him out with warm words of appreciation. Now he had only to wait for 3 o'clock, when his first lender, the military quartermaster, would come to claim his 800 rubles. And he would return it all — not a penny less — just as he had promised the day before!

R' Chaim's faith had stood the test of reality. It had been heated in the cauldron of worldly affairs and emerged purer by sevenfold.

His words took on new meaning, in the most practical sense. "And in the lovingkindness of Hashem, Who has guided and succored me from my youth, I trust in Him and I depend on Him to provide me plentifully with the students' requirements as they become necessary." Hashem's salvation, R' Chaim's lifelong companion, had come once again — quick as the wink of an eye.

Heaven has many messengers. The money is there. All that is needed is a strong dose of faith, to create a sudden new thought in the mind of a Polish *poritz*.

THE CLOWN WHO DIED ... FOUR TIMES

AT THAT LATE HOUR OF THE NIGHT, BAGHDAD'S STREETS WERE deserted. Silence enveloped the city — except for the Jewish Quarter, where the stillness was broken by sounds of revelry. Alfonso Mizrachi, a well-to-do businessman, had concluded a deal that day which promised to bear rich fruit. Never one to let a chance to throw a party slip through his fingers, he decided on the spot to invite his family and friends to celebrate with him.

"We must invite Nissim the Clown," his wife, Sultana, exclaimed. "It would not be a party without him!"

By "Nissim the Clown," she was referring to a certain Jew who had been blessed with a short stature and an overabundance of humor.

Making good use of this latter trait, Nissim had managed to parlay it into a fine source of income. His satirical comments and caustic riddles inevitably made his audiences roll with laughter. At weddings or any other celebration, Nissim's pointed rhymes were in great demand, injecting a bit of color into otherwise humdrum lives.

As is usual with humorists of this type, Nissim was not a man who had spiritual aspirations. His customary place was not to be found in the *beis midrash*, among Torah scholars and G-d-fearing men; rather, the opposite was true. To label him "frivolous" was to understate the matter ... But who cared how much piety a clown had? The important thing was the way he consistently astounded his audiences with his sharp tongue and astute eye, with the help of which he dragged each person's flaws into the light of day — exaggerated to the point of absurdity. The people enjoyed an opportunity to laugh at these examples of human weakness — especially when it belonged to someone else.

That is how it came to pass that Nissim the Clown was standing on a table in Alfonso Mizrachi's house with a full glass of whiskey in one hand, leaving the other free for the energetic gestures that went along with his humorous monologue. Listening to him, the guests laughed until they cried.

But their hilarity disturbed the neighbors' rest. Even worse, the shouts of laughter floated on the wind until they reached the home of the city's Rabbi, the holy *gaon*, Rabbeinu Yosef Chaim, known the world over as the *Ben Ish Chai*.

With a deep sigh, R' Yosef Chaim raised his eyes from the *sefer* he was learning. He walked over to the window and gazed out to see where the noise was coming from. He stood there a while, his keen glance fixed on Alfonso Mizrachi's house. Finally, he sighed again and returned to his seat.

It was the start of a most unusual night in Baghdad.

In Alfonso's home, Nissim the Clown's act had been going on for some time. His host approached and said genially, "Nissim, how about stopping for a while and having something to eat?" He held out a plate of fried fish.

Without pausing even an instant from his amusing monologue, the clown took the plate from him with a nod of thanks. He speared a nice-sized morsel of fish and thrust it into his mouth while still speaking. Uneducated fellow that he was, he had never heard of *Chazal's* warning, "A person should never speak while eating, lest the food enter his windpipe instead of his esophagus." A piece of fish, in which was embedded a bone thin and sharp as a knife, found its way into Nissim's windpipe.

The rhymes and riddles stopped with startling abruptness.

The partygoers stared at Nissim in shock. The clown's face was slowly turning blue and his eyes bulged as his hands clawed frantically at his throat.

"Help! Nissim is choking! A bone is stuck in his throat!" someone screamed.

Pandemonium erupted. People began running to and fro, trying to help the choking man though no one knew precisely what to do in such a crisis. One turned Nissim over while another rocked him from side to side. A third poured water into the clown's throat and a fourth pounded his back soundly in order to free the bone lodged in Nissim's throat. But all he succeeded in doing, apparently, was to thrash poor Nissim's soul right out of his body. A moment later, Nissim was prone on the ground, lifeless.

Aghast, Alfonso felt for the clown's pulse and put an ear to his lips. His face darkened. He felt neither heartbeat nor breath.

"Alas! Nissim died in our home!" Sultana wailed in an unearthly voice.

Her husband glared at her. "This was your idea."

"Mine?" Sultana shrieked.

"Who else suggested that we bring him to the party, if not you?"

"And who served him fish full of bones, if not you?" she countered angrily.

Someone intervened. "It's not bad enough that we have a tragedy on our hands? Do you have to quarrel like children, too?"

"But look what happened! What do we do with the dead body?" Alfonso cried in despair. "Everyone will blame me. Nissim has a wife and children. What will they say? Woe is me!" He burst into heart-rending sobs.

"Not true," declared Rachamim, another guest.

"What's not true? How is it not true?" Alfonso wailed. "The man died in my home!"

Rachamim lowered his voice to a whisper. "I have an idea."

Alfonso's eyes lit up.

A moment later, two strong men hauled Nissim up the stairs to the second floor, where Ovadiah the doctor lived. They propped him up against the wall, facing the door, as though he were still alive. Then they pounded on the door with their fists and hurried back downstairs. Having taken the precaution of removing their shoes first, they made no sound as they ran.

"Who's there?" Ovadiah called from inside his apartment. "Who needs me in the middle of the night?" There was no answer. "There's no rest for doctors, day or night," he grumbled as he groped his way to the door in the darkness.

He found the door and flung it open. "Who are you and what do you want? Why have you come to disturb my sleep?" the doctor demanded. Drowsily, he looked at the figure standing before him.

He didn't like the man's unnatural posture. And why wouldn't the patient speak? Coming closer to investigate, in the darkness Ovadiah did not notice Nissim's outstretched leg. He tripped — and in a flash both men, living and dead, were tumbling down the stairs.

Ovadiah was lucky; Nissim's body cushioned his fall. He emerged at the foot of the steps breathless but otherwise unhurt. But when he crouched over the other man, he saw at once that there was no breath of life. The body was still warm. Ovadiah the doctor believed that he had inadvertently caused the fellow's death!

He dragged Nissim upstairs to his own apartment and shared the terrible news with his wife.

"What do I do?" he asked in despair. "They will try me for killing a man!"

"I have an idea," his wife whispered.

Minutes later, Ovadiah the doctor crept quietly out of his front door once again. Bent almost double under his load, he bore the body out into the street. There he propped Nissim up against a wall at the corner — and fled like the wind.

"*Baruch Hashem*, I got rid of that problem," the doctor sighed with relief.

But Nissim the Clown was not yet due to find rest, even in death.

Opposite the corner on which Nissim had been propped was the shop of Abu Jalal, the personal tailor of the Caliph of Baghdad. The tailor was working late that night. The Caliph planned to embark on a trip through his domain next morning, but two of the items he had ordered from Abu Jalal — a golden traveling cloak and a flowered house robe — were not yet finished. The tailor and his two assistants were forced to toil through the night, cutting and stitching for the privilege of keeping their heads, come the dawn.

The three worked diligently. One of the tailor's assistants was especially sleepy and yawned repeatedly. Abu Jalal lost his temper. "What's this big mouth you keep opening up at me?" he growled. "Are you intending to swallow me whole?"

"I'm tired," whined the assistant.

"And I'm not tired? Go out into the fresh air for a few minutes; that's bound to wake you up. If you continue yawning like that, I'll take that kettle over there and pour boiling water into your big mouth!"

The assistant put down his needle and thread and started going out to the street. He would walk a little, clear his head.

But no sooner had he reached the shop door than a strange sight met his eyes. Someone was leaning on the door, watching him.

In his confusion, the tailor's assistant did not notice the half-closed eyelids or the corpse's glassy stare. In the minutes since the doctor had left him propped against the wall, Nissim the Clown had slipped forward. He was now leaning against the tailor's door, head pressed against the security bars.

The assistant's suspicions leaped to the only logical conclusion: A thief was about to break into the shop! He stepped hurriedly back inside.

"Where's that kettle?" he hissed to his fellow worker.

"What do you need the kettle for?"

"To pour boiling water on the thief!" He pointed at the door.

His colleague jumped up. "A thief? A mere kettle won't be enough!" Without stopping to think, he seized the heavy, sizzling iron that stood ready to press the Caliph's new clothes. He ran to the door and, with a single fluid motion, flung it open and hurled the searing-hot iron right at Nissim's head.

The force of the blow made the "thief" crumple and fall to the ground.

"What happened?" shouted Abu Jalal, alerted by the noise. He ran out to see for himself. When he saw what his assistants had done, his eyes turned round as saucers. "Have you lost your minds?" he shrieked furiously.

"But I only threw the iron at him," the second assistant said, cringing. "I never thought he would die so fast!"

"What's the difference? The important thing is to get rid of the body." The tailor considered the matter anxiously, eyes darting in all directions as if seeking the solution to his problem.

"I have an idea," whispered the first assistant.

Once again, the clown's long-suffering body was dragged to the corner and propped up. The tailor and his two helpers took the trouble to make sure the corpse looked as lifelike as possible standing there.

Out of the darkness came the swaying figure of a drunkard, gripping the neck of his favorite bottle. Through the mists of his intoxication he saw Nissim leaning negligently against the wall of a house. It seemed to the drunkard that the dead man was smirking at him.

"Are you laughing at me?" the drunkard asked, coming closer.

Nissim's lifeless body made no reply. The drunken man took strong exception to what seemed to him a mocking silence. Lifting his whiskey bottle, he delivered a crushing blow to the clown's head.

For the fourth time that night, Nissim toppled onto the ground.

To the drunkard's ill fortune, the city's night patrol chanced to pass that way at precisely this moment. They witnessed the act of the drunkard "killing" the other man with a bottle to his head. The drunk man was arrested.

Next day, the drunkard — now quite sober — was hauled up before a judge.

"It's true that I killed the man," he said. "But I was drunk at the time!"

The judge didn't think much of this defense. "If you turn murderer when you drink, and you drink every day, then you constitute a public menace." And the judge sentenced the "murderer" to death.

Giant posters sprouted all over the city, announcing to the public that on the following Tuesday, at noon, the drunkard would be hanged for the murder of Nissim the Clown.

The posters aroused violent reactions in three different places around the city.

Alfonso Mizrachi, reading one of them, raced home at once.

"The clown died because of you," he told his wife, "and now another innocent man will die. Go turn yourself in to the police. May your death be your atonement!"

His wife, yielding to her husband's authority, placed herself in the hands of the law.

Ovadiah the doctor also read the poster. Someone else was going to suffer the consequences of his own actions! His conscience gave him no peace. It was impossible that an innocent man would pay the price for what he, Ovadiah, had done. He informed his wife and children that he intended to give himself up to the authorities. They protested vehemently to this plan. The commotion was so loud that some neighbors summoned the police. As soon as the uniformed men came, Ovadiah confessed to the murder of Nissim the Clown.

In his spacious shop, Abu Jalal the tailor held a conference with his assistants.

"Only Heaven and we ourselves know who really killed Nissim," he said soberly. "If I keep silent, then I am guilty as well. Let us go to the police and tell them what really happened that night."

The High Court judge was bewildered. He had never encountered a problem quite like this one. Here were four people, each confessing to the same murder! And each of them said he had done it in a different place and under completely different conditions. How to find the truth? Who was the real killer?

The judge puzzled over this question for a long time, but found no solution.

"Only the Jews' *chacham*, R' Yosef Chaim, can help me," he decided at last. That same day, he paid a secret visit to Baghdad's Chief Rabbi.

The courthouse was packed to the rafters. Everyone was very anxious to see how the court would deal with the extraordinary case that had become the talk of the town. Silence fell as the judge stood up and faced the crowd. The air tingled with expectancy as he began to speak.

Then the judge dropped a bombshell.

"Gentlemen, we have before us four people who have confessed to the accidental murder of the same man — and there are clear proofs to convict each one of them. And yet, I say — they are all innocent!"

The courthouse erupted in a shocked and excited babble. The judge pounded with his hammer for quiet.

"Nissim the Clown died for his sins, convicted by Heaven for his frivolous and satirical humor which so easily leads others away from the correct path. I have heard that the Jews have a concept that they call *arba misos beis din* — the four court-inflicted deaths. I declare here and now that Nissim received his punishment in the form of these four deaths:

"*Sekilah* — Stoning: He received this punishment when he fell down the stairs.

"*Sereifah* — Burning: He was burned by the scorching iron.

"*Hereg* — Killing: Nissim was killed by the drunkard.

"*Chenek* — Strangulation: The fish bones choked him at the party."

The vast crowd, Jew and non-Jew alike, began to murmur with admiration at these wise words. But the judge was quick to add, "What I have just said is not my own. It was the holy Rabbi, R' Yosef Chaim, who revealed this truth to me. He is the one who opened my eyes!"

WHY THE REBBE LAUGHED

THE *TZADDIK* OF APTA, R' AVRAHAM YEHOSHUA HESCHEL, WAS renowned in his youth for his holiness and righteousness. He was no less famous for his learning, being well-versed in Torah, sharp and analytical, and astute at rendering *halachic* rulings. R' Avraham Yehoshua started his rabbinical work in the city of Kolovsov. From there he moved to Apta, where he served for eight years before moving on to Yasi, in Romania. At the end of his life, he served as rabbi in the Baal Shem Tov's town of Mezibuzh.

The Apter Rebbe was distinguished from his fellow *tzaddikim* by his special turns of phrase, which translated into parables of great depth and hidden meaning. More than once, the Rebbe stated that this was his soul's tenth visit to this world, and that in a previous *gilgul* he had served as *Kohen Gadol* during the Second Temple era. His intimates, standing close during the Yom Kippur *Mussaf*, would hear him whisper to himself, "And this is what I would say; and this is how I would count." The Rebbe of Mezibuzh, R' Baruch, would say of the Apter Rebbe, "He has a weight of gold in his mouth." And the author of the *Chidushei HaRim* once remarked, "I have never seen a mouth as clean as that of the Apter Rebbe!"

From far and near, on foot or by carriage, people came to bask in the Rebbe's presence. Those who strove to grow spiritually viewed him as their guide in rising upward, while the simpler masses came to pour out their troubles and pain, to tell him of sickness at home, and to beg the Rebbe's blessing for a speedy salvation.

One Shabbos, a newcomer came to Apta. His name was R' Asher Lemmel of Miroslav. He was then but a young man, and a single glance at his pure eyes was enough to tell an observer that he had never in his life strayed from the tent of Torah. Humility and sweetness crowned R' Lemmel like a garland of roses.

This being his first visit to Apta, he was considerably taken aback when he took his place in the long line of men waiting to greet the Rebbe. The Apter Rebbe took one look at R' Asher and broke into a broad smile.

"*Shalom aleichem!*" said the Rebbe. As he extended his hand, there was laughter in his voice. R' Lemmel was startled. It was clear that the Rebbe had somehow recognized him. But from where?

On Friday night, a large crowd gathered in the *beis midrash*, where the Rebbe conducted his *tisch*. As morsels of the Rebbe's food were passed out, the *gabbai* called out, "Asher Lemmel of Miroslav!" No sooner had the name been sounded than the Rebbe's face brightened. And when R' Lemmel came up to take the *shirayim* from the Rebbe's own hand, the Rebbe laughed softly again.

The young man felt uneasy. Why had the Rebbe laughed? He strained to think, but came up with no reasonable explanation.

During *Shacharis* on Shabbos R' Asher Lemmel was summoned to the Torah. As he made his way up to the *bimah* by the most direct route, he passed close by the Rebbe's seat. He met the Rebbe's eyes — and there it was again. The Rebbe was looking at him and laughing.

For Asher Lemmel, Shabbos turned into a day of uneasy brooding. Seeing him, the Rebbe had laughed three times! However hard Asher

Lemmel tried to figure out why, he could not understand the reason for the laughter. Who knew what the holy Rebbe saw in him? R' Lemmel searched his actions and picked through his memories, all the way back to forgotten childhood days, but ended with no more clarity than he had had before.

At last, he made up his mind. On *motza'ei Shabbos*, when he parted from the Rebbe, he would ask outright, "What is my error, and how have I sinned?"

But when *motza'ei Shabbos* came, there was no need to ask. The young man had hardly crossed the threshold when the Rebbe began to laugh merrily. As he laughed, he clapped R' Lemmel affectionately on the shoulder.

"Please, let the Rebbe tell me how to atone!" R' Lemmel cried in despair.

"Why?" the Rebbe asked in astonishment. "What is your sin?"

"I know that secrets stand revealed to the Rebbe that other mortal eyes cannot see. The Rebbe has probably discerned some great flaw in me, and is laughing at my weakness!" R' Lemmel's voice trembled and tears began to trickle from the corners of his eyes.

"Heaven forbid!" the Apter Rebbe exclaimed. "If only there were more Jews like you! A precious young yeshivah man, filled to the brim with Torah and *mitzvos* — what is there for me to laugh at?" The Rebbe paused. "But you are doubtless wondering why I laughed when I saw you."

The young man nodded his head vigorously.

"I will tell you a true story," said the Rebbe. "An old, old story..."

The sun beat on Chananyah ben Gamliel's head as he made his way from his village in the upper Galilee to the city of Jerusalem. The air was as hot as the inside of a furnace. The entire world seemed to have fainted from the heat.

His donkey seemed on the point of passing out as well. It dragged its feet as though there were weights attached to them, and from time to time stopped to fill its lungs with steaming air. But Chananyah did not let the donkey rest for long. "Have pity on me and get me to Jerusalem with great speed," he pleaded. And the donkey, as though blessed with human understanding, began to step more rapidly, as if she had indeed taken pity on her master, so anxious to reach Jerusalem and find atonement.

Chananyah, like his brothers in the Galilee during that era when the Second Temple stood in its glory, was a simple man of the fields, an ignorant farmer. He hardly knew the shapes of the *alef-beis*, and only with difficulty pronounced the words of *davening*. But *yiras Shamayim* (fear of Heaven) burned in his breast!

A mighty awe of his Creator hovered over Chananyah and his brethren, night and day. And if this was the case during the week, how much more so on Shabbos! "The ignorant sense the awe of Shabbos," said our wise men, and they were thinking of simple Jews like Chananyah when they said it.

A shadow of sadness crossed the farmer's face. His spirit was downcast as he remembered, for the thousandth time, the purpose of this journey up to Jerusalem.

It had been a Friday night, and Chananyah, fed up with his own ignorance, had decided to learn a little Torah. He sat at the table with its flickering candle, straining to read from the parchment scroll unrolled in front of him. The weak light made reading nearly impossible, and he kept moving the scroll closer and closer to the candle.

Chananyah had heard about the *halachah* that our Sages set forth about refraining from reading by candlelight on Shabbos, lest one come to adjust the candle, the better to see. He had heard about it, but he did not truly understand the prohibition until he himself stumbled on it. The flame flickered violently in a sudden draft of wind and nearly went out. Hastily, without thinking, Chananyah reached out and adjusted the earthenware dish in which the candle sat. The wick straightened and the weak light began to burn steadily again.

Suddenly, Chananyah realized what he had done.

The entire episode had taken only a second. Chananyah smacked his head, wailing, "Woe is me, for I have desecrated the Shabbos! I have desecrated the Shabbos!"

His family came running at the sound of his cries. They tried to comfort him, pointing out that his action had been completely inadvertent. "It was a total *shogeig*."

"But I was *mechallel Shabbos*," Chananyah kept repeating through his bitter tears. He saw *Gehinnom* opening up at his feet, and the blood drained from his face until he was white as a sheet.

His family managed, with difficulty, to calm him. They reminded Chananyah that the *Beis HaMikdash* still stood in Jerusalem, and that he could sacrifice a sin-offering and find atonement for his sin.

These words breathed fresh life into Chananyah. "I will go up to the *Beis HaMikdash*," he declared joyously. "I will appease my Creator for what I have done to anger Him!"

Two weeks had passed since he had set out on his journey. The days were long and dry, the entire land simmering under a heat wave. There were times when Chananyah wondered if the dusty, winding road went on forever. There seemed no end in sight.

But one day, the hot air turned cooler, and the tall Judean hills loomed at the horizon. After only one more day, Chananyah stood at the gates of Jerusalem.

The *Beis HaMikdash*, glorious in its beauty and uplifting in its holiness, stood out atop *Har HaMoriah*, visible from a far distance.

"I rejoiced when they told me, 'Let us go up to the House of G-d,'" Chananyah murmured as he brushed away an emotional tear. With every bit of speed he could muster, he hurried to join the long line of men waiting to bring their sacrifices.

The *Kohen* looked at him compassionately. "You want a lamb as a sin-offering? And what sin did you commit, my son?"

"I accidentally desecrated the Shabbos," Chananyah replied with downcast eyes.

"'And He is merciful, He will atone for sin.' Come, let me choose you a choice, fat lamb suitable for a sinner like yourself!"

The *Kohen* disappeared from view, only to return a moment later leading an immaculate white lamb.

"Go over there, to that group of *Kohanim* — and may this serve you as an atonement." It seemed to Chananyah that there was a trace of disdain in the *Kohen's* voice as he spoke.

"The *Kohanim,* servants of Hashem, are wholly separated from the material and cannot bear having a sinner in their midst. Not even an accidental one," Chananyah thought. Head hanging, he brought his lamb to the designated place. As the animal tripped lightly after him, its feet tapping on the stones, Chananyah's cheeks burned with shame. He felt accusing stares pierce him from every side. It seemed to him that everyone was pointing at him: "There is the sinner who angered his Creator. He has come to Jerusalem to sacrifice a lamb, and thinks that he will have done his duty thereby. The lamb will be slaughtered, its blood will be sprinkled, and he will be acquitted."

By the time he reached the *Mizbe'ach* (Altar), Chananyah's insides were churning. As luck would have it, the *Kohen* appointed to him was known for his strictness and severity.

"Why and for what purpose have you brought this sin-offering?" the *Kohen* asked with a keen glance. Chananyah wished that the ground would open up and swallow him whole.

"I must know what sin this sacrifice is for!" the *Kohen* repeated sternly.

"I desecrated the Shabbos by accident," Chananyah whispered.

"What, exactly, did you do?"

"I moved a candle."

"And how is it that you came to err in this matter?" the *Kohen* admonished. "Haven't our Sages warned us not to read by candlelight?"

The *Kohen* went on to deliver a lengthy rebuke. Chananyah's eyes filled and overflowed with remorseful tears. Even before the lamb was led to the slaughter, Chananyah had done complete *teshuvah.* Brokenhearted and trembling, he stood by his sacrifice, thinking, "I am the one who should have been slaughtered. It should have been my blood sprinkled on the *Mizbe'ach,* and my fat burned."

"When a person was obligated to add a libation to his *korban,*" the Apter Rebbe continued telling Asher Lemmel, "he had to go to a different part of the *Beis HaMikdash.* The walk from the first place to the second was performed under the public eye. Everyone could observe the sinner as he went by. As the Levites sang, they would suffuse the atmosphere with purity and spiritual loftiness, bringing everyone within hearing distance to love of G-d and total remorse. The sinners would sense the songs piercing their very innards. They almost preferred to hurl themselves on the ground and wither away with awe.

"And then, one Shabbos, that strict *Kohen* himself desecrated the Shabbos inadvertently."

Realizing what he had done, the *Kohen's* eyes darkened. He, the *Kohen* who rebuked and admonished others with his sharp tongue, must now undergo the humiliation of offering his sacrifice like any frivolous sinner.

He brooded until he came up with a clever idea. On the following day, he summoned his favorite student — one of the younger *Kohanim* — and whispered in his ear, "Are you loyal to me? This is what has happened… Now, you go and bear the shame in my place."

A short time later, the student led a snow-white lamb to the Altar. Behind him, at a considerable distance, walked the elder *Kohen,* doing his best to act as though there were no connection at all between himself and the student.

As the young *Kohen* went along with the lamb, his thoughts were not pleasant ones. They were all directed at his teacher. "With your fiery tongue you wish to scorch all the world's sinners, good and worthy Jews, pious and G-d-fearing men who stumbled in their innocence. On these people you heaped humiliating rebuke and scoldings until their ears rang.

"But now, when Heaven has shown you that even a *tzaddik* like you can stumble accidentally into sin — you are seeking to escape your shame. You want your student to pretend that it is *he* who is bringing the sin-offering. You will come up to the *Mizbe'ach* afterwards and quickly offer the animal, and no one will be the wiser."

At that moment, the rope slipped out of the young *Kohen's* hands. The lamb, sensing its newfound freedom, began to race away.

"Catch it!" the student shouted at the top of his lungs. He gestured frantically at the elder *Kohen,* walking behind. "Catch that lamb, it belongs to my Rebbe."

"Quiet!" hissed the older *Kohen*. "Don't shout out loud!"

But his student pretended not to hear. With a lunge, he managed to grab the rope and to pull the lamb around to follow him once more. But just a few steps later, the rope "slipped" through his fingers a second time. Once again the lamb began to run.

The student's shouts reverberated through the courtyard. "Please, merciful brothers, catch my Rebbe's sin-offering before it gets away!"

The lamb was finally captured once more... until the rope mysteriously slipped yet again.

The amusing incident did not quickly leave the onlookers' memories. They would long remember the story of the racing lamb, the young *Kohen* screaming, "Catch my Rebbe's sin-offering!" — while the older *Kohen* pleaded with his student not to shout out loud.

"When you came to me yesterday," the Apter Rebbe concluded, "I recognized you at once. You are a *gilgul* of that student, the daring young *Kohen* who taught his teacher a bitter lesson. One glance at your face, and I immediately remembered the entire episode. That's why I was filled with laughter." The Rebbe paused. "But there is something you should know: You are obligated to rectify your sin. Perhaps that is why your soul was sent back down to this world."

"Sin?" Asher Lemmel asked in surprise.

"Yes. While the older *Kohen* needed to pay for his sins, it was still improper for you to embarrass a person publicly — and in the *Beis HaMikdash*, of all places! Let us talk now about your rectification, your *tikkun*."

THE VILNA GAON
HELPS A CHASSID

THE TOWN OF BILITZ, IN GALICIA, WAS KNOWN FOR THE healthfulness of its clean, invigorating air. Ringed by stately trees, the town was cut in half by a broad river that divided the section called Bilitz from the portion known as Biala-Bilitz. Many tubercular patients and individuals suffering from other lung ailments came there to recuperate. Numbered among them were Torah and *chassidic* leaders from all parts of Galicia and Poland.

As the day edged towards dusk, they would emerge into the bosom of nature to fill their lungs with pure air that wafted among the fields and forests. They would enjoy vibrant Torah discussions as they let their bodies heal from the exhaustion incurred by arduous and unceasing spiritual labor.

One not infrequent visitor to healthful Bilitz was R' Avraham of Sochatchov, author of the *Avnei Nezer*, who had suffered from lung ailments since his youth. Towards evening, when he wished to walk out into the fields and meadows, other illustrious convalescents would accompany him, to bask in the wisdom to be learned even from the Rebbe's most mundane conversation.

One evening, the Sochatchover Rebbe prepared to set out on his daily walk. Accompanying him were the Rav of Bilitz, R' Aharon Halberstam, grandson of R' Chaim of Sanz (the *Divrei Chaim*), and the *chassidic* Rav, R' Yoshe (Yosef) Frankel (father of R' Shabsi Frankel, publisher of the "Frankel *Rambam* and *Shas*"), who were then living in the town.

The three strolled among the trees. When they tired, they sat on a bench beside a broad tree trunk, a gentle breeze playing with their beards. The rabbi of Bilitz, noting the contented look on the Sochatchover Rebbe's face, decided that the time was right to broach his question.

"Pardon me, Rebbe, I wish to ask if it is true that when the Rebbe was a young man reaching marriageable age, a match was suggested with the daughter of a certain prominent Rebbe." He named the Rebbe in question, then continued, "I know that, for various reasons, the *shidduch* did not take place, and that you afterwards married the rebbetzin, daughter of the Kotzker. Is the story true, or is there nothing at all to it?"

The Sochatchover smiled. He nodded his head, and said, "It is true enough. But I have no regrets about the suggested match not going forward. That first Rebbe, a truly elevated person, was 'an important man' — while my esteemed father-in-law, the holy Kotzker, was a 'man of truth' that had no equal. And that makes all the difference."

His two companions sat quietly, holding their breaths. After a short silence, the Sochatchover said thoughtfully to Rabbi Halberstam, "If you wish to know what I mean by 'a man of truth,' let me tell you a story."

THE SOCHATCHOVER'S STORY

After I married (the Sochatchover Rebbe began his tale), I lived for a certain period of time with my holy father-in-law. The awesome Kotzker, whose holiness lit up the firmament and whose utterances made all of Poland tremble, was a destitute man who lived in a one-room flat — which he shared with his daughter and son-in-law. He lived in the room's inner section, while we stayed in the front part. It was in this tiny space that I sat and learned day and night. A thin wooden partition divided both portions.

One day, as I sat learning, there came a knock on the door. I left my *Gemara* and went to open the door. On the doorstep stood a book-seller, a sack bulging with *sefarim* over his shoulder and a pleading look in his eyes.

"Please, buy a *sefer* from me," the man said. "I've been walking from town to town to earn my living, and have arrived now in Kotzk. It is a great *mitzvah* to help me."

"And what do you have to offer?" I asked.

"A very important *sefer*: the *Gra's* commentary on the *Shulchan Aruch*."

"How much does it cost?"

Without hesitation, the bookseller named the very high price of three rubles!

"Three rubles?" I exclaimed. "That's an outrageous price by anyone's opinion! It is a full week's salary for a man. Where do you come to ask so much for a *sefer*?

The bookseller was not flustered by my outburst. "Young man," he said, "this is a very important *sefer*. If you want to buy it, you must pay my price."

Deeply upset, I cried, "In that case, it appears that a *chassidishe* young man cannot buy the *sefer*. The price is too high!"

My shouting brought my father-in-law to the door. "What is the meaning of all the noise?" he inquired.

As the bookseller stood looking on, I explained the situation to my father-in-law. He heard me out, then said, "Buy the *sefer* and pay the three rubles."

A triumphant smile spread over the bookseller's face. Stunned, I asked with great reverence why I should take part in such an outrageous deal.

The Kotzker Rebbe answered, "For a *sefer* by the Vilna Gaon, it is worthwhile paying three rubles."

I was struck dumb. Tranquilly, my father-in-law continued, "And do you know why? Because the Vilna Gaon was a 'man of truth.' If you want to know why I call him that, I will tell you a true story. Listen ..."

THE KOTZKER'S STORY

One of the righteous disciples of the *Maggid* of Mezritch suffered from extreme poverty and destitution. Indeed, who at that time did not suffer from deprivation? But this particular man's lot was one of the most grinding kinds of poverty. His home was devoid of furniture and food, but not devoid of people to feed — especially daughters, with which the man had been blessed in abundance. These girls had reached marriageable age, but not one of them was married because of their father's terrible poverty. No young suitor wanted to marry into the family because there was not so much as a single kopek to serve as the girls' dowry.

In deep distress, the disciple turned to his Rebbe, the *Maggid*, and poured out his troubles. He had grown-up daughters but no money. The *Maggid* said, "Go to Lithuania, to the city of Vilna. There you will find your salvation."

The man was taken aback at this advice. Vilna was hardly a center of *Chassidus*. On the contrary, it was the home of the Vilna Gaon, who together with the other *misnagdim* strenuously opposed *Chassidus*. This was the place in which he was to seek his salvation?

But the disciple had long since accustomed himself to yielding his own opinions to those of his Rebbe, like the Baal Shem Tov's students who had faithfully believed that a G-dly spirit hovered over their Rebbe, permitting him to serve as a conduit for messages from on High. If the Rebbe said to travel to Vilna, fortress of the *misnagdim* — then to Vilna he would go!

The man wasted no time in preparing for his journey. That same day, he borrowed money from friends to cover his traveling expenses, packed a meager bundle with his Shabbos clothes, *tallis*, and *tefillin*, and set out.

When he arrived in Vilna at the end of a tiring and difficult journey, the man began to search for a place where he might lay down his bundle. Seeing a stranger in town in need of lodgings, people directed him to a certain inn where passing merchants stayed. This type of inn was not particularly cheap, but the *chassid* paid out the greater part of his money, put his belongings in his room, got hold of a large *Gemara*, and began to learn.

There was a small *shul* in the inn, where the businessmen and guests *davened*. The *chassid* sat there from morning to night, learning Torah with enormous diligence. The Rebbe had told him to travel to Vilna, but had not said a word about what he was to do once he got there. He was doing, therefore, what his Creator had told him to do: "*V'dibarta bam*, And you shall speak in words of Torah."

Three days passed in this manner. On the fourth day, the innkeeper summoned the *chassid* and said, "Listen, Reb Yid. For my part, you can sit here and learn to your heart's content. I won't bother you; on the contrary, I am earning money for each day that you stay. But you're going to run through all your funds in a short time if you go on this way."

The *chassid* made no answer.

"I understand that you came to Vilna with a certain purpose in mind," the innkeeper continued. "If you will consent to tell me why you've come, perhaps I can help you."

"It is true that I came with a purpose," the *chassid* said. "I am and have always been a very poor man. I have grown daughters at home, and my teacher, the *Maggid* of Mezritch, has instructed me to travel to Vilna, where he says I will find my salvation!"

The innkeeper did not react furiously to the news that his quiet guest was none other than a *chassid* who had dared set foot in Vilna. He did not turn the man away. On the contrary, he respected the guest as a righteous man and an obvious *talmid chacham*. The guest did not waste a moment away from Torah in pursuit of frivolous things, but instead pored over his *Gemara* night and day.

Another man had overheard the conversation between the innkeeper and the *chassid*. Laughing, he said, "In that case, I think it's well worth your while to go to the *beis midrash* of our great Rebbe, the 'chassid' R' Eliyahu. He delivers a *Gemara shiur* there every day. In my opinion, you'll find your salvation there!"

The mere mention of the Vilna Gaon's name made the *chassid* reel. He soon calmed himself, however, and reflected that the comment had no doubt been instigated by Heaven. He left the inn and made his way to the Vilna Gaon's *beis midrash*.

Complete silence engulfed the *beis midrash*, except for the Gaon's voice, reading the *Gemara*, explaining it, and rendering commentary on every word. He rejoiced over the Torah as though it had been freshly handed down at Sinai. Every new question and answer illuminated what came before and further clarified the subject at hand: The Vilna Gaon spoke *Toras emes*, the Torah of truth.

The Gaon reached the *Tosafos*. He was reading aloud the words of *Rabbeinu Tam* to his large audience, when a sudden question occurred to him. It was a difficult question, a query hard as stone, a door made of wood that no carpenter could splinter. Some of those listening tried with all their might to find a solution, but their efforts smashed like waves against obdurate rock.

The Vilna Gaon could not continue his *shiur* until the question was resolved.

The silence in the *beis midrash* became tension-filled. The Gaon sat deep in thought, doubtless reviewing the entire Torah in search of a solution to the puzzle. Nothing he had ever learned was forgotten.

From the corner came a whisper. The newcomer, the *chassid*, had recently heard a *shiur* from his Rebbe, the *Maggid* of Mezritch, in which the identical question had been raised — and answered. The *chassid* whispered his Rebbe's solution to the man sitting beside him.

His neighbor's eyes lit up. A few minutes' thought told him that the answer was the correct one. Unable to keep his excitement to himself, he whispered what he had heard from the *chassid* to the man next to him. The room was soon abuzz. At last, the answer reached the Vilna Gaon's ears. He listened, stunned.

"It is truth! It is truth!" A pause. "Who is the man who came up with this answer? I wish to see him!"

They pointed out the stranger, sitting modestly in his corner.

The Gaon called out to him. "This answer — where did you find it?"

"It is not my own," the *chassid* answered. "I heard it from my Rebbe."

"And who is your Rebbe?"

Steeling himself, the *chassid* answered bravely, "My teacher and Rebbe is the holy *Maggid* of Mezritch, disciple and successor to the Baal Shem Tov, may his merit protect us."

"And where did your Rebbe hear the answer?"

"He heard it from the author himself. *Rabbeinu Tam* appeared to him and gave him the answer!"

The Gaon sat lost in reflection for a time. Then he asked the stranger what his business was in Vilna. The *chassid* related the sequence of events that had brought him to that place. At once, the Vilna Gaon summoned two of his students and ordered them to make their way through the entire town, from *beis midrash* to *beis midrash*, from house to house, and from inn to inn, to collect money for the *chassid* until he had what he needed to respectably marry off his daughters.

"A man such as this," declared the Gaon, "who has a Rebbe great enough to hear an answer directly from *Rabbeinu Tam* himself, is worth collecting money for — a dowry for his daughters!"

Upon his return to Mezritch, the *chassid* understood clearly how true his Rebbe's prediction had been. He had found his salvation in — of all places — Vilna!

⸙

"When my father-in-law, the Kotzker Rebbe, finished telling me this story," the Sochatchover told his spellbound companions, "he went on to say, 'The Vilna Gaon was the leader of those who opposed *Chassidus* in general and the *Maggid* of Mezritch in particular. He knew very well that the guest in his *beis midrash* was a member of the group he despised. And yet, he did not refrain from heaping praise where praise was due, and even helping the *chassid* to his fullest capacity. He was a man of truth!'"

THE SOAP FACTORY MYSTERY

ELKANAH LUDMIR'S SOAP FACTORY WAS NOT AMONG THE largest in the Ukraine, but it was successful enough to comfortably support R' Elkanah, his factory manager, Shaul Chaikin, and twenty other workers. One of the best of these was young Oleg Petrovski.

Oleg was tall, red-cheeked, and the picture of health. Sharp-eyed and energetic, he always seemed to be exactly where he was needed at precisely the right moment — and where was he *not* needed? "Oleg!" was a call heard frequently on the factory floor. He was strong; when a huge barrel of oil had to be lifted, who could do the lifting without straining himself? Oleg, of course. When the machinery broke down and it became necessary to take it apart, piece by heavy piece, who volunteered to scrape away the immovable layers of rust? Oleg!

There was no question about it: Oleg's contribution to the manufacturing process was immeasurably higher than that of any other worker in the factory. From Monday morning until Friday afternoon, Oleg breathed life and energy into the factory. He even slept in one of the rooms there, not returning to his own home until the end of Friday's working hours.

Shaul Chaikin, the manager, noticed that a cloud seemed to darken Oleg's eyes as the time came to return home. He would arrive at work happily enough, but when Friday afternoon rolled around his manner became reluctant and gloomy. Shaul often wished to exchange a word with Oleg on this topic, but Oleg avoided talking about it. And what was there, after all, to relate? That he and his father hated one another, heart and soul? That his father, a longtime drunk, demanded that Oleg hand over every ruble he earned so that he himself might spend it in the nearest tavern? That Oleg was carefully saving up some of his earnings, penny by penny, so that he might set up a home of his own someday.

All the time he spent at home, from Friday afternoon until Monday morning, was one long torture session of shouting and quarreling, always ending with his father beating Oleg bloody. It was his father's good fortune that Oleg was a well-mannered young man who harbored some vestige of respect for his parent; otherwise, he would have seized the stick from his father's hand and hit him back, the way other youths among his people were capable of doing.

One Saturday night, the father grabbed his stick and struck at Oleg with all his might, screaming, "Give me your money!"

In his thirst for the cash, the father redoubled the force of his blows until they were truly murderous. Oleg became genuinely frightened for his life. He took out all his savings — the arduously accumulated earnings of five long years — and handed the bundle to his father.

"You thief!" the older man shrieked hoarsely, eyes bulging with fury. "And you wanted to hide all this from me?"

He tucked the bundle greedily under one arm and made straight for the tavern. Before his eyes danced row upon row of full whiskey bottles, and foaming beer pouring straight from the barrel into his dry mouth.

Oleg watched him go, then burst into tears. All his labor, the hard-earned salary of five years, gone to dust in a single instant.

He tossed and turned, sobbing bitterly, all through the night. As the dawn approached, his father entered the house, swaying and stag-gering in the way of all drunkards. Oleg's spirits sank to a new low. What was the point of such a life?

He got out of his tangled bed and returned at once to the factory. He had a key, because both R' Elkanah, the owner, and Shaul, the manager, trusted him implicitly.

Shaul Chaikin walked into the factory on Sunday morning. This was something he enjoyed. The gentile workers were absent on that day, and the machinery was silent. On Sundays, Shaul would sit with the business ledgers and do his accounting. He patrolled every inch of the factory and noted what repairs were needed.

This Sunday was fated to be different from all the others.

As Shaul stepped onto the factory floor, his eyes were drawn upward as though with a magnet. There, above the giant cooking vat, hung Oleg Petrovski.

A single glance was enough to tell Shaul the whole story. Oleg, depressed of late, had chosen to end his life through hanging.

But why had he chosen to do so in the factory?

This was a question that could be reflected on later. Right now, Shaul had more important things on his mind. They were living in anti-Semitic Russia. If it became known that a gentile had died in a Jewish factory, both he and Elkanah Ludmir would be thrown into prison for many years. The prosecutor might even sentence them to death. In fact, there was no "might" about it — it was practically a certainty! And, on top of that, there was potential for a blood libel here. In that case, the town's entire Jewish population was in danger as well.

Shaul's mind spun and whirred like a wheel. How to get rid of the body?

Then, suddenly, he had the solution. It was Oleg himself, ironically, who showed it to him.

Shaul did not enjoy what he had to do in the following two hours. His gorge rose and his insides churned rebelliously at the strange antics he was forced to perform. But he had no choice. He had to protect his own life, and the lives of every Jew in town. In particular, he must guard Elkanah Ludmir's life. His boss was spending the morning contentedly at home, with no idea in the world of the trouble from which his devoted manager was extricating him.

Shaul worked diligently and deftly. Within hours he was done. Tomorrow, when the great fires under the vats were ignited, the remains would become part of one solid mass of fresh soap that would bear its secret forever in its depths.

Next morning, everyone wondered what had kept the industrious Oleg from coming to work. Shaul made sure to be among those asking the questions. R' Elkanah and the others assumed that Oleg had caught a chill and had taken to his bed for a day or two.

When Oleg did not return home at the weekend, his mother became worried. Ever since the last tremendous row between her husband and son, she had been prey to a growing anxiety. She waited another day or so, and finally went to the police.

The police came to the factory the next day and conducted a thorough search. Two neighbors testified that they had seen Oleg enter the factory with his key on the previous Sunday, early in the morning.

R' Elkanah, in his innocence, disclaimed any knowledge of Oleg's whereabouts. He hadn't seen his worker and had no idea where he might be. Shaul, his manager, said exactly the same thing. It was Shaul's good fortune that the police officers did not press their ears to his chest, where they might have heard the wild pounding of his heart.

Then the two witnesses revised their account. They now claimed to have seen Elkanah Ludmir stab Oleg to death with a long knife! R' Elkanah was brought up before a judge that same day. After several days' imprisonment, the judge informed him of his trial date. R' Elkanah was released on bail.

His first stop after winning his freedom was not his own home. R' Elkanah made straight for his Rebbe, R' Yisrael of Ruzhin, and poured out the tale of his trouble. His story was disjointed, as R' Elkanah himself had no idea what had actually happened to Oleg, or the part that his manager had played. All he knew, and all he could relate, was that Oleg had disappeared, that a blood libel had been instigated against him, Elkanah, and that if he did not succeed in proving his innocence, he was headed for the gallows!

The *tzaddik* assured him solemnly that no harm would befall him.

"And," the Rebbe added, "Oleg will yet be found."

The trial date arrived. Oleg had not been found in the interim. R' Elkanah was taken by carriage, under heavy armed guard, to the large courthouse in Kiev. The local priests in R' Elkanah's hometown had been busy stirring up feeling against the Jews, and they urged their co-religionists to travel to Kiev to attend the trial. They came out in droves, following the prison carriage to the courthouse for the pleasure of hearing the judge sentence the Jew to death.

The line of wagons and coaches following the prison carriage was very long, and it attracted a lot of attention. A group of fishermen, noticing the procession, asked where it was headed. When they heard that the people were on their way to a trial to investigate the sinister disappearance of Oleg Petrovski, they burst into derisive laughter.

"Oleg Petrovski? But he's alive!"

"Alive?"

"*Alive?*"

"Where did you see him?" someone shouted in open disbelief.

The fishermen retorted, "We saw him just now, transporting passengers in his little boat from one bank of the river to the other."

"Are you sure?" the others asked, shocked to the core.

Half-laughing, half-shouting, the fishermen replied, "Don't you think we know what Oleg looks like? May our nets always catch the biggest fish if we tell you that we saw him just moments ago, just a few meters away, standing and arguing with a couple of people who wanted to cross the river and pay less than his usual fare. 'Whoever does not pay twenty kopeks does not cross,' Oleg yelled at them. And you're telling us that he's dead? Are you out of your senses? Go and see for yourselves!"

At these words, the entire procession turned and made for the river. Among the crowd was Oleg's father and the police officers. Even before the group reached the riverbank they could discern, in the distance, Oleg Petrovski's familiar features as he stood tall and red-cheeked, arguing energetically with a group of passengers about his fare.

Stunned, they shouted, "*Oleg!*"

Oleg glanced across at the shouting figures. At the sight of his father, he paled. "Father, what are you doing here?" he called.

The father ran to his son. "You ask me why I've come? Why did you disappear like that, without a word? Everyone thinks that the factory owner murdered you!"

"Why did I disappear?" Oleg screamed. "Because of *you* — that's why I disappeared! I was sick and tired of you, a miserable drunk who stole five years' salary from his own son just to waste it on whiskey!"

The father's joy at seeing his son alive was swallowed in a wave of rage. The blood rushed to his head as he roared, "Is this how you embarrass me in front of all my friends?"

He raised his thick fists and began to shower heavy blows on his son. This time, Oleg did not stand idle, but raised a fist to punch his father back. The police officers intervened to separate the two men. Then, unexpectedly, Oleg burst into tears. "Was it not enough that you beat me day and night?" he wailed. "Can't I even escape you? I can't bear this life any longer. This life is no life. I prefer to end it!"

With that, in front of the entire crowd of dazed spectators, Oleg leaped into the river and sank immediately into its depths.

The Kiev judges considered dismissing the case, then decided for the sake of order — the vaunted Russian bureaucracy — to hold a quick hearing. The case ended with a total acquittal for R' Elkanah, absolving him of all blame.

Overjoyed, R' Elkanah planned to make directly for Ruzhin. His factory manager asked to join him on the trip, and naturally R' Elkanah agreed. Together, the two traveled to see the Ruzhiner Rebbe.

R' Elkanah heaped praise and thanksgiving on Hashem for saving him. Happily, he told the Rebbe, "Your promise that Oleg would be found alive and well certainly came true!" Then he went on to describe the way Oleg had thrown himself to his death in the river, and the resulting court verdict.

The Rebbe rejoiced with him. He was on the point of parting with both men when Shaul Chaikin hesitantly cleared his throat. "Forgive me, Rebbe. May I speak?"

Humbly, Shaul went on, his spirit in turmoil. "I want to ask the Rebbe something. Your *chassid*, R' Elkanah, really knows nothing. He thinks that Oleg actually ran away from his father and was then found on the riverbank. But I know the truth about what happened. I can't believe in fairy tales. It was I who found Oleg hanging from his neck in the factory. With my own hands I dealt with his body; I was forced to turn him into soap, to prevent a terrible blood libel that might have affected every Jew's life." Shaul drew an anguished breath. "Perhaps the Rebbe can reveal to me how one brings a gentile back to life when he's needed?"

The Ruzhiner gazed at Shaul thoughtfully.

"I will tell you a story," he said. "A true story about *Stam Baal Shem*. The story will help you understand how this thing occurred."

Yossel was in grave trouble. The plot of land that he leased from the *poritz*, Janek Favelovitz, was not producing a large income, but the *poritz* — in the manner of all landowners — kept on raising the rent. In vain did Yossel protest that he barely made enough money to feed his wife and children; the *poritz* raised the leaseholder's rent each year, and the Jew's debt grew apace.

After a long waiting period, the *poritz's* patience suddenly ran out. "Either pay the rent in full by the end of the week," he thundered, "or I will throw you and your family off the land!"

Yossel derived a small but definite measure of comfort from the fact that the *poritz* had not threatened to throw them all into his dungeon. Still, he and his family stood in very real danger of losing their sole source of livelihood in very short order.

In great distress, he went to see his Rebbe, who was known as *Stam Baal Shem*. He cried and pleaded with the Rebbe for salvation.

"Heed my advice," the Rebbe said, "and act in a very daring and brazen manner. Go to the *Poritz* Favelovitz tomorrow and demand fearlessly: 'Who made you owner of this property? Show me your documents! Prove to me with legal title papers that you have the authority to charge me rent.'"

Yossel did not sleep much that night. All through the dark hours he tossed and turned, picturing the *poritz* seizing his gun and shooting him, Yossel, in a towering fury. When dawn came, he *davened Shacharis* and begged his Creator to grant him the strength to carry out the Rebbe's instructions.

Davening completed, Yossel went to the *poritz's* stately home. He banged on the door and asked to see the *Graf* in person. The guards, recognizing the leaseholder, told him to wait while they inquired of their master.

Graf Janek Favelovitz was still slumbering soundly at that hour of the morning. The guards' knocking on his door did not rouse him. They redoubled their efforts, pounding on the door with all their might, until the *Graf* was torn from the depths of a sweet dream. He leaped out of bed and ran to the door.

"What do you want?" he shouted at his servants.

"The Jew Yossel has come to see you, sir."

"Yossel's come? He must have brought the money." The *Graf* began to wake up. "Let him in without delay!"

Yossel entered the room with his head held high. A quiet confidence flowed through him, replacing the fears that had haunted him through the night.

"Have you brought the money?" demanded Janek Favelovitz.

"No," Yossel replied calmly.

Enraged, the *poritz* flung aside his pillow and removed a gun. He pointed it at the leaseholder. "Yossel, you're a dead man!"

But Yossel had steeled himself a thousand times the night before against just such a scene. The *Graf* was still dazed with sleep. Yossel smacked his hand aside, sending the gun flying through the window.

"Just a minute, you wild animal," Yossel said through his teeth. "Do you think that I'm a fox in the woods, to be shot at in a hunt? First of all, prove to me that you're the legal owner of this property. Show me your documents! Only when I see that you are the true master of this land will I agree to deal with you."

Yossel himself could hardly believe the words that were coming from his own mouth. He spoke coldly, with unaccustomed courage. His morning prayers, and the Rebbe's blessing, had infused him with a fresh new strength.

The *poritz* seemed utterly stunned. He turned first pale and then red as he stammered, "Wh-wh-who told you that I don't have title papers for this land? Not even my own wife and children know it! Yossel, do me a favor — don't give me away to the police!"

It was impossible to recognize, in the fear-ridden man standing before him, the proud, furious *poritz* who had threatened him with a gun a moment earlier. The landowner's proud spirit had been broken and every vestige of his arrogance swept away.

With an uncanny calm, Yossel said, "When you threatened to have me thrown off the land, I went to see my Rebbe. He is a holy Jew. He is the one who told me that you have no legal claim to this land, or the authority to charge me rent for it, because you have no title papers."

Terrified, the *poritz* sat speechless. Several moments passed as he mulled over Yossel's revelation. At last, he said, "Your Rabbi is right. I don't have any papers. But he is not completely right: I am indeed the legal heir to this property."

He stood up and began to gather his clothing. "Yossel, let's make a deal," he said placatingly. "Let's go together to your Rabbi. If he can see everything with some sort of spiritual power, then maybe he'll agree to take another look around and tell me where the ownership papers are located.

"If we find those papers, then you can live on your plot of land for free for the rest of your life!"

⚬ ⚬ ⚬

Stam Baal Shem showed his two visitors a map of St. Petersburg. "Do you see this section here?" He indicated a circle on the map. "That is where you will find the man who holds the title papers proving your legal claim to the property."

The *Graf* Janek Favelovitz did something that was not at all common among the gentiles, and especially not among the *poritzim*. He girded himself with complete faith in the Rebbe's pronouncement. Without a moment's hesitation he set out that same day for St. Petersburg, with Yossel as his companion.

They wandered through the city for several weeks, until the *Graf* reached the point of despair. The neighborhood that the *Stam Baal Shem* had indicated on the map did not exist. Deeply disappointed and frustrated, the *poritz* made plans to leave the city. "Yossel, you are the only person who knows that I don't have the papers. If you don't make trouble for me — if you don't reveal my secret to a soul — then I will keep my promise to you. I will let you stay on the land, rent free."

Yossel tried to lift the *poritz's* spirits. "Listen, *Graf* Favelovitz, sir. If the Rebbe knew with his holy vision that you have no papers, then he also knows that it is here in St. Petersburg that you will find them. Don't lose hope."

Janek Favelovitz allowed himself to be persuaded. He agreed to remain in the city for several more days.

On the following morning, the two set out to stroll through the city streets. When they began their walk, the sun was shining and the air was pleasantly warm. Then all that changed, seemingly in an instant. The skies darkened with heavy clouds, and a shrieking wind heralded a sudden downpour. The two men were totally unprepared for such a dramatic change in the weather. They ran to and fro, like a couple of street cats, seeking shelter.

In the distance, they spotted a mansion with light coming from the windows and smoke from the chimney. "There's a good place to shelter," the *poritz* shouted hopefully into the noise of the rain and wind. "Yossel, run up and knock on the door!"

Yossel did as he was told.

The door was opened by a maid, well wrapped in a warm shawl. Yossel asked to see the master — urgently.

Presently, standing by a fireplace where orange flames leaped and flickered among the logs, Yossel explained to the master of the house that an honored guest was waiting at the door. The *Graf* Janek Favelovitz was seeking shelter from the storm.

"I would receive him gladly," the master of the house replied. "However, at the moment I have another *poritz* staying here as my guest, and he is already settled into my guest room. If your *Graf* is willing to share the room, he can be my guest as well."

He went up to the door of the guest room and knocked deferentially. An elderly *poritz*, hair and beard white as swans' down, opened the door.

This old *poritz* exclaimed in astonishment, "The *poritz* Janek Favelovitz is here? Of course he can come in. I am his great-uncle! Janek is the grandson of my dear, departed sister."

Two minutes later, the two *poritzim* were joyously embracing.

"Uncle Peter Brodsky!" Janek Favelovitz cried emotionally.

"My Janek!" crowed the old man. He thumped his great-nephew affectionately on the shoulder. "My dear Janek, how did you know to come here at precisely this time? Do you know how many years I have been searching for you?"

"You've been searching for me?" Janek echoed in amazement.

"Certainly, certainly. The title papers for your property are in my possession. I am getting on in years, and may leave this world any day. You would have been shorn of your inheritance. Here — take these documents and guard them well. They prove your ownership!"

As he spoke, the old *poritz* pulled a sheaf of papers from a desk drawer. They were old documents, stamped with the government seal.

When he could speak, Janek asked, "Where do you live these days, Uncle Peter?"

"In Holland."

"Shall I travel back with you and accompany you home?" Janek realized that his great-uncle was very aged and must be looked after.

"No, no," the elderly *poritz* waved away the offer. "Go home with these papers. The first thing to do is to see an attorney and have him confirm your legal claim to the property. When you are the land's legal owner, come see me then, in the Hague."

He handed his great-nephew a small piece of paper with his address in Holland, and the two parted fondly.

After the documents had undergone legal scrutiny, Janek Favelovitz was confirmed as the property's legal owner. Then he and Yossel traveled to the Hague, in Holland, to personally thank the old *poritz*.

On their arrival, they asked people about Peter Brodsky, certain that the whole city must know of him. But not one person they asked knew him. Janek Favelovitz and Yossel began walking up one street and down another, searching for the address they wanted.

Imagine their amazement when they found the house — only to discover that a complete stranger lived in it!

"Peter Brodsky?" the resident asked in surprise. "How strange that you mention his name. He hasn't been alive these fifteen years!"

"Fifteen years?" Janek and Yossel shouted in unison.

"Yes. I bought this house from his heirs immediately after his death. I've been living here for fifteen years."

Yossel and the *poritz* stared at one an other in mingled shock and wonder.

"Now do you understand?" the Ruzhiner Rebbe asked Shaul Chaikin. "If it is possible to bring back to life an old *poritz* who has been in his grave for fifteen years, just to help a Jew pay his rent — how much more so — with a blood libel hanging over the heads of an entire Jewish community — can a young gentile come back to life after being dead only a few weeks!"

Shaul Chaikin gave the Rebbe a shrewd look. "Am I permitted to understand that the story that happened to *Stam Baal Shem* actually happened to the Rebbe himself?"

The Rebbe murmured, "*Nu*, if that's the way you want to tell the story."

THE CHASAN WHO WANTED FOUR FLATS

WHEN GENENDEL, OLDEST DAUGHTER OF BEREL TRIVITCH, reached marriageable age, her father felt as though he had plunged suddenly into a whirlpool. He had never before grasped the meaning of *Chazal's* statement: "Making a match for a person is as difficult as splitting the Red Sea." When he himself had been ready to marry, he found his bride quickly and easily. Now, in trying to marry off his daughter, he found himself stumbling like a blind man in the wilderness.

Genendel was a fine girl of many qualities, and the matchmakers soon became constant visitors in Berel's home. They came in a steady stream, one hardly taking his leave before the next one arrived. They brought with them respectable matches: This one was a good boy, son of a *talmid chacham*; that one, from Zhitomir, already had a teaching certificate; the other young man from Shnipishuk was both amiable and smart. The poor father's head fairly swam with all the various names and suggestions, and he prayed to Hashem to grant him the insight to pick the right husband for his daughter. He prayed, too, that Genendel might marry a Torah scholar whose fear of Heaven preceded his wisdom.

One day, a new matchmaker arrived on Berel's doorstep. He had come from Radom with an enchanting proposal. The prospective groom hailed from Chenistechov, Poland, and was reputed to be a brilliant young man well-versed in all aspects of Torah. He was both physically handsome and unblemished in his *middos*. In short, proclaimed the matchmaker, no less than an *"esrog mehudar"*!

From the first, the matchmaker had asserted that this was one offer that Berel would not be able to refuse. And so it was. Hearing the litany of the young man's praises, the father was prepared to sign on the dotted line right there and then.

"Wait a bit," the matchmaker said, with a twinkle in his eye at Berel's enthusiasm. "I must travel to Poland now to hear what the boy's parents have to say."

The next few weeks ran Berel's nerves ragged. At last, one day, the matchmaker returned. With a broad smile that betokened victory, he exclaimed, *"Nu,* if the *chasan* and *kallah* consent we can break the plate now, may it be a lucky hour!" He paused. "There's just one little obstacle to get out of the way first, though."

"Obstacle? What's that?" asked Berel.

The matchmaker measured Berel with his eyes. "This boy knows his worth. He wants a *hoif* — that is, a complete courtyard."

Berel frowned. "What does that mean?"

"I can see you are not very experienced. A *hoif* is a courtyard surrounded by several apartments — four, as a rule. The *chasan* wants to be able to immerse himself in Torah without worrying about earning a living after he marries. Therefore, he requests this dowry: a courtyard with four apartments. He'll rent out three of them, and he and his wife — your daughter — will live in the fourth. The couple will have a fixed monthly income from the rents, and you will be freed of the burden of *kest* (support)." The matchmaker fixed Berel with a determined eye. "Well? Can we conclude the *shidduch?*"

"Just how much does this *hoif* cost?" Berel asked weakly.

"Oh, something in the region of 5,000 rubles."

Berel nearly fainted. Such a fantastic sum was to be found only in the pockets of the very wealthy. "Who do you think I am, the owner of a fleet of merchant ships sailing all over the world? Or maybe I'm a great lumber man, with forests stretching from Lemberg to Yehopitz? I'm just a simple man, learning Torah and doing a little work. I've set aside a respectable dowry of 200 rubles." Berel caught his breath. *"Five thousand rubles?"*

The matchmaker was not unduly troubled. "Listen, what's more important to you, the money or this special boy? There are not many like him in all of Poland. *HaKadosh Baruch Hu* will help you pay."

At a total loss, Berel picked himself up and traveled to Berditchev.

The holy Rebbe, R' Levi Yitzchak of Berditchev, listened to Berel's account of the matchmaker's proposal. "The matchmaker is not exaggerating the young man's qualities," R' Levi Yitzchak said. "His name is familiar to me — a true gem, a find that does not come along every day. Take out a loan and conclude the *shidduch*, with good *mazal*!"

Berel was weak-kneed. "But I don't know a single rich man who would lend me 5,000 rubles. And not only that, even if I did find such a man, where will I find the money to pay back such an enormous loan?"

"Calm yourself," R' Levi Yitzchak said. "There are men like that. I will provide you with a written recommendation to one of them."

"And how do I pay back the loan?"

"This, too, is no question. You buy merchandise worth 5,000 rubles, travel to the great fair at Lemberg and sell the merchandise at three times the price. You then use one-third to pay back the debt, one-third to buy the *hoif*, and the last third will provide an income for you and your family for years to come!"

Berel had never engaged in the business of buying and selling before. R' Levi Yitzchak sat and taught him the rules of commerce, in meticulous detail.

Berel reached Lemberg on the first day of the big fair. Accompanying him was a large flock of fat oxen, and two men who might have been either cattle merchants or simple shepherds. These men led the herd to a large clearing, surrounded them with a tall wooden fence, and provided the cattle with feed and water. The oxen began at once to recuperate from the rigors of the journey, lowering their heads to munch the fresh green grass. Berel ordered the two men, "Remember, don't come down in price. Sell these oxen for three times what other cattle merchants are selling them for at the fair."

With that, Berel went off to the *beis midrash*, where he sat learning from morning to night. His employees stayed with the cattle, indifferent as to whether customers came or not; Berel had promised to pay them in full in either case.

Potential customers came to inspect the cattle. They marveled at the superior condition of the beasts, and asked their cost. When they heard it, they reeled back. "Are you out of your minds, asking such a price?"

"We are not merchants," the men said. "We are just day-workers. The owner of this herd hired us to stay with the oxen, to make sure none are stolen, and to state their price. If an interested customer comes along, we're to let him know."

The prospective customers left empty-handed, and made straight for the competing cattle merchants at the fair.

A day passed, and then two. Each day, people would come to inspect the oxen, marvel at their superior quality — and then leave without buying, after hearing the inflated price. Everyone agreed that the herd's owner was clearly not a sensible man. He was paying workers, paying to rent space at the fair, and was destined to leave with nothing.

On the last day of the fair, as most of the other merchants were counting their profits and gathering together their unsold goods, not a single ox of Berel's had found a buyer. His workers were untroubled, as their salaries were secure in any case. As for Berel, he continued to learn peacefully in the *beis midrash*.

Suddenly, a minor commotion broke out among the other merchants. The quartermaster in charge of supplying meat for the army had arrived. He had come to purchase oxen for slaughter, to feed the soldiers. As he went from herd to herd, he frowned. Only the weakest and most ill-favored cattle remained to be sold. These were the oxen that no one else had wanted to buy, of inferior quality, scrawny and tough beasts whose meat was not fit for the king's soldiers.

Then the quartermaster came to Berel's herd — and his face lit up. Here were young, fat oxen, a feast for the eyes, each one of higher quality than the one before. The quartermaster approached the two workers, desirous of concluding a deal on the spot ... until he heard the price.

"What's this?" he exclaimed, taken aback.

The workers directed him to the *beis midrash*.

The quartermaster tried to intimidate Berel. "Are you insane? In two hours, the fair will be over and you will lose your entire investment!"

"I don't care," Berel said quietly.

The quartermaster quailed. He held a contract for the royal armies, for which he was obliged to supply a certain quantity of fresh meat. Cleverly, he had found a way to earn a nice little profit for himself. Each year, he'd wait for the last day of the fair, when the cattle merchants were eager to get rid of their remaining stock, even at a loss. Usually, the remaining oxen were a decent lot... but this year, they had been the worst of the worst. This year, his well-oiled plan had failed.

The quartermaster continued to try to bargain with Berel, but his heart was not in it. Inwardly he had already resolved to pay the ridiculous price that this hard-headed Jew was demanding. The expense was nothing when compared to the severe punishment he could expect at the hands of the military authorities should he not fulfill his obligations.

After a lengthy but fruitless debate, the quartermaster paid Berel a full 15,000 rubles for his entire herd of cattle.

Happy and satisfied, Berel prepared to journey home. But first, he needed to thank his benefactor. He traveled to Berditchev, where he gave R' Levi Yitzchak 5,000 rubles, saying, "Here are 5,000 to pay off the debt, 5,000 for the dowry, and 5,000 to the holy Rebbe who set me on the correct path. I know my own worth and the way my luck usually runs. If not for the Rebbe, it would not have been in my power to earn even a single ruble."

On his return home, he hastened to summon the matchmaker from Radom. Not many days later, his daughter became engaged to the brilliant young man from Chenistechov. His friends and neighbors, hearing of his good fortune, rejoiced with Berel. Then the rumors began to spread: Berel had paid a king's ransom as dowry for his daughter. One of his friends came to him and asked bluntly, "Is this rumor true?"

"Yes, it is."

"But — how?"

Berel related the entire story.

That same day, the friend harnessed his horses and rode to Berditchev. "I need the same thing that Berel needed," he told R' Levi Yitzchak. "I, too, have a grown daughter."

R' Levi Yitzchak asked, "Are they also asking you to provide a complete *hoif*?"

Sheepishly, the man admitted that he had not yet been asked to provide such a thing. Yet he wished to marry off his daughter to a *talmid chacham* who could sit and learn Torah without money worries. Why should his portion be any less?

But R' Levi Yitzchak sent him away with a curt, "Where do you come making such requests? Berel came with a practical purpose, and you have not!"

The man had no sooner left than the *tzaddik's* heart began to trouble him. He scolded himself, "For weeks now the sum of money has been sitting in your drawer, waiting for you to do some great *mitzvah* with it. Now this Jew comes along, and you let him leave empty-handed? Perhaps this is the great *mitzvah* you've been waiting for?"

He ordered the man fetched back at once. When the man stood before him again, R' Levi Yitzchak handed him the entire sum that he had received from Berel — 5,000 rubles!

THE BROKEN PROMISE

A LARGE GROUP HAD GATHERED IN THE MARKET SQUARE. A single burning topic was on everyone's lips: the closing of the *mikveh*. On the previous day, police officers had paid the place a surprise visit.

"This looks like the work of Feivish, the talebearer," Berish, the bath attendant, muttered angrily. The police had hung heavy padlocks on the *mikveh* doors and then, as though to underscore the message, had added a large sign proclaiming, "THE *MIKVEH* IS CLOSED."

"But why?" the people wanted to know.

"The Black Plague — have you forgotten?" Berish said angrily. "Feivish told the authorities that the *mikveh* waters are not clear enough. The authorities were only too glad to concur and they ruled that the water is polluted. In fact, they say it may be this very water that caused the Plague!"

In the following days, the Jews came up with an ingenious plan for circumventing the ban on their *mikveh*. They employed the talents of Hershel the Thief — a man who, it was whispered, could open any door. Hershel performed his little trick, and the people were free to immerse themselves in the "locked" *mikveh*.

But Feivish the talebearer was no sluggard, either. Within a short time, he was trotting back to the authorities with the news that the Jews had found a way to outmaneuver the ban. Officials were sent to investigate. Furiously, they attacked the *mikveh* building, destroying the pools and spilling out the water. By the time they left, not a brick of the old *mikveh* was left standing.

The Jewish community reeled. Then, when they had recovered somewhat, community leaders called an urgent meeting to discuss the problem. Matters could not continue in this way. Clearly, a new *mikveh* would have to be built.

"But where will we find the money?" asked Chaim, one of those participating in the meeting. The city's Jews were poor. There were no men of means to be found — except one. He was Shimon, a wealthy manufacturer whose palatial home lay at the outskirts of town. But Shimon was notoriously tight-fisted. He had never, to anyone's knowledge, given charity in his life.

The community leaders debated the question and considered their options. Some suggested that they embark on a fund-raising campaign in the city; another proposed sending messengers to Lodz and Warsaw. But both ideas were deemed impractical. Then the Rabbi stood up. Hesitantly, he said, "Why don't we try to soften Shimon the Miser's stony heart? We can explain to him the urgency of the situation, the great *mitzvah* involved, and the reward that would await him in *Gan Eden*."

No one at that meeting believed that the plan had the slightest chance of working. Still, out of respect for their Rav, they appointed a delegation of solid citizens to visit Shimon's home. Using every persuasive means they knew, they presented their request to him and earnestly explained how vital his help was.

Shimon the Miser understood completely. He consented to contribute the sum of one zloty to the cause.

Enraged, the delegation hurled the zloty to the ground right in front of the rich man's eyes. Then they left his home, acutely disappointed.

The Rabbi of the city realized that the situation was not good. He decided to travel to nearby Kaminka, to ask the *tzaddik,* R' Shalom, for his advice and blessing.

R' Shalom listened to the story. "Have you no source of funds at all?" he asked.

The Rabbi admitted that there was one individual who was capable of donating the full sum. But that individual was a miser whose nature abhorred parting with his money.

R' Shalom thought for a moment. "I have an idea," he said with a smile. "In two weeks, I will come to spend Shabbos in your city and will remain for several days. In all probability, the wealthy Shimon will also wish to come and see me. *Nu,* we'll think of something."

Two weeks later, the Jews of the city turned out as one to welcome their exalted guest. No one stayed at home that Shabbos except the elderly and the infirm. Everyone streamed to the tables that had been set up for the *tzaddik* in the city's largest *shul.*

On Sunday morning, R' Shalom of Kaminka *davened Shacharis* together with the *shul's* congregants. Then the *gabbai* announced that the Rebbe would receive the public. Whoever wished to speak to him would be welcome.

Shimon the Miser was one of the last to come. Perhaps, on some unconscious level, he understood that the Rebbe wished to help him merit the *mitzvah* of *tzedakah.* He put off his visit until he heard that R' Shalom was preparing to leave the city the next day.

Immediately, he went to the Rebbe's lodgings, seeking the great man's blessing.

"What kind of blessing do you want?" the Rebbe asked. "Children, health, a livelihood?"

Shimon considered. "Children? *Baruch Hashem*, I have them. A livelihood? I have enough. But my life has become a *Gehinnom*. I have no peace at home. My relationship with my wife is terrible. She embitters my life and seeks quarrels all day long!"

"The thing to do is to appease her," the Rebbe counseled. "Bow your head and apologize, to make her happy."

Shimon shook his head. "I am a humble person, Rebbe. But the situation is awful. I am finding the woman 'more bitter than death.' I have already appeased her a thousand times, but new fights break out every other day. For at least the past ten years, my life has lost its flavor."

R' Shalom switched tracks. "In that case, you are not required to suffer. Give her a *get* and set her free!"

"*Oy*, Rebbe," Shimon sighed from the depths of his heart. "That's impossible. I was irresponsible when I married her, and wrote a *kesubah* promising her a huge fortune should I ever divorce her."

"Then what can I do for you, my son?" R' Shalom asked in distress. "I cannot find a solution for your problem."

R' Shimon lowered his voice, as though afraid of the words he was about to utter. "There is a solution. The Rebbe might pray that she die."

"*What?*" R' Shalom recoiled as though bitten by a snake.

Again, Shimon sighed. "I am not a cruel man, Rebbe. But I am in over my head. To live with her is impossible, and so is divorcing her. If she were to die, all my troubles would be over."

Closing his eyes, R' Shalom sat lost in thought. At last, he shook his head with finality. "Listen here, my friend. To pray that a Jewish daughter depart from this world is forbidden! Even with respect to completely wicked people, we may only pray that they repent — that the sins end, and not the sinner's life." The Rebbe paused. "But you do have it within your power to behave in such a way that will cause your wife to leave this world."

"How?" asked Shimon quickly.

"The *Gemara* [*Shabbos* 32] says: For sins related to broken vows, a man's wife will die. If a man makes a promise and does not keep it, he can cause his wife, Heaven forbid, to depart this world. Make a vow and do not fulfill it, and the rest will follow on its own!"

"Rebbe," Shimon said urgently. "Please, tell me what to vow."

R' Shalom threw him a shrewd glance. "I've heard that the city's charity collectors have asked you to donate money to build a *mikveh* — and that you have refused."

"True," Shimon averred.

"*Nu*, must I elaborate?" the *tzaddik* exclaimed. "Don't you understand on your own what you must do?"

Shimon left the Rebbe's lodgings with his head awhirl. "What an idea!" he thought in admiration. "I will soon be a free man!"

On his return home, he sent at once for the charity committee. The messenger stressed the fact that it would be very much worth their while to pay Shimon a visit. The delegation flew to the rich man's home as if on the wings of eagles. In their haste, they paid no heed to the lavish gardens stretching across his estate, or the costly beauty to be seen on every side. They hurried up the stairs to the spacious front hall and waited to hear what the master of the house had to say.

"You surely remember that you came here asking me to donate money for a new *mikveh*," Shimon said. "At the time, I gave you one coin, which you hurled to the ground. But I have not asked you to come here in order to remind you of that, but rather to gladden your hearts!"

The delegation wondered where the miser was headed. Shimon pretended not to notice their skepticism. "How much do you need to build the *mikveh*?" he asked.

"One thousand five hundred zlotys."

"One thousand five hundred?" he repeated. "Here it is." Jumping out of his chair, Shimon grasped his *tefillin*. "I hereby vow by these *tefillin* to donate 1,500 zlotys for the city *mikveh*!"

The members of the delegation stared at one another, and at their host, in amazement. Had they heard right?

"So what do you think?" Shimon asked with a broad smile. "Could there be better news than this?"

"No," the other men confessed, radiant. "We never expected such wonderful news!"

Shimon escorted his visitors from the house. "You will receive the money this very day," he promised. "Good-bye."

From the window, he watched the small group make its way to the edge of his estate. Laughter bubbled up inside him. "Let me know when you get the money!" he called gleefully at the spot where the retreating forms had disappeared.

The future suddenly appeared rosy indeed.

During the next days, Shimon monitored his wife's health closely. He waited impatiently for the first sign of a cough or an ache — the first small clue that the Angel of Death was on its way. But she appeared as healthy as ever. His vow, apparently, had made no impression up above.

Shimon had his horses harnessed and traveled rapidly to Kaminka, where he once again entered the Rebbe's room.

"Is it possible?" he complained. "You gave me a 'segulah' that came to nothing. I made a vow, but my wife is still perfectly healthy!"

R' Shalom listened soberly. "Is that so? She's still healthy? Then there's no choice but to pursue the path of peace."

Disappointed, Shimon said, "But I've already gone that route, and it's failed. She simply has no interest in living in peace with me."

R' Shalom waved this away. "What was past is past. We will start a new chapter now. Go home, and tomorrow morning smile at your wife and offer a cheerful 'Good morning!' She will think you've lost your mind, but don't you mind that. Continue to behave in this way, smiling at her, giving her attention, fulfilling her requests — and always be cheerful. Give her the same smile and friendly 'Good morning' every single day."

As the Rebbe spoke, Shimon's heart dropped lower and lower. R' Shalom continued, "The *pasuk* says, 'As water reflects a person's face, so a person's heart is reflected in another's heart.' Someone has to be the first to start a magic circle of mutual feeling. If you let feelings of goodwill and love toward your wife enter your heart, she will also begin to feel them. Then peace will reign in your home, together with the Divine Presence!"

Shimon made the trip back from Kaminka with a leaden spirit. To him it seemed easier to climb the highest peak than to change his habits. Morning after morning, smiling … pleasing … What a dismal prospect. His dream of finding release through a broken vow had come to nothing.

He felt as though a stone was lodged in his throat when he forced out his "Good morning" the next day, and his smile was patently artificial. As for his wife, she gaped at him in astonishment and suspected that he had doubtless hit on a new way to enrage her. But Shimon clung to the Rebbe's advice and continued to behave the way he had been told. And, just as water will wear away the most obdurate stone, the old storehouses of anger and resentment gradually melted away. In their place came friendship and affection and peace.

For the first time in years, Shimon's heart began to wake from its long sleep. The daily "Good morning" emerged naturally now, and his smile became completely genuine.

And then, just as their home was filled with warmth and goodwill once more — Shimon's wife fell ill.

Just when they had put their foolish differences behind them and had begun to feel that their life together was a paradise on earth, Shimon's wife began to suffer from powerful pains throughout her body. They went to see the best doctors, but each one returned the same sober message: "There is nothing we can do. She has only a few months left to live."

Brokenhearted, Shimon returned to the Rebbe in Kaminka.

"Who would have believed it?" he sobbed. "Before, I wanted to see the worst happen. Now I know what a terrible mistake that was! But Heaven is insisting on punishing me. It seems that my prayers for her death were finally accepted. Heaven is about to take away my wife."

R' Shalom placed a gentle hand on Shimon's shoulder. "You must not speak this way. Do you presume to understand Heaven's ways? We have no dealings with such secrets. I'd like to show you a *Gemara*." He went to the bookcase and pulled down a *Maseches Shabbos*. Quickly he rifled through the pages until he came to *Daf 32, amud beis.* "'*Tania Rabbi Nassan* says: Through the sin of [broken] vows, a man's wife dies.'" The Rebbe turned to Shimon. "You made a vow to donate money for the *mikveh*. Did you fulfill that vow yet?"

"Oh, no!" Shimon smacked his head in dismay. "I forgot all about it. It completely slipped my mind!"

The Rebbe laughed, a full-bodied, heartfelt laugh. "The path to your wife's cure is clear, then. Give what you promised, and see how quickly she is restored to full health and strength!"

R' Chaim of Sanz would tell this story, concluding, "It goes without saying that the wife recovered. But we must definitely state that R' Shalom of Kaminka was not only a *tzaddik* — he was also a brilliant man!"

A FOUNTAIN OF WEALTH

TWO MEN WALKED TOGETHER. THEY WERE BOTH CALLED Naftali and they were both *tzaddikim*. One was R' Naftali of Lizhensk, grandson of the holy Rebbe Elimelech of Lizhensk; the second was R' Naftali of Ropshitz. The two walked together collecting *tzedakah* for poor Torah scholars. From house to house they went, amassing charity, penny by penny.

R' Naftali of Ropshitz noticed a carriage approaching from the other side of the street. "Now you'll see something interesting," he exclaimed to his friend. "Riding in that carriage is a rich man — R' Yosef. I think that Hashem has just brought the answer to our prayers. That man is going to hand us his purse and ask us to take as many gold coins as we want!".

"Who is he?" asked R' Naftali of Lizhensk. "I've never heard of such generosity before."

"In another moment, you'll have the answer to your question."

The horses galloped toward them, pulling the ornate carriage ever closer. Riding inside was a man dressed in the height of fashion, his clothes sewn by an expert tailor and a gold chain peeking from his waistcoat pocket, where a gold watch rested. The man's face was hearty and well fed, and his eyes sparkled. In short, he had the appearance of a person of cheerful temperament to whom life has dealt a kindly hand.

Seeing the two *tzaddikim* by the side of the road, R' Yosef immediately ordered his coachman to halt. He descended from the carriage and joyfully shook their hands. *"Beruchim haba'im b'shem Hashem!"* he exclaimed. "Welcome! What business brings the *tzaddikim* to my city?"

"We are collecting money for *tzedakah*," R' Naftali of Ropshitz explained. "It is for the benefit of the righteous poor who are not able to make ends meet."

At once, the rich man pulled a bundle of money from his waistcoat. Shining among the notes were a goodly number of gold coins. With a happy, generous air, R' Yosef cried, *"Baruch Hashem* that I have merited participating in a *mitzvah*! Reach out and take as much as you please. Don't hold back and don't feel sorry for my money."

Both men were deeply moved — not to mention astonished — at this tremendous generosity. Even R' Naftali of Ropshitz, who had heard much of R' Yosef's openhandedness, was speechless. After all, hearing about something does not compare to seeing it with one's own eyes.

"Why are you staring at me like that? Why don't you help yourselves?" R' Yosef urged. "I promise you that I mean what I say. I was not joking when I told you to take what you want. And in case you're afraid that I'll feel the lack of money, let me tell you this: However much you may take, you will not harm me by as much as a penny's worth. It's a case of one person benefiting while the second incurs no harm. So go on — take!"

"How can it be?" ventured R' Naftali of Lizhensk. "We know people who are blessed because they give *maaser* money. But someone who gives everything and lacks nothing? That is something we have neither seen nor heard of before!"

The rich man invited them to climb into his carriage. He seated them beside him on the upholstered seat and ordered the coachman to travel at a leisurely pace toward the fields surrounding the city. When the carriage was moving slowly among the vineyards and trees, R' Yosef began to speak.

"I see that you are amazed at this, and that you are concerned lest the source of my money be impure. Let me tell you how I merited my wealth, and you will agree that its source is blessed indeed."

Yosef had always lived in poverty. He supported his family in the most meager fashion by selling thick salted pretzels, known as "*beigelech*." As people became used to seeing him always wandering the street with his tray of pretzels, he naturally became known as "Yosef the Pretzel Man." Out of the small amount of money he earned, he had to pay the bulk to the baker who baked the pretzels; the remaining profit could be counted in pennies.

To supplement his income, he added a new line to his business. Every Friday, he would go into the kitchens of the wealthy. There he would set to work sifting flour, adding eggs, kneading dough, and preparing fine *challos* for Shabbos. (In those days, only the rich could afford to eat *challos* that had been baked in their own homes from white flour. Poor and even middle-class folk ate *challah* made without eggs, from the flour that was left over after the white flour had been sifted.)

For a time, this sideline improved Yosef's financial picture. The rich men in whose homes he baked *challah*, taking pity on his lined, hard-working face and on his children's hunger, paid him over and above the wages he asked. More than one would add some vegetables, a few eggs, a jug of wine, and another of milk.

The "good years" in Egypt lasted seven years; Yosef's lasted only six. Some of his "well wishers," envious of his good fortune, managed to spread cunning lies among his patrons, and ended by pushing him back into his former situation. His wife, realizing that it was impossible to support the family on pretzels alone, decided to lend a hand. She hired herself out as a maidservant in the homes of the wealthy, where she washed their clothes, scrubbed their floors, and, on Fridays, whitewashed the walls and polished the floors in honor of the Shabbos.

Her back ached from the difficult and endless labor, while Yosef's legs were sore from his ceaseless trudging with his tray of pretzels, which began at sunrise and ended when the stars came out. And still their income was scant; between them, they managed to earn only pennies. They could not afford to buy anything. There was one winter coat in their home; when Yosef wore it his wife would stay home, and when she wore it Yosef was forced to remain indoors because of the intense cold.

But neither one complained. They accepted their lot with love and did not question Hashem's will.

An even harder ordeal awaited the faithful couple. The three-week mourning period beginning with the 17th day of Tammuz arrived — a time when pious Jews do not paint their homes. During the final days of that period, they do not even wash their clothes. Both Yosef and his wife remained at home, weak and hungry, for they did not possess so much as a crust of bread for one meal. Yosef's legs were aching and sore, and he had to carry himself around on crutches.

At last, Yosef roused himself. "Why sit home doing nothing?" he thought. "I'd better go outside. Perhaps Hashem will send me something out there."

He went into the street and wandered about for a time. Suddenly, he heard a commotion. It was the sound of an approaching crowd, voices raised in excitement and celebration. A large number of men passed Yosef, all hurrying toward the market square. Yosef stopped one of them.

"Where is everybody going, and why all the excitement?"

The man answered over his shoulder, as his feet continued step-ping quickly along. "Haven't you heard? The great Rebbe, R' Zusha of Anipoli, has come to visit our town!"

Yosef had never heard of R' Zusha. He returned home and told his wife the news: A *tzaddik* had come to town and everyone was running out to greet him.

"In that case," asked his wife, "why did you return home?"

"What would you have had me do?"

"What everybody else is doing. Of such men it says, '*Tzaddik kata-mar yifrach,* A *tzaddik* flourishes like a date palm.' Why is a *tzaddik* compared specifically to a palm tree? The palm offers its frond as a *lulav,* its branches for *s'chach,* and its fruit for honey and eating. We benefit from the tree, therefore, both spiritually and physically. A *tzaddik* is the same. No one who comes near a *tzaddik* can fail to ben-efit. The *tzaddikim's* benevolence toward their fellow men benefits others both spiritually and physically.

"My heart tells me that this guest, R' Zusha, is such a man — one who distributes alms to the poor. Go ahead, tell him about our diffi-cult situation," Yosef's wife counseled. "He will doubtless give you a gift of a few pennies to sustain us."

"How will the *tzaddik* sustain us?" Yosef countered. "What will he give me? He himself is a guest at other people's tables!"

But his wife was undeterred. "Go anyway. Maybe he has a few pennies in his pocket. Go quickly, before he gives it all away."

"That's right," Yosef decided. "Many poor people will run to him and empty his pockets, leaving me with nothing. There's no use in my going at all."

"Go anyway. If he can't give you money, he will at least give you a blessing!"

Yosef heeded his good wife's advice and hobbled off on his crutches. The *tzaddik's* wagon proceeded slowly to the market square, the crowd following. The moment the wagon rolled to a halt, the Rebbe was inundated by the eager throng's enthusiastic greetings and requests for *berachos.* By the time Yosef finally made his labored way to the square, he found a huge number of people, young and old, sur-rounding R' Zusha's wagon. People shoved and jockeyed to get close to the wagon. Parents clutched their children's hands, lest they be lost in the crowd, while many others climbed up onto rooftops and other high places for a glimpse of the holy Rebbe.

Yosef stood to one side, afraid to submit his frail body to the press of the crowd. He could not approach any closer through the packed horde. Despite the efforts of some men to impose order, access to the Rebbe was impossible.

Suddenly, R' Zusha's voice rang out. "R' Yosef! R' Yosef! Come here to me!"

Yosef heard the call, but entertained not the slightest suspicion that it had been meant for him. He watched a long line of "Yosefs" form — Rabbis and Torah scholars, wealthy men and community supporters. All of them passed before the *tzaddik*. R' Zusha listened to them and replied to their requests, but did not tarry with any one of them.

"*Yosef Hashem aleichem!*" he quoted. "None of these men is the one I wanted. Isn't there another Yosef among you?"

Yosef understood at last that the Rebbe meant him. "My name is Yosef," he called in a feeble voice, as he began to hobble slowly into the heart of the crowd. When he reached the wagon, the Rebbe's face lit up. "Come closer!" he cried. "You're the one I called for!"

Yosef climbed onto the wagon. R' Zusha greeted him warmly. Holding the poor man's hand tenderly in his own, he gazed at Yosef for a long moment. "How do you support yourself?" he asked at last.

"I have no livelihood," Yosef answered sadly. "There is no bread in my house, and no clothing to wear. That is why I have come to Your Honor."

R' Zusha summoned his assistant. "Bring me a jug of honey-water," he ordered.

The assistant did as he was told, returning with a jug of honey-water and several large glasses. R' Zusha poured a tall glassful and handed it to Yosef, saying, "Drink it all up."

Yosef was not accustomed to drinking so much. Still, as the holy Rebbe faced him expectantly, he tilted up the glass and drained it to the last drops. R' Zusha exclaimed, "*L'chaim*, R' Yosef, *l'chaim*! What do you have at home?"

"My house is completely empty," Yosef admitted. "Just yesterday, I sold the last of my meager belongings in order to feed my hungry children."

"But something must be left," insisted the Rebbe.

Yosef thought. "Yes, I just remembered. There is one small box at home."

The *tzaddik's* countenance brightened. He took three coins from his pocket, totaling about twenty cents in value, and gave them to Yosef.

"Take these coins. When you get home, put them into the box, and from this day on you and your family will have abundant money for the rest of your lives. Whenever you need money, just reach into the box and take what you want!"

"I am Yosef the Pretzel Man," the wealthy philanthropist explained to the two illustrious Rabbis seated beside him in his carriage. "The Rebbe's blessing came true. The moment I put the three coins into the box, it became filled to the brim with coins. From that day on, I have known no want and have become a rich man. As much money as I take from the box, it continues to overflow with money, like an underground spring that grows ever stronger. I thank Hashem, Who has granted me the wisdom not to be short-handed when it comes to giving charity. And, indeed, why should I be stingy? As much as I take out, more money always flows in.

"That is why I urged you to take as much money out of my purse as you wish. It is not from me that you are taking it, but from the bountiful blessing of the *tzaddik*, R' Zusha of Anipoli, may his memory protect us all!"

THE WRONG MOSHE

"Yankel," THE *GRAF* SAID TO HIS JEWISH LEASEHOLDER, "your situation is very serious.

"Yaakov the Innkeeper's hair was already streaked with white. At his landlord's words, he suddenly looked twice his age. His erect posture became stooped and his eyes grew sunken. The *poritz* had been walking around with a face like a thundercloud for some weeks now. Yaakov was keenly aware of his debt to the Polish landowner, and the *Graf's* remark just now had sounded like the knell of doom. In a quavering voice, he asked, "S-serious? Why?"

The *Graf's* glance was cold as ice. "I met with my business manager the other day. He tells me that you have yet to pay a single ruble in rent for the entire past year! a hundred also bought twenty calves from me — plus two strong horses, a hundred chickens, seventeen bales of hay, and twenty bushels of turnips." He paused. "Have my figures been accurate so far? The total comes to 475 rubles, and we aren't done yet. Yankel, what do you intend to do about this?"

Yaakov trembled. The staggering sum of 475 rubles was not even the full extent of his debt! He didn't know how he was going to pay even a tenth of that amount, let alone the whole sum.

"Yankel," the Polish *poritz* continued sternly, "I have given much thought to the question of how to deal with you. You have been living on my property for the past ten years."

"And I have paid my rent faithfully in every one of them — till now," Yaakov broke in. An instant after he'd spoken, he regretted his outburst.

The *Graf's* eyes narrowed with cold-blooded cruelty. "Until now, I've dealt with you with extreme lenience. You are wrong! Your previous debt is not fully paid. You still owe me half the previous year's rent, bringing the total to a year and a half in all. And that is apart from the additional debts I've listed." He paused purposefully. "If you pay the full debt within thirty days, you can stay on the land and continue to run your inn as usual. However, if you do not pay me what I am owed, in one month's time you and your family will be banished from this town — forever!"

❧

Yaakov the Innkeeper was no common man. He had discovered the light of *Chassidus* years before, and from time to time made the trip to acquire wisdom at the court of his Rebbe, R' Shneur Zalman, author of the *Tanya*. In general, he made it a rule never to ask the Rebbe for help in the material areas of his life; all his requests when standing before the Rebbe dealt with spiritual aspirations. But now, with the threat of banishment hanging over his head, he saw no other choice than to travel to R' Shneur Zalman and ask his advice. With lightning swiftness, he saddled his horse and made his way to Liozna.

With a grieving spirit he poured out the tale of his woes. He explained that his debts had swollen because his expenses far outstripped his income, and that until now he had managed to pay the debt little by little, thanks to the *poritz's* patience. Now, that patience had run dry.

"If I don't pay it all back within thirty days," Yaakov pleaded, "my family and I will be thrown out into the street! I'll be forced to become a lowly beggar, going from door to door asking for handouts."

R' Shneur Zalman blessed the innkeeper from the depths of his heart, then asked, "What else do you wish from me?"

The question, Yaakov believed, had been asked from genuine *ruach hakodesh*, a Divine spirit. For how else would the Rebbe have known that there was, indeed, a favor that Yaakov wished to ask of him? In a broken voice, he presented his request.

"There is a wealthy Jew by the name of R' Moshe Peschovitch who has ready access to the *Graf's* house. This man has a tremendous influence over the *Graf*, so that nothing in the *poritz's* household takes place without R' Moshe's consent. If he asks the *Graf* to give Yankel the Innkeeper more time, there is no doubt in my mind that the *Graf* will listen.

"The problem is that I am only a simple Jew, and R' Moshe is a wealthy and well-respected one. I don't have the courage to go and speak to him myself. But if the Rebbe would write him a letter asking him this favor, R' Moshe would certainly not refuse. I've often heard him speak of the Rebbe with great admiration."

The *Baal HaTanya* did not delay for a moment. Sitting down at once, he dipped his quill in ink and dashed off a quick but detailed letter to R' Moshe Peschovitch. He folded the letter, placed it in an envelope, and handed it to the innkeeper.

"Go on your way, and may *Hashem Yisbarach* grant you success!" the Rebbe said, pressing Yaakov's hand warmly. Yaakov left the Rebbe's house in a joyful spirit.

In his happiness, he never thought of glancing at the envelope to see to whom it was addressed.

But the next day, before leaving Liozna, Yaakov did look at the envelope. To his dismay, he saw that the Rebbe had written, "*For his honor, R' Moshe Eizekovitz of Rovna,*" instead of "*R' Moshe Peschovitch of Kovno.*"

"If it's only the envelope that's wrong, that's not such a problem," he thought. "I can find some excuse to hand R' Moshe the letter without the envelope." He hesitated for a long moment before opening the envelope. Pulling out the letter, he read the first line — and the world turned black before his eyes. The letter, like the envelope, was directed to one "*R' Moshe Eizekovitz of Rovna.*"

What increased Yaakov's anxiety a hundredfold was the fact that he happened to know R' Moshe Eizekovitz of Rovna. The man had absolutely no connection with the *poritz* who owned Yaakov's plot of land, though he, like R' Moshe Peschovitch, owned a large tavern and inn. How in the world could R' Moshe Eizekovitz be of any use to Yaakov in his hour of need?

Running all the way, Yaakov returned to the Rebbe's house, letter in hand. He would beg for an urgent appointment with the Rebbe. At the door he found R' Shneur Zalman's son, the holy R' Dov Ber, who would later take his father's place as Rebbe. Recognizing Yaakov, he said, "You were just here yesterday. What do you mean by asking to see the Rebbe day after day?"

Yaakov explained the mistake in the letter, but R' Dov Ber shook his head with finality. "No. My father does not make mistakes. His eyes are wide open to see all that is necessary. My advice to you is this: Go give the letter to the person to whom it is addressed, and all will end up for the best!"

⁓ᴑᴄ⁓

Yaakov saddled up once more and rode into Rovna. Going directly to the inn owned by R' Moshe Eizekovitz, he handed him the Rebbe's letter without a word of explanation.

The prosperous Jew read the letter in wonderment. "I do not know this *poritz* of yours at all. How will it help if I give him advice?" He eyed Yaakov narrowly. "I suspect that you forged this letter yourself, and mistook me for someone else who is close to the *Graf*."

"Heaven forbid!" Yaakov exclaimed, jumping to his feet. "If I were permitted to swear to you, I would swear that our holy Rebbe himself wrote this letter with his own hands. But the second half of your remarks are true. There is another man with a name that is similar to your own — R' Moshe Peschovitch of Kovno. I asked the Rebbe to write the letter to him, but the Rebbe put your name in instead. The Rebbe's son advised me to place my trust in the Rebbe and bring the letter here, to you!"

R' Moshe Eizekovitz reread the letter, then sat lost in thought. "Even if I wished to help you," he said at length, "I do not know how I can do it. I have never met this *poritz* of yours, and he has never met me."

Yaakov sank into gloom. He stood in the inn's front hall, gazing sadly outside. Night had fallen over the town hours before, and a faint glow of candlelight gleamed from every window. The dark streets were peopled with shadowy figures hurrying home.

R' Moshe Eizekovitz turned to Yaakov. "Sit down and have some supper. After that, you can sleep here in my inn tonight. Tomorrow morning I will see what I can do for you. It is not a good idea to refuse a request from the holy Rebbe!"

The two ate supper together, recited the Grace After Meals with great devotion, said *Krias Shema*, and went to sleep.

They had scarcely dropped into sound slumber when a loud pounding at the door awakened R' Moshe. He ran to the door, shouting, "Who's there?"

"A *poritz*!" came the answer in an authoritative voice. "Open the door, for I am tired and hungry!"

The innkeeper threw open the door at once. The *poritz* and his retinue swarmed into the inn, ten men in all. Loudly, they set up a clamor for food and drink.

R' Moshe was used to this. His nights had long been like a broken wall through which anyone might enter at any time. He lit an oil taper, fired up the ovens, set the tables, and warmed some food for his unexpected guests.

The raised voices woke Yaakov. It seemed to him that one of the voices was familiar. Curiously, he left his room and stepped out into the hall.

"I wasn't mistaken," he whispered to himself, eyes wide as saucers. "It's my *poritz*. He has come here on the very night that I brought my letter to the 'wrong' R' Moshe!"

For a few minutes he stood motionless, watching the group feasting at the tables. At the earliest opportunity, he motioned the innkeeper closer and whispered excitedly, "Listen! That is the very *poritz* that the holy Rebbe asked you to speak to about me!"

R' Moshe was dumbfounded. "Are you sure?"

"Sure, I'm sure! Don't you think I'd recognize the *poritz* whose land I've been living on for ten years?"

"In that case," R' Moshe said in amazement, "this is surely the Hand of G-d! It is no coincidence. Both the letter and the subject of the letter came to me in the same day. It is a sign of Divine Providence. Quick, return to your room before the *poritz* sees you. I will put my mind to work and see how I can act on your behalf."

The next morning, when the *poritz* awoke, R' Moshe was assiduous in his attentions. He set the table with warm, freshly-baked bread, jugs of frothing milk, and a selection of fine cheeses. The *Graf* and his men ate their fill. At last, the *poritz* stood up, patting his full stomach contentedly. "Jew, what is your price?" he asked.

R' Moshe smiled. "You don't owe me a cent."

Taken aback, the *poritz* thought the innkeeper was joking. "Ten people were here with me. We ate two full meals. We slept in your beds and enjoyed the warmth of your ovens. All that costs money! I did not intend to receive it as a gift. Tell me what I owe and I will give it to you."

R' Moshe would not budge. "Honored *poritz*, let me explain why I do not wish to accept a penny for my hospitality. You see, I have a brother who is an innkeeper, like myself. I would ask only this: that you keep him close to you and treat him well."

"Gladly," responded the *Graf*. "And who is your brother?"

R' Moshe smiled. "His name is Yaakov, and he is the innkeeper in your village. He has leased his land from you these past ten years."

A flush of rage suffused the *Graf's* face. "Aha! You're talking about my Yankel? I know him well, that Yankel. He owes me a large debt, and because he has not paid it I've decided to take away his inn and give it to my Moshke's brother-in-law instead."

R' Moshe pleaded, "Please listen to me, honored *poritz*. It is true that my brother Yaakov did not pay his latest debts, but you must admit that he has never failed to pay before!"

"True," the *Graf* acknowledged reluctantly.

Encouraged, R' Moshe continued. "Every year, with great effort, Yaakov manages to pay off his debt. Only in the last two years have things been difficult for him, and his income has diminished to the point where he's found it impossible to pay what he owes. Because of this, Your Honor grew enraged and spoke of banishing him from his inn. Yaakov is an honest and dependable man. If you let him stay, G-d will help him and he will faithfully repay his debts."

The *poritz* thought for a while. Presently, he asked, "Where is Yankel these days? It's been a while since I've seen him."

"Do you miss him?" A broad smile spread over R' Moshe's face.

"A little," admitted the *poritz*. "To tell the truth, in general I've found Yankel to be quite a pleasant and loyal fellow."

Smothering his laughter, R' Moshe said, "I can arrange a meeting within minutes, if Your Honor wishes!"

"What? How can you do that?"

"You see, he, too, visited me recently." Raising his voice, R' Moshe called, "Yaakov, come here. The *poritz* wishes to see you!"

With slow, hesitant steps, Yaakov entered the room. Seeing the *poritz*, he rubbed his eyes in astonishment. Then he took the *Graf's* outstretched hand and warmly shook it.

Just minutes later, the three were sitting around the table, talking animatedly. The *Graf* said, "Yankel, I see that the same blood runs in your veins and in your brother Moshke's. Like you, he is a good-hearted fellow. He has fed and hosted me as well as ten of my men for free. In his honor, I will deal well with you. I will renew your rental contract on my land for another five years and supply free wine and liquor for your inn. As for your debt, you can pay that back over time, when things get easier for you. Don't worry about it. If not this year, then pay me in two years, or even three."

The new contract was immediately drawn up and signed, before the *poritz's* enthusiasm had a chance to cool off. As he handed it to his "Yankel," he confided, "You should know, Yankel, that I've always liked you. It would never have occurred to me to send you away. But a certain Jew who is an intimate of my house — Moshke Peschovitch is his name — had asked me to give your inn to his brother-in-law."

A SHOWER OF BLESSINGS

TWILIGHT SHADOWS COVERED THE TOWN OF KUZHMIR. IN the *beis midrash*, all was plunged into gloom until someone lit a few candles in simple brass holders.

The table bore the remainders of a meager meal. Crusts of black bread sat waiting for some hungry soul to polish them off. Several dozen men sat around that table, shoulder to shoulder, giving no thought to leftover food or other material concerns. Every sinew was focused on the white-bearded man in the center. It was apparent that the man was not well-to-do. In fact, his tattered coat and battered hat told their own tale of poverty and lack.

"You knew R' Levi Yitzchak?" asked R' Yechezkel in wonder.

"Certainly," replied the old man. "He lit a Chanukah candle in my home. He ate my bread and slept in my bed!"

"In that case, please tell us about him," begged the Rabbi, the holy R' Yechezkel of Kuzhmir. "On R' Levi Yitzchak's *yahrtzeit*, we want to hear a little from someone who had the privilege of actually knowing him."

"I was young then," the man said. "In those days, my beard was black as coal. I lived in a small village near Zelichov."

A freezing wind howled through the snowdrifts that concealed everything in sight. The man walking down the road stopped to mop the sweat from his brow. Even on such a frigid day it was possible to feel warm. When the heart is alight with the joy of doing a *mitzvah,* it heats the rest of the body with flames of holiness.

R' Levi Yitzchak glanced at the houses that made up the distant village. He was especially interested in the windows of those homes. Tiny lights twinkled there. The small flames danced in every passing breath of air, rising and falling and then rising again. It was the fifth night of Chanukah. Time to press forward and find lodgings, so that he, too, might light the Chanukah candles!

R' Levi Yitzchak quickened his pace until he reached a small hostelry. Its owner was not a man of substance, but Chaim Chaikel would happily give his last pennies to help support the village's poor. R' Levi Yitzchak knocked at the door and was received joyfully.

"Rebbe, I have been waiting since Succos! All summer long, I collected penny after penny. I have a respectable sum for you!" He handed a small bundle to R' Levi Yitzchak.

The *tzaddik* thanked him. "Would I be able to light Chanukah candles in your house?"

"Here? In my house?" Chaim Chaikel repeated, as if in a dream. "What a question!"

R' Levi Yitzchak set about preparing for the *mitzvah* with his usual vigor. He rolled wicks, poured oil from a small bottle that he carried with him, and recited the blessings with such fervor that the very walls of the humble house shook. Chaim Chaikel's neighbors came running to watch the *tzaddik* light his Chanukah candles.

R' Levi Yitzchak's charity-collecting work was made easier that night. Instead of having to go door-to-door, the villagers came streaming out to Chaim Chaikel's house with their donations.

"One *mitzvah* brings another in its train," quoted R' Levi Yitzchak radiantly. "Because you agreed to take me in, Chaim Chaikel, you've become a partner in the *mitzvah* of *tzedakah* taking place here tonight." He paused. "Would you be interested in meriting a third *mitzvah*?"

"Which is that?"

"I had planned to continue on my way tonight. But the road from Zelichov was long, and I arrived here late. Darkness has covered everything and the roads are blocked because of the heavy snow. I do not wish to resume my journey tonight. May I spend the night here in your home?"

"What a question, holy Rebbe! Only someone with a heart of stone could let the Rebbe go out into such a night," Chaim Chaikel exclaimed. He spoke rapidly, as if afraid his illustrious guest might change his mind. "Would the Rebbe consent to sleep in my bed? I have no other."

He led his guest to his bed. "The Rebbe will sleep here," he said. "And I," he added quickly as R' Levi Yitzchak began to gesture his refusal, "will spread my coat on the floor and sleep on it."

All of R' Levi Yitzchak's objections went unheeded. Chaim Chaikel, filled to the brim with the joy of the *mitzvah* that had unexpectedly come his way, was determined to make the most of this extraordinary opportunity to host the *tzaddik* properly.

The Chanukah lights had died down when host and guest lay down to sleep. Chaim Chaikel was still as a mouse, careful not to disturb the Rebbe's rest by any noise or movement of his own. For himself, sleep was impossible.

R' Levi Yitzchak was not asleep, either. He lay quietly in the darkness, waiting. When the silence assured him that his host was asleep, he rose carefully and quietly from his bed and began to pace the room.

In the morning, Chaim Chaikel got up from his resting place on the floor and parted warmly from R' Levi Yitzchak. On his arrival at *shul,* he was bombarded by eager questions about the previous night.

He answered enthusiastically, "*Rabbosai*, what can I say? This is no man, but an angel. From the moment he believed me to be asleep, he began to pace around the room, over and over. Sometimes he hummed a sweet, joyous tune almost under his breath, and at other times he sighed as though his heart were breaking as it shared in the *Shechinah's* pain in exile. Neither one of us closed an eye all night long. But I know what he did, while he has no idea that his secret lies open before my eyes!"

Five months passed. Chaim Chaikel made his way past fields of golden wheat. The long winter was behind them, and Pesach as well, and the earth was offering its bounty in abundance. Chaim Chaikel's destination was the *poritz's* mansion, perched in lonely splendor high above the simple cottages of the village, and nestling among lovely landscaped gardens.

The moment Chaim Chaikel entered the *poritz's* presence he sensed a change. Until now, he and his landlord had been on friendly terms. Now the *poritz* glowered at him balefully.

"Chaikel, I am not renting you the hostelry any longer!"

Chaikel's heart plummeted. "But — why?"

"You've been behind in your payments for years. By now you owe me an enormous amount of money. Every time you're late with your payments you cause me a real loss. Enough!"

Chaim Chaikel was not a man to give in without a struggle. He attempted to argue, which nearly caused the *poritz* to explode with anger. "If you don't leave my house at once, I will have the dogs set on you!" he thundered.

At a total loss, Chaim Chaikel left the mansion and started down the hill. He wandered for hours in a fog of confusion and despair. Then, all at once, he remembered.

"I'll go to the holy Rebbe, R' Levi Yitzchak!" he thought in a flash of inspiration. "After all, I recently did him a favor. He will know how to pay me back with a favor of his own."

No sooner had he hit on the plan than the villager put it into action. Before long, he was spilling the story of his troubles into the *tzaddik's* ear.

R' Levi Yitzchak's heart ached for the good man who stood in danger of losing the source of his livelihood. At all costs, he must not be allowed to fall prey to the ruthless *poritz*.

"Wait here a moment," he told Chaim Chaikel, and stepped into the next room. When he returned, he was holding a sealed envelope.

"Take this to the *poritz*," R' Levi Yitzchak ordered. "Tell him that I sent you."

Happily, the villager took the envelope and began to retrace his journey back to the *poritz's* mansion.

It was not long, however, before fresh doubts and worries began to assail him.

"How can R' Levi Yitzchak write a letter to the *poritz* when he doesn't even know who he is? And how in the world is the *poritz* — a gentile and the son of gentiles — to recognize the holy Rebbe's name? What is the meaning of this mysterious letter?"

Finally, his curiosity overcame him. Chaim Chaikel opened the envelope and peeked inside.

"B-but the page is completely blank!" he gasped. In shock, he turned the paper over, from side to side and then upside down. There was not a single word written on it!

"*Oy*," he groaned. "If I go to the *poritz* with this blank page, he'll decimate me on the spot!"

For a moment, he toyed with the idea of returning to the Rebbe's house to ask the meaning of this strange letter. Then he thought the better of it. For one thing, he was acutely embarrassed at having to admit that he had opened it up. And another, more important, deterrent was this: He knew that R' Levi Yitzchak would not have done such a thing without a reason. There must be some deep significance in this smooth, blank page.

For the rest of the long way back, Chaim Chaikel kept his spirits up with musings on faith and *bitachon*. He decided not to tarry on the way or even stop off at his own home, but to go straight on to the *poritz* that very day. Humbly, he asked the servant who opened the door if he might see the *poritz* just this once.

"Chaikel!" roared the *poritz*. "I hope you know what you're doing. You must have come to pay your debt. If not, you'll leave here with your ears boxed!"

Without a word, Chaim Chaikel proffered the envelope he had received from R' Levi Yitzchak.

"Why are those drums beating so loudly?" he wondered to himself. Then he realized that the pounding drums he heard was actually his own heartbeat, thundering in his ears. His terror mounted as the *poritz* opened the envelope and glanced at its contents.

"This is the end," Chaim Chaikel thought in resignation.

To his astonishment, the *poritz* stood for some moments reading the letter from beginning to end.

The *poritz* looked up. "This letter was sent by R' Levi Yitzchak?" he asked Chaim Chaikel once again. Dumbly, Chaim Chaikel nodded his head. Speech was impossible; his tongue was stuck to the roof of his mouth. He stood as one paralyzed as he watched the *poritz* reread the letter a second and then a third time.

The *poritz* began to walk around the room with a measured tread, breathing heavily as though plunged into deep thought. Finally, he stopped.

"Chaikel," he said, his voice unexpectedly gentle, "you are an honest man. It's true that you've been late with your payments, but you have integrity. What good would it do me to rent my land to tricksters and cheaters who would surround me with lies?"

"And — and the debt? What of that?" Chaikel whispered, his throat dry as paper.

"Chaikel, what are you worrying about? All debts are canceled!" the *poritz* broke into hearty laughter. "The land is yours for the next ten years, on the condition that you pay your rent on time!"

Chaim Chaikel's legs almost buckled beneath him. Walking slowly, as one in a dream, he returned home. There he filled a jug with fresh butter, added some rounds of his best cheese, and went to deliver his grateful offering to R' Levi Yitzchak for the help he had afforded through his miraculous letter.

R' Levi Yitzchak received him with a radiant countenance. Upon hearing the outcome of Chaim Chaikel's meeting with the *poritz*, however, his face darkened.

"Only ten years?" he exclaimed in dismay.

Chaim Chaikel hastened to reassure him. "Ten years is a very nice amount of time. And all the debt has been canceled! Could there be anything better than that?"

"Tell me the truth," R' Levi Yitzchak said persuasively. "Did you by any chance open the letter on your way?"

Chaim Chaikel nearly swallowed his tongue. Red-faced, he admitted that this had indeed been the case.

"*Oy, oy, oy*," sighed R' Levi Yitzchak. "I stored a great power in that letter! You did something very foolish. Had you not opened it, the *poritz* would have given you the land for your entire lifetime, and to your sons and grandsons after you! When you yielded to your curiosity, you caused a shower of blessings to evaporate into thin air. You did this with your own hands."

By the time the old man had finished his tale, the Kuzhmir *beis midrash* was plunged into full darkness. The listeners sat as though hypnotized.

"And what happened to you after those ten years?" someone wanted to know.

The old man heaved a heavy sigh. Wordlessly, he pointed at his tattered hat and threadbare coat.

R' AHARON IS HUNGRY

R'AHARON, THE KARLINER REBBE AND DISCIPLE OF THE *Maggid* of Mezritch, was like a ladder perched on the ground with its head in the clouds. Even when walking the roads, his mind did not have the leisure to dwell on the natural beauty surrounding him. His entire being was absorbed in unceasing devotion to the Divine.

But even such a body requires some modest attention from time to time. In order to survive as a worthy vessel for the soul, the body needs at least a bit of fuel. For three days, R' Aharon had walked without tasting a morsel. To quench his thirst, he had drunk water from the sparkling springs he had passed, but no food had passed his lips.

Suddenly, on the third day, R' Aharon felt a tremendous weakness overtake him. He was consumed with a ravenous hunger. If he did not eat something soon, he realized, his soul would simply leave his body.

Looking back over his shoulder, he saw a small town lying behind him. Lost in his thoughts, he had not noticed it when passing earlier. Now he turned around on the road and retraced his steps to enter the town. Perhaps there were some Jews there who would take pity on him and assuage the raging hunger that threatened to steal away his very life.

It was high noon. The burning sun stood at the zenith of a cloudless sky. No one was about; everyone was busy with his or her work. R' Aharon went from house to house, knocking on doors, but no one opened.

Then he saw a smoking chimney. It belonged to a house standing on the main street. Here, no doubt, was a hostelry of sorts where a traveler might find a hot dish always simmering on the stove. A freshly-baked loaf of bread should be easy to get in this place. Here he could appease his ravenous hunger.

At the end of his strength, he went to the door and rapped weakly.

The door remained closed.

"It's because I'm so weak. They didn't hear my knock," he thought. Gathering the remnants of his energy, he knocked again, twice as loud this time. And still, the door remained closed in his face. R' Aharon began to pound on the door. This was a matter of life and death.

Suddenly, the door swung violently open. The aroma of cooking food wafted through the doorway — a delicious fragrance that only served to double R' Aharon's desperate appetite. A Jewish woman, eyes shooting sparks of fury, screamed, "Are you a thief? What business do you have pounding down my door? Have you come to break my house to bits?"

R' Aharon swallowed the humiliation in silence. He apologized, explaining that he felt ill, having tasted no food for three days.

Still angry, the woman snapped, "Is it my fault that you haven't eaten for three days? What has my door done to deserve such treatment?"

"The door has done nothing," R' Aharon replied softly. "I am pleading for your compassion. Please, give me something to eat, a bit of hot food, perhaps, before I faint."

But she was not yet ready to relinquish her rage. Raising her voice, she shrilled, "Do you have any money to pay for a meal? Your tattered clothing tells me that you're a beggar!"

R' Aharon tried again to arouse her pity. "It is true that my pockets are empty. I am asking for a gift. Please, from the goodness of your heart, just a little food to appease my hunger."

"Leave my house at once!" Not content with shouting at the top of her lungs, the woman advanced and slapped R' Aharon on the face several times with the strength of her heavy hand.

R' Aharon turned slowly away and left while he still had the strength to move.

He had not gone far when he heard a voice call urgently, "Reb Yid, please wait!"

Turning, he saw one of the villagers — a neighbor of the woman he had just met — who had emerged from his house just in time to see her treatment of R' Aharon. His first impulse had been to dash over to the hostelry and shout, "You wicked woman, how dare you strike a fellow Jew?" But, afraid of creating strife, he waited until she had slammed the door before dashing after R' Aharon.

This villager had noticed the radiance of R' Aharon's countenance, and knew something of the nature of hidden *tzaddikim*. He immediately invited R' Aharon into his home, where he gave him food and drink to restore his spirit.

The woman slammed the door behind her unwelcome visitor, still muttering about the insolence of beggars trying to take away the fruits of her labor. Suddenly, she felt a terrible heaviness course through her limbs. Her head felt as though it were being split in half, while her hands and feet were like petrified wood. Her eyes glazed over and her tongue became hard as stone. Complete paralysis overtook her entire body.

For a minute she stood there, swaying on her useless legs like a tree sliced through at the base with the woodman's axe. Then, with a resounding crash, she toppled over. She lay on the floor like an inanimate rock, unable to move a muscle. Only her darting eyes gave witness to the fact that she still breathed.

The house was thrown into an uproar. The woman's children came running when they heard the crash. They were appalled to find their mother — a strong, sturdy individual — lying immobile on the ground with unearthly groans rising from her throat. They tried to lift her, but her eyes bespoke the enormous pain this effort cost her. They put her down.

The family was at a loss. A son suggested one course of action and a daughter offered another, while their mother stared at them in mute pleading that tore at their hearts more than the wildest screams might have done. It seemed to them that she was silently begging, "Save me, please, I'm dying!"

"What do we do?" they asked each other in despair.

The mother wanted to roll around on the floor in her agony, but she couldn't move a muscle. This total inability to control her own limbs added bitter fuel to the flames of her anguish, until she wished she could simply die on the spot.

But not a syllable escaped her lips.

Presently, the door opened and the man of the house stepped inside.

His heart nearly stopped at the sight that met his eyes. His wife was lying on the floor, motionless as stone. Around her stood their sons and daughters, wringing their hands and weeping.

"What happened to Mother?" he bellowed in terror.

They told him what had happened — how, suddenly, without any prior warning or symptoms, their mother had become completely paralyzed and collapsed with a crash.

The husband was made of different stuff than the wife. He knew that the world did not run itself haphazardly. He knew that there is justice and there is a Judge, and that a healthy person does not suddenly collapse on the floor, half dead, without some sort of reason. It was not a doctor that he sought in this crisis, but the sin that cried out for repentance.

"What happened here before that?" he demanded.

Shamefaced, they said, "A Jew came asking for some food. He said he hadn't eaten for three days. But Mother chased him away angrily, and even slapped him on the cheek."

"Woe is me!" cried the hostel-keeper. "Now all is clear. She was repaid in kind for her wickedness and cruelty."

He saddled up his horse at once and, accompanied by one of his sons, galloped away in search of the Jewish beggar who had come seeking food to sustain his starving body.

Fortunately, R' Aharon had not gone far. After satisfying his hunger at the neighbor's house, he had lingered a little while before they set him on the road leading away from town.

"There he is!" cried the son.

"What is wrong with you?" the father scolded. "Are you blind? Can't you see his holy face? Why are you shouting like that in front of a holy man, as if he were a nobody?" Mournfully, he yanked a handful of his own hair. "And this *tzaddik* is the man my wife chased away! Woe is me!"

He leaped from his horse and humbly approached R' Aharon. Amid copious tears, he described the punishment that had struck down his wife after she had raised her voice and hand to R' Aharon. He begged the *tzaddik* to forgive her. He pleaded with R' Aharon to come back home with him and beseech Hashem to have compassion on his wife, to send her a speedy recovery.

R' Aharon did not refuse. "*Gam anosh latzaddik lo tov,*" he quoted *Mishlei* (17:27), which means, literally, *One who is not good will punish even the righteous.* "Our Sages have interpreted this to mean that it is not good for a *tzaddik* if someone is punished because of him. *Tzaddikim* have added an allusion from *Tehillim* (41:12), '*B'zos yadati ki chafatzta bi — ki lo yaria oyvi alai.'* They homiletically interpret this to mean, 'This is how I know that You are pleased with me: You have not punished my enemies because of me.' In other words, how can I know whether or not I have found favor in Hashem's eyes? If no harm befalls my enemy because of me."

They returned immediately to the hostelry. R' Aharon walked up to the woman, who still lay motionless on the floor.

"Why did you strike me?" he asked her.

"She can't talk," the children told him.

Ignoring them, R' Aharon repeated his question.

With shocking suddenness, the power of speech returned to the woman's paralyzed throat. To the children's shame and terror, she began to recite in a choked voice all the sins she had committed during her lifetime, ending with the events of that day. The *tzaddik* listened impassively. When she had finished, he said, "I have not yet received an answer to my question. Why was I punished by your blows today?"

The woman launched a fresh account of additional sins that she had forgotten to mention the first time around. But R' Aharon was not yet satisfied.

"What other sin did you commit?"

With embarrassed glances at her husband and children, she stammered, "It's — it's been years since I've stopped going to the *shochet*. I fooled everyone and secretly slaughtered the chickens and geese myself."

"Now we know!" R' Aharon roared in anguish. "You fed innocent Jews non-kosher meat. For years, you have caused hundreds of Jews to sin. Who knows what manner of spiritual damage you've caused! And I myself came and asked for something to eat — *treifeh* food! That is why it was decreed that I must be struck. How could this mouth ask for a meal in a *treifeh* place?"

"Rebbe, I have sinned," wailed the woman. "Please design a plan of repentance for me!"

"*Teshuvah* consists of *Vidui* — acknowledging your sin — remorse over the past, and resolutions about the future," R' Aharon told her. "You have acknowledged your sin and expressed remorse over it. If you will undertake never again to do this thing in the future, to improve your behavior and to keep your door open for guests and passersby, you will be cured."

The woman repeated after him, word for word, promising to improve her behavior and to repent with all her heart.

The *tzaddik's* promise was fulfilled. The woman was restored to complete health. And until her final day on earth, she would relate to guests at her hostel how sinners are punished in this world, and how they receive their reward if they abandon their evil ways — a truth for which she could vouch as a personal witness.

HUMILIATION WITH LOVE

O NE OF THE FIRST *CHASSIDIM* TO FLOCK TO THE COURTYARD
of R' Meir of Premishlan was R' Yirmiyah of Brigel. R' Yirmiyah
had family *yichus*, being the grandson and great-grandson of
disciples of the holy Baal Shem Tov. He had extraordinary personal
yichus as well. He was a *talmid chacham* and a model of *Chassidus*
whom others admired and imitated, knowingly and unknowingly.

R' Yirmiyah spent long periods of time beside R' Meir of
Premishlan, absorbing into the depths of his own soul the Torah
and *mussar* that his Rebbe dispensed. And R' Meir esteemed him in
turn. R' Yirmiyah was one of the most honored guests in
Premishlan. Aryeh, the Rebbe's assistant, knew that when R'
Yirmiyah came, he was not to be made to wait in line with the rest.
The Rebbe's door was always open for him. R' Yirmiyah was hon-
ored with an important *aliyah* when it came to reading the weekly
Torah portion, and his seat was near R' Meir's when they sat at
the table.

R' Meir revered and respected his disciple, R' Yirmiyah. This
much was abundantly clear to all who came to Premishlan. He made
no attempt to conceal the fact. The Rebbe's face would light with
pleasure when he heard that R' Yirmiyah was coming to town. And
when he related words of Torah, he turned often to his prized student,
as though addressing nobody but him in all the vast crowd.

All this was well known in Premishlan. Imagine then the shock of
Aryeh, the Rebbe's assistant, at R' Meir's reaction one day. Seeing R'
Yirmiyah's carriage pulling up at his accustomed lodgings, Aryeh ran
to inform the Rebbe of his beloved student's arrival.

"R' Yirmiyah's come?" R' Meir said coldly. "Well, for my part, he
can turn right around and go back where he came from!"

A stunned silence fell in the room. Aryeh stood with his jaw hanging open, speechless. When he had recovered somewhat, he asked, "Shall I summon him to greet the Rebbe?"

"No, no, there's no need," R' Meir said, with a finality that left no doubt that something had changed, and dramatically.

Astonished as he was at the Rebbe's surprising answer, Aryeh did not have the leisure to stand and ponder the situation. There was too much work waiting to be done. Not long afterward, R' Yirmiyah himself entered the house and asked to see the Rebbe.

"Wait a minute, please," Aryeh said. Going into R' Meir's room, he announced, "R' Yirmiyah is here." Hesitantly, he added, "He asks if he may greet the Rebbe."

"Why should he come in here?" R' Meir demanded sternly. "He does not need to be near me!"

The Rebbe's other helpers were shocked at this most unusual reply. As for R' Yirmiyah himself, he was heartbroken. What had he done to warrant this reaction?

"Perhaps the Rebbe is preoccupied with some important matter and is not free to see you just now," one of the other *gabbaim* consoled the distraught *chassid*. But this, as they both knew, was cold comfort. R' Meir had always shown his esteem for R' Yirmiyah by making himself available to him at any time, even at his busiest.

R' Yirmiyah sought another explanation. "Is the Rebbe not feeling well?"

But this possibility, too, fell flat. The Rebbe was feeling fine and was receiving petitioners as usual.

R' Yirmiyah stood by the Rebbe's door and waited a long time. Surely, when R' Meir stepped out, he would notice him and remember his former love for his student and his student's holy fathers, disciples of the *Besht*.

But when the Rebbe emerged from his room and noticed R' Yirmiyah waiting impatiently, he turned his head aside and did not so much as glance into his face.

A seedling of protest sprouted in R' Yirmiyah's heart.

Those close to the Rebbe tried to restore things to the way they had been. One of them entered the Rebbe's room and mentioned that his beloved student was waiting humbly outside.

Furiously, R' Meir exclaimed, "What does he want from me? Who needs him here? For my part, let him return home!"

He had spoken in a loud voice, and the angry words reached R' Yirmiyah's ears. Finally, the Rebbe relented slightly. "Go tell our *meyuchas* that if he will deign to grant me a little time when I've finished receiving people, he can come in then."

For long hours, R' Yirmiyah stood by the door along with the masses who had come to petition the Rebbe. He stood, and was shamed.

Seven times, he wanted to make his escape. He could not understand the humiliation that was being heaped on him. But each time, one of the Rebbe's *gabbaim* seized R' Yirmiyah and urged him to remain. They soothed him and appeased him, assuring him that the Rebbe would almost certainly begin behaving in the old way toward him soon. When R' Yirmiyah would finally go in to see him, he would find out what had happened.

The hours passed. Everyone who saw R' Yirmiyah waiting in line gazed at him in wonder, as if they could not believe the evidence of their own eyes.

Each one of these wondering glances pierced R' Yirmiyah's heart, which felt as though it were crumbling with shame. His face repeatedly changed color. Every new person who saw him this way only increased his mortification.

"It's all worthwhile," he consoled himself. "In the end, all will be sweet and good. I will present myself to the Rebbe in awe and trembling, and I will learn why this is happening. The Rebbe will doubtless compensate me for the scorn he has unjustly heaped on me today."

But his mortification was not fated to vanish when he stood face to face with the Rebbe. R' Meir had not changed his stance at all. He extended the merest tips of his fingers in greeting, and said very clearly, "Go in peace. I am very busy with more important business!"

A most bitter pill to swallow.

Remembering all the hundreds of other greetings he had received in this room, the Rebbe's face wreathed in smiles, R' Yirmiyah decided on the spot not to stay for Shabbos as he had planned. He would return home at once.

In the morning, however, he reconsidered.

"Perhaps his other concerns weighed down the Rebbe's spirit so that he found relief only in rejecting those closest to him. Shabbos will bring peace. On Shabbos, he will reveal his former love for me. I will stay and honor him."

On Friday night, R' Yirmiyah hurried to take his usual place at the table. The Rebbe's helpers took pains to seat him as close to R' Meir as possible. They did not understand the Rebbe's recent attitude and could not bear R' Yirmiyah's disgrace.

R' Meir walked in. Raking the room with his eyes, he spotted R' Yirmiyah seated near the head of the table. With a sharp look, he declared aloud, "I don't understand all the honor given to *rebbishe* grandchildren. So what if their ancestors were great men? What is their personal *yichus*? They pat themselves on the stomach and say, 'I am great, I am holy.' And Meir'l says, 'You are arrogant!'"

A frightened silence fell on the room. Every person present keenly sensed R' Yirmiyah's pain and shame, as though it were their own.

As if his first comments were not enough, in his Torah discourse the Premishlaner Rebbe spoke scathingly of "grandsons" who relied on their fathers' exalted status while they themselves were devoid of spiritual content. He spoke with his gazed fixed on R' Yirmiyah, as though to say, "Let there be no mistake as to whom I am referring!"

The same scene repeated itself during all three Shabbos meals.

On *motza'ei Shabbos*, R' Yirmiyah decided to depart at once, without the customary parting visit to the Rebbe. He had had his fill of humiliation. From the moment he had arrived, several days earlier, the Rebbe had not ceased to heap scorn on him.

But in the end, he yielded to a stronger urge, and went to part from the Rebbe as usual. Even if he were not to stand up for his own honor, he must at least fight for that of his fathers. What sin had they committed, that their grandson should suffer such mortification?

In due time, he was permitted into the Rebbe's room. When he left a few minutes later, he was aflame with rage. R' Meir had received him with extreme coldness, his eyes half closed. Before his *chassid* had the chance to speak, the Rebbe murmured, "Good-bye, good-bye," and dismissed him. R' Yirmiyah wanted to ask what had turned the Rebbe against him in such a marked manner, but R' Meir did not let him say a word. A finger flicked toward the door, its message unmistakable.

R' Yirmiyah walked out with one certainty in his heart: He would not be returning to Premishlan. Apparently, the Rebbe had swallowed some slanderous tale against him without verifying its truth.

Still churning with rage, R' Yirmiyah made his way back to his lodgings. He was halfway there when he heard the rattle of wheels and the clip-clop of horses' hooves. Raising his eyes, he saw a closed carriage coming his way. A moment later, a familiar figure descended from the carriage. It was the Premishlaner Rebbe's son-in-law, the *tzaddik* R' Chaim Avraham of Mikoleib, who also happened to be R' Meir's great-nephew. R' Chaim Avraham's father, the *tzaddik* R' Shlomo Redlich, had been a son-in-law of the *tzaddik* R' Aron Leib of Premishlan, R' Meir's father. R' Chaim Avraham had taken his father-in-law's place after his death, leading his congregation in the city of Mikoleib for many years.

"Why the downcast face?" R' Chaim Avraham asked, thrusting out a jovial hand to shake R' Yirmiyah's. "You look very angry!"

"Do you want to pour salt on my wounds?" R' Yirmiyah asked furiously.

"I have only just arrived, and I have no idea what's been happening here. But your face tells me that a great rage fills your heart. As the wise man said, when your heart is troubled, speak to someone about it," R' Chaim Avraham said persuasively. "Let us sit down together, have a little something to drink, and hear what's going on."

But R' Yirmiyah was in a hurry. Right there on the street, he related to R' Chaim Avraham what had happened to him on his visit to Premishlan. He concluded, "Know this: I will not come here again. I have committed no sin, no crime. I have not changed from the man I was the last time I was in Premishlan. There was no reason for your father-in-law to humiliate me the way he did."

"Wait a little," R' Chaim Avraham begged. "Don't run away yet. I will go in to my father-in-law and find out what happened."

"No!" shouted R' Yirmiyah. "I'm not looking for any favors. I don't need go-betweens. I am leaving now."

And he was as good as his word.

R' Yirmiyah's wagon quickly put some distance between himself and Premishlan. He was still furious. He was in no mood to accept any explanations or justifications. From now on, he would join another *chassidic* court. There was no lack of *tzaddikim* and devoted servants of Hashem; he would find another Rebbe who, if he did not treat R' Yirmiyah with any special tokens of respect, would at least not heap abuse on him.

The horses galloped rapidly, pulling the wagon after them. They approached the crest of a hill. The driver yanked on the reins to slow the team on the curving mountainous road, as was his usual practice.

But the horses, normally well-trained, suddenly refused to obey. As though seized by madness, they continued to gallop unrestrainedly through the night. The result was inevitable. At a sharp curve in the road, the horses plunged over the side of the mountain into the abyss below. The wagon went along with them.

R' Yirmiyah never had a chance. He fell in a broken heap at the bottom of the mountain, with no breath of life left in his body. The driver survived, with only superficial wounds to show for the tragic episode.

The bad news traveled quickly back to Premishlan: The accident's victim had been R' Yirmiyah. The *chassidim* began to argue amongst themselves as to who should bear the sad tale to the Rebbe. At last, unwillingly, his son-in-law, R' Chaim Avraham of Mikoleib, strode into R' Meir's room with shadowed eyes, to tell him of the tragedy.

"Do you need to tell me this?" R' Meir asked. "Do I not know of this awful thing that has happened? Meir'l does not need people to come and tell him such things."

He looked at his son-in-law and sighed. "I knew, my son, before it happened," he said sorrowfully. "A terrible decree was laid on our dear friend, R' Yirmiyah. Meir'l saw this bitter fate and tried to have it erased. That was why I poured all that shame and humiliation on him.

"Who can judge the value of shame? It is a veritable *Gehinnom*, all on its own. A small dose of mortification in this world is worth several years of *Gehinnom*, and can banish severe decrees.

"But he grew angry and fled. All his sufferings were for naught. They were for naught — they helped him not at all!"

There was a brief pause. Then the Rebbe resumed softly, with a sigh, "Chaim Avraham, you know your father-in-law. Is it my way to shame people? Had R' Yirmiyah had an ounce of sense, he would have understood that I had his welfare at heart. But his pride stood in the way. He did not comprehend that it was well worth his while to accept this kind of humiliation with love!"

TO SPEAK FROM THE GRAVE

NIKOLAI, THE WICKED RUSSIAN CZAR, PERSECUTED R' Yisrael of Ruzhin mercilessly. By the skin of his teeth, R' Yisrael managed to escape the czar's clutches and, after much travail, succeeded in reaching the city of Sadigur, in Austria. But even here, he was not permitted to live his life in peace.

One day, an important *chassid* by the name of R' Yosef of Toporov came to see the Rebbe. R' Yosef was a man of illustrious lineage; on his father's side he was the grandson of the *Maggid* of Zlotchov, and on his mother's he was related to the *Ohev Yisrael* of Apta. He himself, however, did not seek to wear the crown of leadership, being an enthusiastic Ruzhiner *chassid*. When the Rebbe had lived in Ruzhin, R' Yosef had traveled there. Now that the Rebbe had moved to Sadigur, R' Yosef followed.

The moment he set foot in the Rebbe's courtyard, R' Yosef noted something different in the faces of the *gabbaim*. Their expressions were somber, their eyes filled with pain.

Fearfully, R' Yosef asked, "Is the Rebbe well?"

The *gabbaim* assured him that the Rebbe was not sick. It was not ill health that was causing them to live under a cloud.

"So what happened?"

"For the last few days, the Rebbe has shut himself away in his room. He asked that he not be disturbed. While the door is not bolted, nobody comes in and nobody goes out. The Rebbe's request is stronger than any lock. Nobody knows the reason for this, but it's clear that something serious is weighing on him."

R' Yosef was very close to the Rebbe, and was considered almost a member of his household. "I'm sure I'll be permitted to go in to see the Rebbe in a little while, and then the situation will improve," he told the disconsolate *chassidim*.

"That is just what we hoped!" they said, brightening. "Knowing how close you are to the Rebbe, we wanted to ask you to see him and try to learn the reason for all this."

R' Yosef washed his hands, recited several chapters of *Tehillim* with great fervor, prayed for the success of his mission, smoothed his beard and *peyos*, and tentatively approached R' Yisrael's door. If the Rebbe's courtyard was holy, then his room was the Holy of Holies.

With pounding heart, he knocked on the closed door. It was a feeble knock, scarcely heard.

"Who is there?" the Rebbe's voice asked from within.

"Yosef of Toporov," he answered, teeth chattering.

"And what is it that you wish?"

"I request permission to enter."

He heard the Rebbe's footsteps walking to the door, but it opened only a crack. A hand emerged to shake his own. *"Shalom aleichem."*

R' Yosef was no fool. He understood by the minimal way in which the door had opened that it was about to shut again. And so, as the Rebbe extended his hand, R' Yosef offered not only his own hand — but his foot as well. The foot slipped into the crack between the door and jamb. When the Rebbe tried to close the door, R' Yosef's instep was squeezed unmercifully. But the door would not shut.

A slight smile illuminated the Ruzhiner Rebbe's face. He liked his *chassid's* devoted obstinacy. He threw the door wide open and called, "Welcome, R' Yosef of Toporov!"

A sigh of relief swept through the small crowd of *gabbaim*. R' Yosef of Toporov had been blessed with a charm, a *chein*, that lent grace even to his *chutzpah*. Seeing it, one had to smile.

But if the *chassidim* outside were celebrating R' Yosef's victory, R' Yosef himself, in the Rebbe's room, did not share that feeling. He sensed the full weight of his impulsive action. He felt like a silly child, not a mature and thoughtful *chassid*. As he gazed at his Rebbe, he found himself suddenly tongue-tied. He could not think of a thing to say.

For his part, the Rebbe did not seem eager to break the silence. On it stretched, seemingly endless.

At last, R' Yosef groped for something, anything, to end the painful quiet. "Does the Rebbe permit me to speak?" he asked.

R' Yisrael nodded his head in assent.

"The twelfth chapter of *Mishlei* states, 'When there is worry in a man's heart, he should suppress it.' Two *Amoraim* in the *Gemara*, R' Ami and R' Assi, were in disagreement as to the meaning of this verse. One said that a person should put his worry out of his mind, and the other said that he should discuss it with others. If the Rebbe agrees with the first opinion — that it is better to distract oneself from one's worries — then it would seem appropriate for his door to be opened to the people who wish to come as usual and pour out their woes. And if the Rebbe agrees with the second opinion, then he ought to discuss his worry with others." He drew a breath and added, "I am ready to hear what is on the holy Rebbe's mind!"

R' Yisrael's lips lifted in a small smile. He nodded, as though to say, "You have scored a victory, my son."

✦✦✦

Sadigur and Chernowitz were neighboring cities whose fortunes changed together. In the sweep of history, they belonged first to the Austro-Hungarian empire, then to Romania, and after that to a third country.

At that time, there lived in Chernowitz a well-known *maskil*, a proponent of the so-called Enlightenment movement. Like many such religious rebels, he was versed in *Tanach* and other Jewish wisdom. From time to time, this *maskil* would appear in public, spouting his anti-Torah notions. Then he decided to put his speeches into writing. Finally, when he had amassed enough collected writings to publish a book, he had the appalling effrontery to approach the Ruzhiner Rebbe for an approbation!

With a cynical smile that said he knew exactly how much distress he was causing the Rebbe, the man awaited his reply.

The Ruzhiner Rebbe had a regal bearing. At that moment, however, enraged at the wicked, vulgar creature standing before him with that insolent smile, he shouted with all his might, "Leave my house!"

The *maskil* was undaunted. All the unkosher meat he had eaten had dulled his sensibilities and turned his heart to stone. The shout, emanating from the depths of holiness, passed over him without leaving a ripple. He moved closer to the Rebbe, wearing the same scornful smile.

"Rebbe, I have large-scale plans for distributing this book — with your approbation inside. If the *chassidim* hear that you have approved it, they will flock to buy my book. That way, we will all profit: My pockets will fill with gold, and the unenlightened *chassidim* will have their eyes opened at last to the wisdom I offer in my writings."

"Absolutely not!"

The wicked smile did not leave the *maskil's* face. Taking yet another step closer to the Rebbe, he whispered, "Rebbe, ever since you fled from Russia and made your way through devious means to this city, there has existed a thick file with your name on it — a file containing several serious accusations against you. At present, the file resides in the state courthouse. It has been kept under wraps for the time being — your *chassidim* knew whom to 'sweeten' in order to make sure that those accusations don't see the light of day. But they won't succeed in silencing *me*. I will make very certain that your file is dealt with — and promptly, too!"

The last drop of blood drained from the Rebbe's holy countenance. Encouraged, the *maskil* continued, "Rebbe, if this seems overly harsh to you, I am prepared to hold my tongue — for a price."

"How much do you want?" sighed the Rebbe. If they were talking about a financial deal, something could be worked out.

The *maskil* took a bottle of ink and a feather pen from his bag. Holding them out to R' Yisrael, he said, "Let the Rebbe write an approbation for my book. *That* is my price!"

The Rebbe shrugged his refusal. Furious, the *maskil* snapped, "In that case, I know very well into which ear to whisper my little story. This is the end of your stay in this city!"

Wisely, the Rebbe decided to defuse the immediate crisis by calming the other man's anger. He said, "Come back in a few days. I'll see what I can do."

"Reb Yossel, you know how difficult and dangerous was my journey to Sadigur — how much I've gone through since the Russian government began to persecute me," the Ruzhiner Rebbe told R' Yosef of Toporov. "And now that I've finally arrived in this place and achieved a bit of peace, this wicked man has threatened to overturn it all. For days now, I have been wracking my brain trying to find a way to keep him from placing my family and myself in danger. Perhaps it is permissible for me to give my approbation to his despicable book, because there exists a definite danger to life if I do not. On the other hand, what a desecration of Hashem's Name would emerge from such an action!"

R' Yosef thought a moment before he replied.

"With all due respect, I do not understand why the Rebbe can't do as the *maskil* asks. What's so bad about that? After all, what is his purpose in publishing this book of his? If you'll say that it is in order to spread his heretical notions — well, he is already doing that without the help of any book. He goes around among the people, gathering crowds of the idle and empty-headed, and peddling his ideas to whomever will listen.

"No, his goal is this: After his death, he hopes that people will read his book and quote his 'wisdom.' In other words, he would like to be able to 'speak from the grave.' *Nu*, is it so difficult for the Rebbe to yield to this modest request, and let him speak from the grave right now?"

The light of laughter filled the Rebbe's face. He liked R' Yosef's remarks.

"Is that what you say, Reb Yossel?" he murmured. Then, raising his voice, he called out for his *gabbaim*, with instructions to summon the *maskil* to his home at once.

The *maskil* was delighted. "I knew he'd give in," he crowed to the Rebbe's messenger. "And why not? His life is precious to him." He galloped like the wind from Chernowitz to Sadigur.

But his arrival at the Rebbe's home was a disappointment. As he stood there expectantly, the Rebbe merely asked the *maskil* not to request something that he, the Rebbe, could not fulfill. R' Yisrael spoke persuasively, offering a flow of words that must surely find their way into the other man's heart.

But the man's ears were sealed. Insolently, the *maskil* replied, "Rebbe, I came here to get your approbation for my book, not to listen to a sermon!"

"But what good will my approbation do you?" the *tzaddik* pleaded. "My *chassidim* will surely understand that it was wrested from me against my will, and those who've never heard of me will be unmoved by anything I might write."

"I meant what I said," the *maskil* insisted stubbornly.

"In that case," sighed the Rebbe, "go ahead and print your book at the printer's in Chernowitz. Before the printing is completed, bring it to me."

Wearing a triumphant smile, the *maskil* left the Rebbe's home and galloped back to the high road leading to Chernowitz.

It was late at night when he reached the bridge that spanned the river. A deep blackness covered everything. The darkness concealed from the traveler's gleeful eyes the fact that the bridge was trembling for some reason. Moving at a brisk pace, man and horse stepped onto the wooden bridge.

The horse was the first to sense danger. It stopped short, lifted its head, and snorted in terror.

"Why are you stopping?" the *maskil* yelled, raising his whip. But the horse would not budge. It stood as though frozen in place. The rider whipped it viciously once and then again, but still the horse refused to move.

Suddenly, it felt the entire bridge shaking. It danced from side to side like a drunkard. The *maskil's* eyes filled with fear and confusion. He tried to turn the horse around and run while there was still time.

At that moment, with an ear-splitting crack, the wooden slats broke.

The supports splintered like toothpicks, and the entire bridge split into a hundred pieces that fell slowly into the fast-running river below. Horse and rider were thrown from the heights into the rushing water, where they quickly drowned.

The powerful current washed the corpses of man and beast up to the riverbank, like some debris that no one wanted.

The noise of the splintering wood reached a nearby village. The villagers rushed to the spot — and rubbed their eyes in disbelief. The bridge was gone.

The *maskil's* untimely demise, right on the heels of issuing a threat to the Rebbe, made a story that spread like wildfire through the streets of Sadigur. In the dead of night, the Rebbe's *gabbaim* raced to the inn to tell R' Yosef the news.

"R' Yosef is asleep," protested the innkeeper.

"So what? Wake him up!" they cried joyfully. "He can sleep later. Our news can't wait a moment!"

They burst into R' Yosef's room. Shaking him by the shoulder, they cried, "Wake up, R' Yossel, wake up! The accursed *maskil* has met his just deserts and has drowned in the river under most unusual circumstances. May all of Hashem's enemies meet a similar fate!"

R' Yosef washed his hands, roused fully from his deep slumber at the news. But the next moment, an expression of mock-anger crossed his face.

"And for this you woke me up?" he roared.

"Yossel, do you love your sleep that much? We didn't know," they laughed back at him.

R' Yosef plumped the pillow and placed it beneath his head. "Heaven forbid," he replied tranquilly. "I'm no sleep lover. It's just that your news is no news to me at all. The moment I left the Rebbe's room, it was clear to me — clear as the noonday sun — that that *maskil* would not succeed in carrying out his wicked plot. I knew that his lips would soon be speaking from the grave. Only I didn't realize that they would speak from the depths of the water first."

HOLY FLAMES

THE BLANKET OF SNOW THAT HAD COVERED THE TOWN BEGAN to thaw. Under the benign influence of the spring sun, tender young buds began to appear, amid bright green grass. Every heart was filled with gladness at the sight. The festivity could be felt in the very air: Pesach was approaching, along with the gentle breezes that the spring brought in her train.

Shlomo gazed through his factory window. "Ah, Pesach is coming — and where am I?"

It seemed to him that he had never enjoyed such a successful year. His factory, which produced whiskey and pure alcohol, hummed busily from morning until night but still did not manage to keep up with the orders that kept pouring in. "When *HaKadosh Baruch Hu* wishes to make a person rich, nothing can stand in the way," Shlomo's friends in town said with satisfaction. The wealthy Shlomo was respected by all his neighbors, Jew and non-Jew alike, for his good nature and his willingness to help all and sundry. Everyone benefited from his growing fortune. Even the *poritz*, owner of the town, had heard of Shlomo's cleverness and had appointed him his personal adviser.

Anxiously, Shlomo peered again at the streets of his town. Everyone he saw was hurrying with that special urgency preceding Pesach. Only five days remained before the onset of the holiday.

"And I haven't even sold my *chametz* yet!" he though worriedly.

Each year at this time, Shlomo would climb aboard his carriage and ride over to the next large city to sell his *chametz* to the Rabbi there. There was no lack of gentiles in his own small town, and there were also enough learned men who knew how to conduct the sale of *chametz* in proper accordance with the *halachah*. Despite all this, however, the Jewish residents of the town preferred to travel to the larger city to sell their *chametz*. The Rabbi of the city was blessed with numerous daughters, and the money the townspeople paid in exchange for his services was helping to create a dowry for their future marriages.

Shlomo wanted to travel to the Rabbi this year, as well. But pressure had built up in the factory and he was required to stay and supervise his workers as they toiled to meet the demand for their product on the eve of the holiday.

The next morning, after *Shacharis*, Shlomo strolled over to his neighbor and friend, Wolf the Baker, and they chatted together for a few moments. In the course of the conversation, Shlomo asked, "Wolf, are you planning to travel to the city to sell your *chametz*?"

"Certainly," replied Wolf.

"Perhaps you can do me a favor?" Shlomo explained how difficult it was for him to leave his business just now; the trip to and from the city entailed a full day. Wolf agreed promptly to Shlomo's suggestion. He was going to the city in any case. Why not help out a fellow Jew?

Shlomo gave Wolf a *kinyan* that made Wolf his representative in selling Shlomo's *chametz*. Then the businessman sat down and compiled a long list of where all of his *chametz* was located: in his factory cellars, on the two factory floors themselves, in the attics, in the vats and kettles. In short, all the *chametz* he owned, everywhere he owned it.

The first two days of Pesach came and went. The town's Jews celebrated the holiday joyously, but Shlomo was beset by an inexplicable anxiety. On the first day of *Chol HaMoed*, he saw Wolf in *shul* and tried to greet him. But Wolf averted his eyes as though he didn't see Shlomo coming. In another moment, he was gone.

Shlomo was surprised. Still, being in the habit of judging his fellows favorably, he decided that Wolf had probably not noticed him, being preoccupied with thoughts or dreams of his own.

After *Maariv* that night, Shlomo waited for Wolf at the *shul* door. To his astonishment, he saw that the baker had managed to get there before him, and the back of his neck was all that was visible as he hurried away through the night. A suspicion arose in Shlomo's heart — a suspicion that he did not wish to explore.

On the following day, Shlomo lay in ambush for Wolf on the path leading to *shul*. He was there well before *Shacharis*, so that Wolf would not again anticipate him and escape. Seeing the baker coming, he called, "Good morning to you, my friend Wolf!"

Wolf started up in confusion. His eyes darted wildly and his face grew pale. For a second, he seemed poised to run. But Shlomo was too quick for him. He seized Wolf's arm and asked, "What's the matter with you, my friend? Why are you running away from me? What harm have I done you?"

Wolf drew several labored breaths before he could speak. "Heaven forbid. You have not harmed me in any way. The... the opposite is the case. I... I..." His voice faltered and died.

"What are you stammering about?" Shlomo demanded. "Tell me quickly what's happened. Don't drag out the suspense!"

Wolf took another deep breath, and sighed, "I've been avoiding you because I've been uncomfortable. Shlomo, I didn't sell your *chametz*. I simply forgot all about it!"

Shlomo's heart began beating like a drum. He shrieked, "*You didn't sell my chametz?*"

"It flew out of my mind," Wolf said apologetically.

"And you call that 'uncomfortable'? You were obligated to let me know the minute it happened!"

"Please understand," Wolf pleaded. "I was so ashamed, so upset at the damage I've done to you..." With that, he turned tail and raced back the way he had come.

"He'll be *davening* alone this morning, no doubt," Shlomo thought with a flash of bitter humor. Then Wolf's last words echoed in his brain: "*The damage I've done to you.*"

Shlomo's prayers that morning issued from a broken heart. His agile mind quickly plumbed the depths of the situation. After *davening*, he returned home with bowed head and stood in the kitchen as one whose entire world has crumbled around him. His wife, busy preparing breakfast, glanced up and noticed his dejected posture and stricken eyes.

"What happened?" she asked in alarm.

In a broken voice, Shlomo told her, "Wolf forgot to sell my *chametz*."

His wife was not as distressed as he was. "What's the big tragedy? Go sell it right now to the first *goy* you see!"

"Impossible. You can only sell *chametz* before Pesach. Each and every minute, I am transgressing the law of *bal yira'eh u'bal yimatzeh* ('You shall not see or find [*chametz* in your possession]')."

"So what do we do?" she asked, for the first time fully aware of the awesome dimensions of the problem.

"So what do we do?" he echoed. "We burn."

"Burn what?"

In the *Gemara* chant, he replied, "We burn the *chametz*."

"So go burn the *chametz*," she agreed. "That's the solution. The world won't turn over."

Shlomo walked slowly over to his wife. "You don't understand. My factory is entirely *chametz*. It is *chametz* from top to bottom."

For an instant, she stood thunderstruck. Her mind refused to absorb the implications of what her husband was saying. Then, gathering the strength that she had inherited from her womanly Jewish ancestors, in whose merit the entire nation was redeemed from slavery in Egypt, she raised her voice and said, "So go burn down the factory!"

Shlomo's heart filled with joy at this proof of his wife's greatness. But what a bittersweet joy it was… He thought a moment, then said, "I am afraid that I will burn it with a heavy heart. I'll be thinking all the time about the vast property that is being destroyed. Therefore, I am going to hire a band of musicians to play merry melodies near the factory, so that I can fulfill the *mitzvah* joyously!"

All that day, Shlomo ran around like a person caught up in a feverish madness. He scoured his own and all the neighboring towns for musicians. By nightfall, he had found what he sought.

The news had spread. By dusk, all the town's Jews had gathered by the whiskey factory to watch the coming spectacle. Shlomo gave the musicians the signal to start playing. Then, to the merry sound of clarinets, flutes, and drums, he walked over to the factory door, a burning torch in his hand.

He thrust the torch at the wooden door. The dry wood ignited at once — but Shlomo was not content to let matters rest there. He went on to burn the door frame and the surrounding wooden supports. Within minutes, the fire had spread throughout the building. Fed by the alcohol, tongues of flame climbed high into the night sky, illuminating it with an orange-red glow that could be seen for miles.

When he saw his factory thoroughly burning, Shlomo climbed up and cried out emotionally, "My friends and brothers, this is a happy day for me! I never thought I'd be given the opportunity to fulfill the literal letter of the law of burning my *chametz*. Let us dance joyously because we are performing Hashem's will!"

He seized the hands of two of his neighbors. Lifting his voice in glad song, Shlomo began to dance.

⚬

Hearing the music and revelry, and seeing the flames, several of the town's non-Jewish residents came running. They stood watching the scene with incredulous eyes. Never before had they witnessed such a sight: The whiskey factory was going up in flames, while its Jewish owner not only exhibited no signs of wailing or distress, but was actually crowing with delight. On top of this, a band of musicians was playing lively Jewish songs for the large circle of Jews who were dancing merrily around the burning building.

"What's going on?" they asked someone with avid curiosity.

When they finally grasped the reality that the factory owner was actually planning to destroy all of his property and that he had renounced his ownership of it all, the non-Jews raced to the warehouses that stood near the factory proper, and which had not yet been touched by the flames. Shouting with triumph, they pulled out several barrels of whiskey and sat down to drink by the light of the flames, amid the music and song.

It wasn't long before word of the free whiskey spread to the other gentiles in town. They came at a run. The courtyard, ablaze with reflected firelight, quickly filled with drunken gentiles and celebrating Jews.

The *poritz's* personal secretary stepped out of his master's mansion and began to walk toward the town. It was his custom to get some fresh air at that time of day. Imagine his surprise when, instead of the usual crisp, spring-scented night air, he found his lungs filling with the acrid smell of smoke. Coming closer to the source of the smell, he soon spotted the fire itself. He heard the music and the drunkards' gleeful shouts. Without ado, he raced to the site of the fire to find out why no one was lifting a finger to try to save the burning factory. It was only then, as he stood face to face with the scene, that he began to understand just what had happened here.

While he still had breath left, he ran back to the *poritz*. Gasping for air, he related what he had seen on the other side of town.

The *poritz* did not believe it. "Impossible!" he declared. "Shlomo is no fool."

But the secretary stood firm in his story. At last, the *poritz* decided to find out the truth for himself. He sent for Shlomo to come to him at once.

✌✍

Politely, Shlomo put aside the secretary. "Don't you see that I'm busy right now?" He pointed at the circle of dancers from whom he had just parted. His face still shone pink from the exertion. "I have the privilege of fulfilling a commandment for the very first time. Only when the flames have died will I have time to visit the *poritz*."

When the secretary brought this answer to his employer, the *poritz's* face reddened with anger. For some time, he sat and thought about ways and means of punishing his adviser. Finally, when the last of the flames had died and nothing was left but gray ash and glowing, red-hot cinders, Shlomo arrived at the *poritz's* house.

"You've shamed me!" the *poritz* screamed furiously. "What have you done?"

Respectfully, Shlomo explained the importance of the *mitzvah* of burning *chametz*. But the *poritz* refused to listen. He shouted, "If you were a private individual, I wouldn't care if you went insane and burned down all your property. But everyone knows that you are the *poritz's* adviser. You have made me appear a complete fool, who takes advice from a madman!"

Shlomo tried to answer, but the *poritz* cut him off. Harshly, he declared, "I hereby confiscate your home and banish you and your wife from the town. You must leave this place at once, or I will shoot you on the spot!"

All of Shlomo's protests and pleadings were to no avail. That very night, he and his wife were forced to leave town.

Tzaddikim afterwards declared that Shlomo's act roused a great commotion in Heaven. A simple, small-town Jew was prepared to give up everything he owned and to see his family exiled, all in order to fulfill his Creator's law!

In a year's time, Shlomo's wife gave birth to a son who lit up the world with his holiness and his Torah. He grew up to become the holy Rebbe, R' Chaim of Chernowitz, who wrote works which won renown throughout the land: the *Be'er Mayim Chaim* and *Sidduro Shel Shabbos*, which are learned by large numbers of Jews the world over.

THE TORAH IS NOT IN HEAVEN

WHEN THE LARGEST PORTION OF HIS LIFE HAD PASSED without the blessing of children, the *Chacham* Sasson Papo began to think about the future.

He and his wife, Flora, had merited a good and prosperous life, but they were no longer young. In a matter of years they would depart this world — childless. He had arranged payment for ten Torah scholars who would recite the *Kaddish* for them, but as time passed, who would remember him and his work? They had not left behind anyone to bear their name. In a year or two, they would be forgotten as though they had never existed. But the Torah states, "And his name will not be erased from Israel."

The *Chacham* Sasson thought hard and long. And, one day, Hashem sent him an inspiration. He knocked at the door of R' Saadyah Nuri, a *sofer stam* living in Baghdad, and made his request.

"Please write me a beautiful *Sefer Torah*, from which the Torah portion will be read in *shul* every Shabbos. In this way, mine and my wife's name will be remembered down through the generations."

The scribe wiped his ink-stained hands on a towel. "When do you want it to be completed?"

"As soon as possible!" the *Chacham* Sasson exclaimed. "No man knows when his time will come. I want Flora and myself to enjoy the *simchah* of the *hachnasas Sefer Torah*."

Calmly, the *sofer* said, "R' Sasson, what are you saying? You are still a vigorous man, *bli ayin hara*. With Hashem's help, you and your wife will have many more good years. Why entertain such morbid thoughts?"

The *Chacham* Sasson pulled a bundle of banknotes from his pocket. He handed the money to the surprised *sofer*. "R' Saadyah, I know that writing a *Sefer Torah* is an expensive undertaking. That is why I have brought you 300 dinar. I've been saving up this money, with great effort, for many years." He smiled. "And now, my son, sit down and write for me, day and night — until the *Sefer Torah* is finished!"

The scribe was dumbfounded. Three hundred dinar was more than four times his usual fee. Not in his wildest dreams had he expected to turn such a profit — and before he had even lifted a finger!

There was a problem. R' Saadyah had several previous commitments on his time. Three Torah scrolls remained to be written ahead of R' Sasson's, and he still had not finished the one he was currently working on. The *sofer* should have had the integrity to tell the *Chacham* Sasson, "Take your money to some other scribe, for my time is limited and I will not be able to give you what you want."

But the money blinded him like a bribe. He took the bundle of banknotes and promised the *Chacham* Sasson Papo that he would complete his *Sefer Torah* in one year, no more.

Most of the money was spent even before the year was up. That is the way of money; it melts like ice cubes on a hot summer day. Counting his banknotes, the *sofer* found that less than a tenth of the original sum remained. In the interim, he had managed to complete the first of the *Sifrei Torah* he was under obligation to write. He was now under intense pressure from the two other men who had ordered theirs before the *Chacham* Sasson Papo.

Twelve months passed. The *Chacham* Sasson came to the *sofer's* home and asked, "Well, what's the status of my *Sefer Torah?*"

He had not expected to hear that it was finished; he had noticed the way R' Saadyah had been avoiding him in the street and in *shul* whenever R' Sasson came near. However, in his innocence he was certain that the *sofer* must surely be in the middle of *Sefer Vayikra*, at the very least. Hearing from R' Saadyah Nuri that his *Sefer Torah* had not even been started, he was furious.

"How can that be?" the *Chacham* Sasson asked angrily. "I paid you more than anyone else in Baghdad, and this is how you treat me?"

The *sofer* stammered an apology, but the *Chacham* Sasson was in no mood for explanations. "From this day on, you are to leave all your other pursuits and write just for me. Understand?"

"I understand perfectly. Everything will be just fine," R' Saadyah assured him. But the moment the *Chacham* Sasson left, R' Saadyah sat down to continue writing the *Sefer Torah* he had been working on previously. This was for another man, Tziyon HaKohen Mashiach, who was also childless but who had had the good fortune to order his *Sefer Torah* before the *Chacham* Sasson Papo. Apart from this, Tziyon had been astute enough not to pay for all the work in advance, but in installments, as the *sofer* completed portions of the scroll.

Six more months went by — and, still, R' Saadyah had not yet dipped quill into ink to write a single letter of the *Chacham* Sasson's *Sefer Torah*. One day, R' Sasson's patience ran dry. He came to the *sofer's* house in a towering rage. The window panes rattled with the force of his shouts. If R' Saadyah did not begin writing his *Sefer Torah* that very day, the *Chacham* Sasson threatened, he would summon him to a *din Torah* before the *gaon* R' Moshe Chaim (grandfather of the *Ben Ish Chai*).

R' Saadyah wiped his ink-stained hands on an old towel and told his irate customer calmly, "Why do you speak of beginning to write the *Sefer Torah*, when I am already near completion?"

The *Chacham* Sasson was astonished. "You're not deceiving me?" he asked suspiciously.

"Heaven forbid! You've been beating down an open door. Only a few more panels, and your *Sefer Torah* will be done. I will sit and write for two days, night and day, and on the third I will complete my work. You can invite the congregation to a feast in celebration of the *hachnasas Sefer Torah.*"

The *Chacham* Sasson Papo left the scribe's home amid profuse apologies. He heaped a shower of blessings on R' Saadyah's head. For himself, there was much to do. He must invite the congregants to the *hachnasas Sefer Torah.* His wife would do the cooking, preparing fish and meat and all manner of delicacies in honor of the occasion. In just a few days, his *Sefer Torah* would be brought to the *shul* amid great song and rejoicing. His heart expanded with joy and pride.

Had the *Chacham* Sasson known what the *sofer* was planning, he would have fainted on the spot. For the moment, however — to his contentment — he had no idea of the convoluted thoughts spinning around in R' Saadyah Nuri's mind.

In advance of the festive *hachnasas Sefer Torah* came a much less festive, and much more secret, *hotzaas Sefer Torah.*

In the dead of the night, when all of Baghdad was sound asleep, R' Saadyah the *sofer* stole into the *shul.* Because he was often called upon to repair the Torah scrolls, he possessed a key to the building.

Stealthily, like a thief in the night, he sneaked into the darkened *shul.* A small candle feebly lit the scene as he approached the Holy Ark. R' Saadyah opened the doors. By candlelight he groped through the Ark until he found what he was looking for.

In a corner of the *aron kodesh* stood a wooden case containing a *Sefer Torah* that he had written for the *Chacham* Menasheh Zakkai. The *Chacham*, a community leader, had not been blessed with children. After his wife's death about three and a half years before, he had ordered a *Sefer Torah* from R' Saadyah Nuri. The *Sefer Torah* had entered the *shul* amid song and dance, and for some weeks afterward the weekly portion was read from it. However, some two months after the donor, the *Chacham* Menasheh Zakkai, passed away, the *Sefer Torah* was put aside and had not been opened again for a solid year.

R' Saadyah was not a thief. But he had allowed himself to make rash promises that he could not fulfill, and one sin inevitably drags another in its wake. Tonight, he had lowered himself to the sin of stealing a *Sefer Torah* from the Holy Ark.

He opened the wooden case, removed the Torah scroll, wrapped it in a *tallis*, and carefully carried it home. With every step, his eyes darted fearfully from side to side. To his relief, the streets were deserted. There was no one to witness his nefarious deed. R' Saadyah brought his booty safely home, and placed it inside a secure wooden closet.

On the following day, he put the *Sefer Torah* into a new wooden case — a special, ornamental one that he had bought for the *Chacham* Sasson Papo. At the appointed time, he invited the happy man to his house to take possession of his completed *Sefer Torah*. (The custom of writing in the last letters in public was not followed then, thus sparing the *sofer* added complications and explanations.)

The *Chacham* Sasson's *hachnasas Sefer Torah* was talked about in Baghdad for many days afterward. It was a celebration the like of which had not before been seen in that city. The *Chacham* Sasson Papo threw a huge banquet for all his friends and acquaintances, making sure to invite all the wise and respected members of the community. Baghdad's elders and scholars streamed to his home to honor the Torah, and to exalt the Holy One who had bestowed it on His people.

The signal was given. A huge crowd set out to accompany the *Sefer Torah* from the *Chacham* Sasson's house to the *shul*. An enormous procession of men, women, and children celebrated with tremendous enthusiasm. The *Sefer Torah* was carried beneath a silken canopy through the streets of Baghdad, to the accompaniment of song and dance that inspired even the local Arabs to join in. There was joy in the air.

When the *Sefer Torah* reached the *shul* courtyard, the *gabbaim* and elders of the congregation came out to meet it, each carrying a Torah scroll in his arms. The *shul* doors were thrown open, and almost immediately the place filled to capacity. Everyone stood watching, shoulder to shoulder, as the *Sefer Torah* was carried inside. Their voices uplifted in jubilation, the enormous crowd circled the *bimah* seven times. The *Chacham* Sasson Papo danced at their head, the precious *Sefer Torah* in his arms and ecstacy in his heart.

Then the *Chacham* Sasson went up to the *bimah* and reverently placed the *Sefer Torah* upon it. He honored his friends by calling them up to the Torah, and all of them responded with generous donations in the Torah's honor.

At last, when the Torah reading was done, the scroll was placed inside the Ark and the celebrants dispersed to their own homes.

Two wooden cases stood side by side inside the Ark, one full and one empty. Except for R' Saadyah the *sofer*, nobody knew what had happened under cover of the night's darkness.

Two years later, the *Chacham* Sasson Papo fell ill with his final sickness. His soul departed this world and went to its eternal rest.

A short time later, his nephew, the *Chacham* Salim Ben Rachamim Papo, had a terrifying dream.

In the dream, he was standing in *shul,* facing the open Ark. The *Sefer Torah* case that his uncle had donated was open, and his uncle was lovingly caressing the scroll. Suddenly, the *Chacham* Menasheh Zakkai came and tried to take the *Sefer Torah* from him. The *Chacham* Sasson demanded angrily, "How can you take my *Sefer Torah* without permission?"

Now it was the *Chacham* Menasheh Zakkai's turn to be surprised. "How can a person have the nerve to tell someone that something belongs to him, when it doesn't?"

The two former friends stood facing one another in a fury. Each one declared that the Torah scroll was all his — until their cries ascended heavenward and reached the Throne of Glory. Then a heavenly voice announced, "The Torah is not in heaven. Pure souls, you don't need the Heavenly Court. Your dispute must be judged in an earthly court, before the city's Rav, R' Moshe Chaim. Let him judge between you."

The *Chacham* Salim woke up with a start, heart thumping and head awhirl. He sensed that this had been no ordinary dream. In the morning, after *Shacharis*, he went to R' Moshe Chaim and related the dream to him.

R' Moshe Chaim was a wise and clever man who knew how to distinguish between a foolish dream and one that carried the seeds of truth. He sent for the *shamash* of the *shul* and asked him whether the *aron kodesh* contained a *Sefer Torah* that had been written for the *Chacham* Menasheh Zakkai.

"Yes," answered the *shamash*.

"And it also contains a *Sefer Torah* that was written for the *Chacham* Sasson Papo?"

"Yes."

"Go to the *shul* at once and check whether both of the *Sifrei Torah* are there," the Rabbi ordered.

The *shamash* hurried to carry out the command. He opened the Ark — and there were the two scrolls. Taking pride of place in the center was the *Sefer Torah* that had been written for the *Chacham* Sasson Papo; resting in a corner was the one written for the *Chacham* Menasheh Zakkai. The *shamash* hurried back to the Rabbi and confirmed that both Torah scrolls were indeed where they were supposed to be.

The rabbi's brow knitted. "What can this mean?" he whispered to himself. "Can one of them have become flawed?" To the *shamash*, he said, "Please bring me the *Chacham* Menasheh Zakkai's *Sefer Torah*."

Once again, the *shamash* made his way to the *shul*. He reached into the corner for the case containing *Chacham* Menasheh Zakkai's *Sefer Torah*. But when he lifted the wooden case, he started up in confusion. The case was so light that it felt empty. Opening it with trembling hands, he ascertained that it *was* empty. He stared for a moment, then ran like the wind back to the Rabbi. Breathlessly, he related what he had discovered.

R' Moshe Chaim had uncanny insight. He did not for a moment suspect that this had been a case of simple theft. He ordered the *shamash* to make all haste to the home of the *sofer*, R' Saadyah Nuri, with instructions to have him come to the Rabbi's home at once.

"We found an empty case in the *aron kodesh*," R' Moshe Chaim stated flatly, the instant the *sofer* set foot in the Rabbi's home. He did not give R' Saadyah any time to catch his breath or recover from his hurried walk. "The *Chacham* Menasheh Zakkai's *Sefer Torah* is missing. Perhaps you know where it might be?"

Terror seized the scribe. His eyes darkened and his face grew very pale. Fear closed his throat so that no word could escape.

"Silence is like a confession!" the Rabbi thundered. "Open your mouth and tell me at once where the missing *Sefer Torah* is!"

The *sofer* tried to rescue the tattered shreds of his dignity. "I took the *Sefer Torah* home to check it," he said.

"In that case," R' Moshe Chaim declared skeptically, "the *shamash* will go home with you right now and fetch it here."

R' Saadyah saw that the game was over. He broke down and confessed what he had done — how he had removed the original *Sefer Torah* from its case and sold it to the *Chacham* Sasson Papo. Under the Rabbi's grilling, he finally admitted that he had never actually written the *Sefer Torah* that the *Chacham* Sasson had ordered from him.

"Are you a *sofer* or a businessman?" the Rabbi scolded. "It is the way of merchants to take from one and sell to another while their pockets are empty. Is this fitting behavior for a *sofer* engaged in divine work?"

The *sofer* stood abashed and ashamed. R' Moshe Chaim continued to enumerate R' Saadyah's sins: "Not only have you stumbled on the sin of stealing, but you have caused a quarrel in the World of Truth between two upright and pious men who intended only to fulfill the *mitzvah* of writing a *Sefer Torah*. You have disturbed and confused their peace. Both are clinging to the same *Sefer Torah*. The first is claiming that it belongs to him, along with all the merit of the accompanying *mitzvos* — reading it aloud in *shul* and reciting all the blessings over it. At the same time, the second man is claiming the very same thing! How shall I judge between them? Look what you have brought about with your despicable behavior. They trusted you, and you deceived them!"

The *sofer's* spirit quailed and his knees sagged. He fell to the floor, weeping bitterly. "Woe is me, that I did such a thing! Forgive me! Grant me atonement!"

He sobbed for a long time, regretting his misguided actions from the bottom of his heart. Seeing that R' Saadyah's remorse was genuine, R' Moshe Chaim suggested a course of *teshuvah* — the first step being to rectify the damage he had done by writing a *Sefer Torah* for the *Chacham* Sasson Papo immediately. When the scroll would be completed, the Rabbi and the *shamash* would quietly introduce it into the Ark at *shul,* taking care to protect the *sofer* from public shame.

As for the quarrel between the two souls in the World of Truth, R' Moshe Chaim ruled as follows: "*Shnayim ochazin … yachaloku.*" (When two people come to *beis din* claiming ownership of the same object, they must divide it.) In other words, the blessings over the Torah, as well as the gifts and monetary pledges made over the second *Sefer Torah*, would accrue to *Chacham* Sasson Papo because the people involved had intended to honor him. But the merit of all other blessings, gifts, and pledges would belong to the owner of the first *Sefer Torah*, the *Chacham* Menasheh Zakkai.

After the *sofer* left his house, the Rabbi remarked to the *shamash*, "Now I understand the significance of the words, 'Torah is not in Heaven.' The Torah was handed down from Heaven at *Har Sinai*, so that it may be observed. The Heavenly Court is not required to judge matters that belong to this earth even when the matter at hand is the case of a stolen *Sefer Torah*, and the two disputants have come to reside in Heaven."

TWO HOURS
— FOR A LIFETIME

E VEN AS A YOUNG MAN, THE HOLY REBBE R' DOVID TZVI
Shlomo of Lelov harbored intense spiritual yearnings. He longed
to learn the paths to spiritual elevation from the great men of his
generation. From his home in Jerusalem, he cast an eye on the Jewish
communities across the sea — communities whose leaders spread
Torah and guided their flocks along life's proper road. The young man
longed to serve his Creator, and he was convinced that the best way
he could do it was by taking up the wanderer's staff and crossing the
great ocean.

He undertook the long trip, ending up in Vienna, capital city of
Austria — and home of R' Aharon of Karlin, author of the *Beis Aharon.*
R' Dovid went to see the Rebbe. He later related that with his first
"*Shalom aleichem*" he felt a powerful bond to R' Aharon. On the spot,
he made R' Aharon his Rebbe.

R' Dovid's very soul became bound up with that of his Rebbe. As
R' Aharon once told him, "You and me, me and you, now and later."

After he had accepted R' Aharon as his teacher, R' Dovid continued his plan of becoming acquainted with the great men of Poland
and Galicia. His first stop was Sanz, and the Rebbe who had authored
the *Divrei Chaim.*

R' Dovid reached Sanz on *Rosh Chodesh.* In *shul,* R' Chaim of
Sanz led the congregation in reciting the *Hallel.* As he listened, R'
Dovid felt close to melting from the sweetness of the *tefillah.* When
the Rebbe reached the words, "*Pischu li shaarei tzedek,* Open up the
gates of righteousness for me" — it was as though a thunderstorm

had passed through the *shul*. Another two or three minutes of listening to the Rebbe praying in the voice of the angels, R' Dovid believed, and he would be forced to renege on his commitment; he would have to rend the delicate strands that bound his soul with that of R' Aharon of Karlin.

"I sensed such a spiritual satisfaction, such a divine sweetness in the Sanzer Rebbe's *tefillah*, that I knew one thing clearly: Should I continue to hear his *tefillah*, I would never leave," he later explained with a smile. "I would have contradicted the decision to 'acquire a Rav' for myself that I had already made beforehand."

As we try to walk in the footsteps of these giants, let us tell a story that will illustrate the exalted power of the Sanzer Rebbe's prayer. It was related by the Pshevorsker Rebbe, R' Leibish Leizer, of Antwerp.

Here is the story he told.

After the Second World War, R' Leibish Leizer lived with his family in the Polish city of Wroclaw. His father was the renowned Rebbe, R' Yankel of Antwerp, who had passed away the year before. His mother, the rebbetzin, was the daughter of the famous R' Itzikel of Pshevorsk.

The present Rebbe, then but a youth, went with his mother to see an old Jewish doctor by the name of Dr. Kahn. This doctor, who went about bareheaded, appeared to be an irreligious man — a phenomenon sadly common among physicians in those days, while a *mitzvah*-observant Jewish doctor was a rare find indeed.

Imagine the surprise of mother and son, then, when with the sinking of the sun the elderly doctor excused himself and went off to one side. He replaced his white doctor's coat with a suit jacket, put on his hat, then stood in a corner of the room, a small *siddur* in hand, *davening Minchah* with feeling and devotion.

When he was done, he noted the astonishment that his patients were trying hard to conceal. Smiling, he said, "You are surprised to see a doctor *daven*? I want you to know that I did not do it in your honor, because you look religious. Heaven forbid — I am not an actor." He paused, then added reverentially, "I have seen prayer — a single prayer — that has changed my life!"

And he went on to tell them about it.

I grew up in the city of Katowitz, in Galicia (the doctor said), an offspring of an extremely secular family. My grandfather — my father's father — was a totally irreligious Jew, but some spark had remained alive in his soul, so that once a year, on Yom Kippur, he would go to pray in the synagogue. My father moved even further away than his father had done, and it was difficult to distinguish him from a gentile. He behaved like a gentile and bore the outward appearance of one.

My father was a merchant who dealt in the purchase and sale of various goods. In his line of work, he was always traveling. It was common for merchants in those times to do much of their traveling by train, where my father inevitably ran into a goodly number of Jews. In the course of conversation with them, one name kept cropping up: the name of a certain Rebbe whom the people referred to with awe as the "*Vunder Rabbiner*" (the "Wonder Rebbe").

Curiosity finally pierced the thick hide that cushioned my father's heart from all that was holy. Though his ears had long been sealed shut against the most delicate persuasions that might insinuate themselves into his soul, his mind was still alive. And his mind told him that there was something special taking place in the city of "New Sanz" — something worth his while to see. A wondrous Rebbe lived there, and my father sought the challenge of meeting him, face-to-face.

On his next trip to the Leipzig fair, the merchant Kahn took along his son (yours truly!). I was only 12 years old at the time. He made sure to plan an itinerary that would take us through the city of "New Sanz," where we would stop long enough to satisfy his curiosity about the Rebbe he had heard so much about.

My father did not live his life according to the Jewish calendar; he used the Gregorian calendar instead. So he had no way of knowing that it was the month of Elul, the month of compassion and forgiveness. In Elul, R' Chaim of Sanz prayed in public in the city's largest *shul,* instead of in his own, smaller one. When the Kahns, father and son, arrived at the Sanzer *shul,* they were amazed to find it empty.

"The Rebbe?" the children repeated, eyes wide as they took in the strangers' non-Jewish garb. "Don't you know that it's Elul?"

"Meaning — what?"

"In the month of Elul, the Rebbe *davens* in the big city *shul,*" the children explained eagerly. A few of them were happy to accompany the strangers from one *shul* to the other.

On their arrival at the large city *shul,* the Kahns found the congregation in the middle of a service, with the Rebbe himself leading them in prayer.

"Forgive me," quavered the old Dr. Kahn, as tears coursed down his cheeks. He was living in a different time now. Only his aged body remained in Wroclaw; his spirit had flown back to Sanz — a Sanz of seventy years ago — during the holy Rebbe's last years on this earth.

Father and I pressed into the crowd of praying people (the doctor continued his tale). We wanted to see the Rebbe up close. We were unable to see his face, as he stood with his back to us, his head covered with his *tallis.* But we heard his voice, and we saw his holy form, even if only from the back.

It seemed to us that we were seeing an angel. To all outward appearances, he was only a frail old man — but the impression that burrowed deep into our hearts was that of an angel! He prayed with such holy emotion that his voice penetrated the air like claps of thunder. The entire *shul* vibrated from his *tefillah* — literally. From time to time, the Rebbe's left foot would pound the ground, in an outpouring of endless longing. Only later did we learn that it was that very foot that was ill and caused him severe pain and suffering.

What can I say? We were plucked out of our secular, material world and lifted all at once into a very rarified atmosphere. For a long time, we stood there as though held fast by iron chains, unable to move. We forgot where we were and knew only one thing: We wanted to keep listening to that amazing voice, and that holy prayer.

Suddenly, silence descended. The Rebbe had finished *davening*. Only then did we rouse ourselves, as though from a deep sleep, and remember that we were visitors in a strange city.

"The train!" my father recalled, glancing frantically at his watch. "If we don't hurry, we'll miss it!"

We ran breathlessly to the station, where we just managed to catch the train we wanted. And, as it turned out, I also managed to "catch" the train of my own life.

At first, we could not speak. The mad dash to the station had robbed us of breath, along with the fear of missing the only means of transportation that could carry us out of a strange city. When we had recovered somewhat, both my father and I discovered that the brief experience we had just undergone had given our slumbering Jewish souls a dramatic awakening. We suddenly felt that the man we had just seen was an authentic Jew, and that this was the way a Jew ought to live; our own lives were mired in a quicksand of lies and materialism.

"I am already too old," my father said sadly, "too old to change. But you, my son, can still do something."

From that day, I knew no peace. That single episode had shaken me to my depths. I was only a child of 12, but I decided that I would change. I sought a teacher and guide to *Yiddishkeit*. They say that a person who desires to purify himself is granted Heaven's help. Heaven helped me find a pious Jew, a wise and faithful man.

I came to him eagerly, stammering, "I w-want you to t-teach me to be like them!"

"Like who?" asked the man.

"Like one of those *chassidim* who belong to the Sanzer Rebbe's group," I said with determination. I felt a unique and powerful sense of identification with those men. My entire soul longed to be like one of them!

The man understood. He spoke with me a little, and when he had reassured himself that I was not joking, he sat with me every day, teaching me the principles of Judaism. I learned it all from the very beginning, just the way a 3-year-old child learns in *cheder*. Most importantly, he taught me how one observes the Shabbos, what "kosher" means, how to put on *tefillin*, and how to *daven*.

To *daven* ... that was my primary ambition. To pray like the old Rebbe!

There were other passages and trials waiting for me in life. When I grew up, my father sent me to Berlin to learn medicine. If I had managed, back in Katowitz, to observe a few *mitzvos,* in Germany this became all but impossible. Berlin was an outstandingly gentile city. I studied with gentiles, and the few Jews that I met there were not, to say the least, stringent about *halachah*. To keep Shabbos and eat only kosher food became one of the most difficult goals I have ever undertaken. And, truth to tell, there was more than one time that I found myself in crisis, almost ready to throw my hands up in despair. Why did I have to be the only religious Jew in all of Berlin?

At those moments, a curtain would suddenly open in my soul, and once again I would see the holy Rebbe praying. I would hear the thunderclap of his voice in the New Sanz *shul,* reverberating in my own mind and throughout Berlin. I heard R' Chaim cry out to his Creator, like a baby who had never sinned and weeps longingly for his beloved Father. I saw his foot beating the ground with amazing life force.

That crystal-clear memory was stronger than all my present trials and tribulations! The Rebbe had passed away years before, but his image lived clearly in my memory, never leaving me for an instant. Time and again, that image helped me conquer the temptation to yield to the vicissitudes of life.

"Seventy-two years have passed since then," Dr. Kahn concluded. "I have never abandoned the *mitzvos* that I learned as a youth from that pious Jew. I've never skipped a single *davening*, however difficult. That single event that I witnessed as a child of 12 in the city of New Sanz placed its stamp on me forever. They were two hours that changed the course of my life!"

THE PEDDLER'S LUCK

MENDEL THE PEDDLER'S FEET WERE WELL USED TO wandering. Through the weary years, they walked up hills and down again, through valleys and forests. Over his shoulder he carried a heavy gray sack. In this sack lay the source of Mendel's livelihood.

At each stop he would pull out his wares: rags and combs, tools and pins and writing implements. All day long he walked the roads, buying and selling, selling and buying. He never stopped, never grew disgusted with the exhausting work. Day after day, week after week, months after month, year upon year. This was Mendel's job.

For many years he roamed from village to village throughout Romania, crossing vast expanses on foot, the eternal bulging sack over his shoulder. Beneath the brim of his cap, a pair of innocent Jewish eyes twinkled out of a face darkened by years in the sun. His long beard showed signs of age, and he wore it like a badge of honor. Mendel looked like a Rabbi who had mistakenly wandered into the wrong profession. Seeing him, one would be forgiven for thinking that he was on his way to his *shtender* to chant over a *Gemara*.

Mendel went from door to door, from Jewish home to non-Jewish home alike. At one place, he became interested in the fate of an old goose coop he found lying in the yard as though abandoned.

"It seems to me that last year, when I passed this way, I saw that same coop lying in the yard, unused. Perhaps I can have it?"

The housewife, seizing her chance to earn a bit of ready cash, told him that the price of the coop was twenty lei (Romanian currency).

"Twenty lei?" Mendel repeated in surprise. "You should pay *me* twenty lei for clearing that heap of rubbish out of your yard!"

As he spoke, he turned and began to walk quickly away.

"Wait!" the housewife called after him. "How much are you willing to pay?"

"Five lei, not a penny more," he threw over his shoulder.

"Fifteen."

"Five!"

"All right, let's leave it at ten. But I want all the money in advance."

Once again, Mendel turned to leave. The housewife saw that stubbornness would lose her a certain five lei which she had never expected to see. She had had no use for that old coop for some time now.

The deal concluded, Mendel took out his bundle of money and counted out five lei. He parted with the sum with a sigh. "That old thing is not really worth more than a lei and a half," he told the housewife, who was feeling foolish for having agreed to such a low price. "I doubt if I'll even find a customer for such a broken-down coop."

Under Mendel's dextrous fingers, the coop underwent a miraculous transformation. Old slats were removed and new ones nailed into place. The coop was given a new lease on life. In the next village, Mendel sold it for a nice profit.

In this way, various pieces of old furniture passed through the peddler's hands. Rusted old carriages missing one wheel — or even two ... ancient, battered copper kettles that had lost all likeness to their original appearance ... and all sorts of "bargains" that people had thrown away as useless. After Mendel's treatment, they were restored to their youthful glory. No wonder, then, that he was afterwards able to sell them for a relatively good price.

Mendel was a faithful Vizhnitzer *chassid*. Every few months he made sure to travel to the city of Groswardein, home of his Rebbe, R' Yisrael of Vizhnitz. Whenever he was in the neighborhood, he made sure to stop in at his Rebbe's courtyard. The Rebbe always greeted him warmly and blessed him with a peaceful life, a good livelihood, and success in his endeavors. Mendel would leave feeling strengthened both spiritually and materially.

On this visit, as always, Mendel handed the Rebbe his *kvittel*. The Rebbe studied it, then glanced up into Mendel's face. R' Yisrael's gaze was veiled, but the words he spoke could not have been clearer.

"*Zolst upgehitten veren fun goyishe hent!* May you be saved from non-Jewish hands!"

Mendel walked out feeling bewildered. On his *kvittel* he had written a long list of requests, but the Rebbe had addressed none of them. Instead, he had offered a blessing unlike any he had ever given before. Though Mendel had longed to ask for an explanation, fear and awe had effectively tied the peddler's tongue.

On leaving the Rebbe's courtyard, the matter troubled Mendel for a while. He tried to unravel the mystery behind the Rebbe's strange words. But Mendel had never been one to worry himself overmuch about the future. He put aside his wondering and went back to work.

The meeting with the Rebbe, and the Rebbe's strange blessing, were pushed to the back of the peddler's mind, all but forgotten.

Several weeks passed.

Mendel neared the outskirts of the Romanian village of Nehi-Kolosh. There were no Jews in the village, which was situated in an isolated spot, far from the big cities. The sun beat mercilessly down on the peddler's head as he trudged along, perspiring freely. He did not know which felt worse: his aching feet or his parched throat, beset with a raging thirst.

Weak and tired, he passed from door to door, collecting outstanding debts from the gentiles living there, old customers of his. At dusk, he knocked on Cleo's door. Cleo owed him a substantial sum.

"Good evening!" Cleo exclaimed at seeing Mendel. "Of course I'll pay you what I owe you. But where's the fire? You're soaked in sweat — you look terrible. Rest tonight, and tomorrow I'll pay my entire debt, I swear!"

The peddler shook his head. "I can't stay in your house." He pointed at a cross hanging on the wall. "That is forbidden for me."

"Who invited you to sleep here?" Cleo retorted. "Go out to the barn. It's large and airy. We'll spread some blankets on the fresh, sweet-smelling hay and you'll sleep well there. Don't worry — if Nicholas, my son, hasn't found a more comfortable bed than that, surely a Jew like you will find it comfortable, too!"

Exhaustion tugged at Mendel with insistent fingers. He didn't argue with Cleo.

After *davening Maariv*, Mendel ate something and then lay down to sleep. But despite his deep fatigue, sleep continued to elude him. He was bewildered. This had never happened to him before. He usually had no trouble dropping off at once. All he had to do was lay his head down on the pillow and he was lost in sweet slumber. What was happening tonight?

He turned from side to side, rolling around like a bale of the hay he was lying on. An hour passed, then two, and still Mendel was awake.

Soundly asleep on a nearby pile of hay was Nicholas, Cleo's grown son. Unlike Mendel, Nicholas had had no trouble dropping off. His snores testified to that.

At midnight, Mendel's patience evaporated. If he didn't sleep tonight, tomorrow he'd be as useless as a drunkard and would lose a sizeable portion of his daily income. No! He must sleep at least a little. But, try as he might, sleep would not come.

Suddenly, Mendel remembered a saying of our Sages: "*Meshaneh makom, meshaneh mazal*" — that is, a change of location can bring in its train a change of fortune. Perhaps those wise men had been referring to sleep as well. Maybe, on a different mattress, sleep would finally come to end his suffering. He thumped on Nicholas's back. Nicholas snorted, gasped, and mumbled, "What? What happened?"

"Nothing, don't get excited," Mendel said. "I can't sleep. Will you switch places with me?"

Nicholas grew angry. "And if you can't sleep, do you have to drag me into your bad luck?"

"It's all to your advantage," Mendel coaxed. "My haystack is softer."

Finally, muttering and grumbling, Nicholas switched places with Mendel. Not a moment later, his snores were once again resounding through the barn.

As for Mendel, he lay as wide awake as ever.

Finally, some time in the wee hours, he gave up. "This night is obviously not meant for sleep. I'd better get up now, while it's still dark, and walk over to the next village to collect my debts there in the morning."

He wasted no time. Mendel got up, slung his sack over his shoulder, and stepped out of the barn into the darkness. Picking his way with care among the stones, he forgot completely about the money that Cleo owed him. Mendel was filled with gratitude to Hashem for giving him the idea to set out for the neighboring village now, at night, and not to wait for morning. A brisk walk through the crisp night air was far preferable to trudging along beneath the heat of the summer sun.

Mendel was not the only person who had trouble sleeping that night.

Inside the house, Cleo tossed and turned for hours. He could not calm down.

"That Jew has no shame. Here he comes, a year later, asking for his money! He himself is rich as a sultan. His pockets are dripping with treasure." His mind calculated feverishly: The peddler collected his debts all day long — why, Stephen the lumber merchant alone owed him hundreds — and would come away with a fortune.

With startling abruptness, just before dawn, Cleo leaped out of bed. It was time to put into action the plan that had been turning over in his twisted mind all night long.

"Cleo, what are you doing?" his wife demanded, as Cleo stood by the large stove, filling it with dry logs. "What do you want with the oven in the middle of the summer? You must have dreamed about winter and snow!"

"No dream," growled Cleo, "and no sleep. I'm going to burn that Jew in this oven!"

His wife stood speechless. "What are you saying?" she hissed at last. "Why have you killed the Jew? He's a good man!"

"Hush, will you! I haven't killed him yet. I'm going to do that now. I will burn his body in the oven. With his money, I will be able to pay all my debts — and we'll live like kings!"

Leaving her behind, open-mouthed in astonishment and dismay, Cleo tiptoed out to the barn. In his hand was a long, wicked-looking knife. The barn was dark, but he knew his way. Cleo made straight for the haystack on which he had made up the Jewish peddler's bed. And then, without glancing into the man's face or hesitating an instant, he plunged the knife with all his strength into the man's back. He pulled the knife out and stabbed again, just to make sure. Then he hurried out of the barn; Cleo had no desire to watch a man in the throes of death.

A few minutes later, he returned. Dragging his victim by the heels, he made for the oven.

As he stepped out of the barn, the moonlight shone full on the dead man's face. For the first time, Cleo saw it clearly. The breath left his own body with a gasp.

"Nicholas!" he shrieked. "Nicholas, what have I done?"

Alerted by his screams, his wife came running. In the next instant, her wails rose into the night air, to mingle with her husband's.

Mendel walked on, oblivious to the drama being played out behind him. As he walked, he whistled a merry tune.

"Stop!"

The sudden, authoritative call took the peddler by surprise. Turning, he saw two armed police officers. "What are you doing here in the middle of the night?"

Trustingly, Mendel explained the circumstances that had brought him to that spot that night. The officers, however, clearly did not believe a word of his story. After all, thieves spoke just as convincingly.

"What kind of old grandmother's tales are you babbling?" they scoffed. "You couldn't sleep, and that's why you're lugging around that heavy sack? Hah! Where are you coming from?"

"From Nehi-Kolosh," Mendel answered, resigned.

"All right — let's go to Nehi-Kolosh. We'll see whom you cleaned out there!"

Long before they reached Cleo's house, they heard the unearthly wailing of the man and his wife.

"See?" one of the policemen sneered, jabbing Mendel in the back. "This innocent Jew says he couldn't sleep. Those two have probably just found out how much he stole from them. That's why they're screaming like that."

Approaching nearer, they began to discern what Cleo and his wife were saying. They stopped to listen.

"I told you not to harm the Jew," the wife shrieked, beating her own forehead in despair. "Look what you've done! You cruel murderer, you greedy, bloodthirsty creature — you've killed your son with your own hands!"

"Quiet, woman!" Cleo roared. "What can I do? I killed Nicholas by mistake. I didn't mean to do it. We can't bring him back to life again. But if this comes to the ears of the authorities, they'll lock me up in jail. We'd better spread the tale that the Jewish peddler murdered our son and then ran away."

The two policemen looked at one another and nodded their heads in unison. This was the sweetest moment for any law-enforcement officer — to hear a criminal describe exactly what his plans are. Moving as one, they burst into the house, apprehended Cleo, and began to beat the truth out of him. In short order, they had the whole sorry story from Cleo's own lips.

"Jew," the police officers said to Mendel, "your luck was with you tonight. If you hadn't happened to run into us, things would have been very different for you."

Mendel wanted to tell them who was really responsible for his good fortune, but the policemen did not precisely consider themselves Vizhnitzer *chassidim*. As soon as he was able, Mendel thought, he would seek out a fellow Jew to whom he could relate the whole astonishing tale.

"May you be saved from non-Jewish hands."
Exactly!

BLESSED BREAD

ONE OF THE MOST PROMINENT *CHASSIDIM* WHO GRACED THE Karliner Rebbe's courtyard was R' Elazar Sofer. He lived in the city of Stolin, and would visit R' Aharon of Karlin for the Jewish festivals, for various Shabbosos, and at every chance he got.

Early one morning, before sunrise, R' Elazar woke as usual, washed his hands, and noticed a strange, sluggish sensation in his limbs. He felt as though he hadn't slept at all. With difficulty, he managed to stand up — and then quickly lay down on his bed again, exhausted and devoid of strength. Seeing him thus, his wife became alarmed. Had he fainted, or worse? Hurrying over to him, she was relieved to see that his eyes were open.

A little later, the doctor pronounced his diagnosis: Ague!

This all-purpose name covered a dozen different illnesses, about all of which the doctors knew very little. Most of them came along with high fever. R' Elazar burned and writhed in pain. But the worst pain came from the knowledge that his illness had removed all possibility of visiting the courtyard of the holy Karliner Rebbe.

At first, it was believed that his illness would pass fairly quickly. A week, or two at most, and R' Elazar would be back on his feet. To the concern of his family and friends, however, there was no improvement in his condition. On the contrary, he seemed to be getting worse. R' Elazar lay in bed like a stone, burning with fever, his eyes like glowing coals in his wan face. The illness ravaged his body for two full months, sapping his strength until he was so frail he could not lift an arm or leg.

As the festival of Shavuos approached, a group of his *chassidic* friends prepared to travel to their Rebbe, R' Aharon of Karlin. Before their departure, they visited R' Elazar to say good-bye.

"When do you leave?" R' Elazar asked.

"Today," one of the *chassidim* said. "We hope to reach the Rebbe before nightfall, so that we can *daven Maariv* with him and count the last of the *Omer* together."

From somewhere, a bottle and glasses appeared. "*L'Chaim!*" chorused the *chassidim,* raising their glasses to the sick man. "It's too bad you can't join us. But don't worry. As soon as we reach the Rebbe, we'll give him your name and ask for his blessing for a speedy recovery."

"*It's too bad you can't join us.*" The words echoed in R' Elazar's mind like painful hammer blows. It was the first time in a very long time that he would not be with the Rebbe for Shavuos. He could hardly bear it.

Suddenly, like a lightning bolt illuminating the dark, he was struck by a thought. *Who says I can't?*

"What do they mean? I also intend to see the Karliner Rebbe this year!" he blurted to his wife when his visitors had left.

"Elazar, what's going on?" She stared at him.

She thought at first that he was delirious with fever. It soon became apparent, however, that her husband was thinking very clearly. She tried to dissuade him from considering the wild scheme, but faith is stronger than the most cogent logic. R' Elazar burned with faith in his holy Rebbe.

The woman realized that she was fighting a losing battle. In despair, she tried to draft stronger powers to deal with her husband. She went to the Stoliner Rebbe, R' Moshe, who was universally respected and known to all as R' Moishkele. He sent a message to the sick man saying, "If you desire life, do not do foolish deeds. An ill man like yourself, traveling in a wagon over such a long distance, is endangering his life!"

R' Elazar understood at once who was behind the Rebbe's emotional plea. His answer to his wife was final: "If I do not travel to Karlin for Shavuos, my life will have no flavor!"

A hired wagon stood in front of the house. R' Elazar's wife labored to load the wagon with an abundance of pillows and blankets. When she had seen that nothing would stand in the way of her husband's determination, she had resigned herself to the prospect and was now doing her best to help him. If he must make the journey, let him at least do so in whatever comfort she could provide.

"Don't hurry the horses too much," she warned the driver. "Don't forget for a minute that you're transporting a dangerously ill man!"

"Don't worry." The driver held his head up proudly, "You may rest assured that I will drive as though the king himself were my passenger."

"Oh, if only he weren't going at all!" The woman burst into uncontrollable tears. "He's so stubborn. My heart is filled with such anxiety."

A different kind of anxiety filled R' Elazar's heart. Usually, whenever he would go to his Rebbe, he would travel via Pinsk, where he would visit his father. The wagon driver, an old friend of his father's, would surely not allow him to journey to Karlin without the customary stop in nearby Pinsk to see his father first. But once his worried father saw his condition, he would not let R' Elazar leave his house. R' Elazar would be put straight to bed and would not get to see the Rebbe at all.

A cunning plan sprouted in his brain. As the wagon jogged along, he struck up a pleasant conversation with the driver. From time to time, R' Elazar proffered a drink from a bottle he kept in his bag. When the driver was nicely full of wine, R' Elazar extracted a promise from him that he would drive directly to Karlin without stopping at R' Elazar's father's house in Pinsk.

"Then where shall I take you?" the driver asked foolishly.

"What a question! To the Karliner Rebbe's house. There is a large hall there, where *chassidim* gather to be welcomed by the Rebbe. There is *always* a bed in one corner of the room. We'll put some of my pillows and blankets on that, and I will lie there."

The driver nodded his head in comprehension.

The wagon, accordingly, passed Pinsk without stopping, and went directly to the Beis Aharon *beis midrash* in Karlin.

"My dear brothers! Who wants to merit a big *mitzvah*?" shouted the driver into the hall, which was filled wall-to-wall with *chassidim*.

"What happened?" the *chassidim* asked.

"Come outside with me," the driver beckoned, like one with a secret.

Several men followed him outside. Seeing R' Elazar lying in the wagon, shaking with a high fever, they were stunned. When they had recovered from their first shock, an uproar ensued. If the driver had thought he would win praise for his daring act, he was due for a disappointment.

"Have you lost your mind?" they scolded him roundly. "How could you bring such a sick man here? Is this crowded, noisy *shul* any place for a sick man? Take him to his father's house in Pinsk at once!"

But their rebuke fell on deaf ears. The driver, well fortified with wine, paid not the slightest heed. R' Elazar had prepared him for just this reaction. The ill man pointed to the bed, and the driver carried him there. When he had seen R' Elazar settled comfortably with his pillows and blankets, surrounded by a crowd of anxious *chassidim,* the driver beat a hasty retreat.

Someone ran to inform the Rebbe that R' Elazar, desperately ill, had arrived. But the *Beis Aharon* did not react at all.

Sudden and complete silence descended as the Rebbe entered to welcome his *chassidim.* The commotion that had filled the large room a moment earlier gave way to a respectful quiet as the Rebbe made his way from man to man, welcoming each. Then he reached R' Elazar's bed.

The expectancy in the air was so thick one might have been pardoned for believing it could be cut with a knife. Every person present waited tensely to see how the Rebbe would speak to the sick man. Would he sharply berate R' Elazar for his foolhardly act — or praise him for his devotion?

To their astonishment, the Rebbe did not say anything. He stood and gazed thoughtfully down at R' Elazar for several minutes. Then, still without a word, he left the place and returned to his room.

All during that festival of Shavuos, R' Elazar was in an exalted frame of mind. Though confined to bed and unable to so much as walk across the room because of the severity of his condition, he was not deprived of the flow of holiness that all his friends and acquaintances enjoyed. The doors of the great hall stood opposite those of the *beis midrash*, and he could hear the *tefillos* taking place there over the holiday. He listened intently as the Rebbe roared out his *Akdamos*; even the *Yom Tov Kiddush* after the service reached his ears clearly.

After *Kiddush*, the men washed their hands for the holiday *seudah*. This meal hardly deserved the title. The Rebbe's court was not a wealthy one, to say the least. The number of *challos* available did not match the large number of *chassidim,* and only a small group merited eating actual *challah*. The rest received coarse brown bread, with a pinch of salt to dip it in. This — brown bread and salt — constituted their meal. But their souls, replete with spiritual satisfaction, sensed no lack as a steady stream of Torah teachings reached them from the senior *chassidim*.

The exalted atmosphere and the burning *chassidic* dialogue drew R' Elazar like a magnet. With the last of his strength, he rose from his bed and made his way to the table. He wanted to be able to hear some of the things that were lighting up his friends' faces. The *chassidim,* mesmerized by the table talk, did not notice that the Rebbe had emerged from his room. With his hands on either side of the door, the Rebbe stood framed in the doorway, regarding the crowd. Then he moved forward and approached the head of the table, where a deep *chassidic* discussion was taking place, the meager food forgotten.

"Eat, *kinderlach*, eat!" the *Beis Aharon* urged his *chassidim*. "Eat the bread and salt. Anyone who needs a cure and a salvation — you all will be saved!"

R' Elazar had not tasted regular food for months. Coarse bread such as this had been strictly forbidden him by his doctors. Now, hearing the Rebbe's words, R' Elazar picked up and ate a small piece of brown bread, while announcing enthusiastically, "I believe with complete faith that from this bread I will have a complete recovery!"

The taste of the dry bread was strange to him, and it was difficult for him to swallow. But, held fast in the grip of his unshakable faith in his Rebbe, swallow it he did. He took another small bite, and managed to get that down, too.

Many eyes gazed at him wonderingly. What would happen now?

What happened was — the incredible. Little by little, as he nibbled the bread and swallowed it, R' Elazar felt his strength slowly returning. Before his friends' amazed eyes, the color returned to the sick man's pallid cheeks, and his carriage became slightly more erect. Gradually, as the hours passed, all sign of his illness disappeared. By the second night of the festival, not a sign of his lingering "ague" was left!

On the following day, the second day of Shavuos, when some meat and fish were distributed among the crowd, R' Elazar was among the few who were privileged to receive some. He consumed his portion with gusto!

But the greatest surprise was reserved for the next day, *Isru Chag*, when the group of *chassidim* from Stolin decided — in view of their slim budget and empty wallets — to make the return trip from Karlin, a journey of several hours, on foot. And who led the procession of energetic walkers but R' Elazar Sofer, the man who had been so dangerously ill.

A GLASS OF FINE BEER

NISSAN THE BARTENDER HAD NEVER KNOWN ANY OTHER profession. In the small village close by the city of Square, his father had leased the tavern and hostelry from the local *poritz* thirty years before. After the father died, his son Nissan inherited the business. All day long, he poured whiskey and beer into tall mugs for the gentile farmers. He managed to earn a meager living thereby, and to pay his yearly rent to the aging *poritz*.

An upright and pious man was Nissan. He prepared the kegs of beer with his own hands. With time, he became something of an expert in the field, and his product earned a fine reputation.

As the years passed without change, Nissan felt secure. He would live out his days in the village tavern, a steady source of livelihood always on hand. True, his income was not large, but it came without too much trouble and in a respectable fashion.

But the sun rises and sets, and little by little people grow older and the days of their lives are spent. The *poritz*, too, aged day by day, until the time came when his soul left his body and he died. He left the world childless, with no son to inherit his property. He bequeathed it all instead to his nephew, son of his brother.

The nephew was living in Paris at the time, where he was studying for a degree in philosophy. He was in no hurry to leave. For a while, as he completed his studies, the village remained unattended. Then, his education finished, he traveled to the village to claim his inheritance and place his own stamp on it.

Almost at once, the winds of change began to blow through the peaceful village. They were not benevolent winds.

The young *poritz* was not a good-hearted man. He instituted new, autocratic measures. He mistreated the villagers and exiled those who did not please him. All the joy went out of the villagers' lives as they waited tensely to hear what new edicts the *poritz* would come up with each day.

If the village folk in general feared the *poritz*, Nissan feared him doubly. His heart pounded as he wondered whether his new master's cruel hand would fall on him next.

It never occurred to Nissan that it would be a Jew who would bring about his downfall.

The Jew came from the city of Balilubka, and he heard that there was a tavern in the village that turned a nice profit. He made an appointment with the young *poritz* and proposed to lease the tavern from him at twice the usual rent.

The *Graf* sent at once for Nissan. "A certain Jew from Balilubka is competing with you. He is prepared to pay me twice what you pay. Because I am a fair man, I do not demand your answer at once. I will give you two days to consider the matter and decide what to do. If you wish to give me three times your usual fee — fine. If not, the Balilubkan will take your place."

A dark curtain seemed to fall over Nissan's eyes. He threw himself on the floor at the *poritz's* feet and pleaded through bitter tears for himself and his wife and children. "As it is, I barely make ends meet. I make just enough to live on, no more. Where am I to find three times the rent?"

But the stone-hearted *Graf* merely repeated: "You have two days. Either pay three times the rent, or leave the village."

In desperation, Nissan traveled to Balilubka to see his competitor. "What have I done to you," he cried, "that you are turning my life upside-down?"

But the other man shut his ears to Nissan's pleas. He would not say a word, except to point out the door leading from his house.

From Balilubka, Nissan traveled to Berditchev, where he poured out his heart to R' Levi Yitzchak. He explained how one of his own people was causing him such harm.

At once, R' Levi Yitzchak had a message sent to the other Jew.

"With the authority of our holy Torah, I order you to appear before me for a *din Torah* together with Nissan, and to refrain from doing that which should not be done!"

But the man was coarse and uncaring. He did not travel to Berditchev; in fact, he did not even trouble himself to answer the summons. R' Levi Yitzchak sent an additional sharp warning: "If you do not come at once, your end will be bitter."

Even now, the brazen-hearted Jew did not come. A few days later, he traveled back to Nissan's village, where he leased the tavern and hostelry from the young *poritz* at twice the rent that Nissan had been paying. Nissan was forced out of his home that very day.

He returned to Berditchev and cried piteously before the Rebbe. "I now have no way to support my family!"

"Do not cry," said R' Levi Yitzchak. "*Hashem Yisbarach*, Who has been with you until now, will not abandon you. Travel throughout the region and look for another tavern. Perhaps you will find another one, even smaller, that will still suffice to provide your sustenance."

Nissan obeyed the Rebbe's instructions. From village to village he went, until he did find a small tavern, which he leased from the local *poritz*. He sent at once for his wife and children.

Nissan set to work at the only profession he knew. He prepared his drinks and brewed his beer, and Heaven rewarded his efforts with blessing. Word began to spread through the area that Nissan's whiskey and beer were top quality, with a taste that was unparalleled. From far and near, farmers began to stream to his tavern.

Meanwhile, the new tavern-keeper in Nissan's former village enjoyed a good beginning. The whiskey poured like water into his customer's thirsty throats, and the gentile farmers kept coming back for more.

But the success was short-lived.

One day, two months after Nissan had been sent away, a large and boisterous group of farmers entered the tavern. "We're thirsty!" they bellowed. "Bring us good beer and whiskey — and lots of it!"

No sooner had they begun to take their first generous gulps of their drinks when a change came over the farmers' faces. They spat out the whiskey and the beer. "This stuff is rotten. It stinks!" In a fury, they hurled their glasses to the floor, and the noise of splintering glass mingled with the farmers' angry curses.

The bartender, alerted by the commotion, came out to see what was going on. "B-but I poured you my best beer and my finest whiskey," he said, trembling.

One of the gentiles thrust a brimming glass under the Jew's nose. "Smell it," he ordered in a shout. "I'll eat my hat if this stuff doesn't smell like sewage water!"

The tavern-keeper took a cautious sniff — and wrinkled his nose in disgust. "Heavens, you're right! How did this beer get to smell like that? Perhaps the glass wasn't clean."

He went from glass to glass and then to the barrel of beer, and from every one rose the same foul stench of decaying bodies.

The next day, he went to a nearby town to fetch a fresh supply of beer and whiskey. This time, he did not trust anyone else to do the job for him. He sniffed each barrel before he bought it, and the good scent of fine whiskey and beer calmed him. With the barrels in his wagon, he returned to his own village, and his tavern.

But the very next day, the farmers complained again that their drinks stank as though dead men were buried inside. Aghast, the owner put his nose to the barrels once more — the barrels that had smelled fresh and pleasant just the day before — and found that the farmers had not lied. The same foul stench rose from them.

In a panic, the tavern-keeper traveled to yet another town, paying good money to bring the best whiskey back with him. But the curse did not depart. The moment he crossed his threshold with the barrels, they began to stink horribly. The man was in despair.

Longing to assuage their thirst with decent beer and whiskey, the farmers began to ask around, inquiring where they might find some. It was not long before it came to their attention that Nissan, the former tavern-keeper and bartender in their village, was now working in a different village not far away. The reputation of the drinks he served was sterling. Nissan was selling fine whiskey and excellent beer at inexpensive prices.

The farmers headed that way without delay.

The new influx of customers brought a welcome addition to Nissan's income. As the wheel turned, Nissan began to grow prosperous, while his competitor's fortunes sank ever lower.

The distraught tavern-keeper went to the *poritz* and complained that the local farmers were taking their business elsewhere. The *poritz* summoned some of them and asked, angrily, why they weren't buying their drinks at their own village tavern.

"What can we do?" the farmers complained. "His whiskey stinks — literally!"

"What?" shrieked the irate *Graf*. "Whiskey cannot become spoiled. I have never heard such nonsense in my life."

The farmers' claim, however, was simple enough to prove. They brought the *poritz* a glassful of the stuff sold in the tavern. One sip — and one sniff — was enough to convince him that the stuff was undrinkable.

Meanwhile, the new tavern-keeper kept very busy. He traveled to the farthest ends of the land, buying and bringing back new barrels of whiskey and beer. He tried different brands and paid for the very best quality. But the *tzaddik's* curse entered the barrels the moment they came into his possession. Like the Egyptians' water that turned to blood in their hands, the stench of the drink made it impossible for anyone to swallow.

For two solid years, the tavern-keeper tried his luck. He traveled, he bought, he tried to sell his whiskey. But no one would drink it. The Jew sank a veritable fortune into his tavern, but ended up with his head in his hands. Before long, he was destitute. There was no money with which to pay his landlord, the *poritz*, the rent he owed.

One day, the *poritz* was invited to a party thrown by the *poritz* who owned the village where Nissan now worked. The two friends chatted for a while on various topics, until the subject of "drink" came up.

The *poritz* from the village near Square sighed heavily. "My Jew promised me the world. He said he would pay me double the usual rent! But in the end, not only did he not pay double, he doesn't even have the regular amount to give me. I regret having sent away the former tavern-keeper."

"Well, Nissan, *my* tavern-keeper," boasted his friend, "is a good and loyal man. Even if you would lend him several thousand rubles, you could sleep easy knowing that he is an honest man who will return every cent. Everything he does seems blessed. People come from all around to drink his excellent beer and whiskey."

"Nissan?" The first *poritz* pounced on the familiar name. "Let me see him!"

He walked into the tavern, and paled. "Yes, that's Nissan — the man I sent away." For a moment, the *poritz* hesitated. Then he walked over to Nissan, apologized for his earlier actions, and asked him to return to his former tavern. Just days later, the Jew from Balilubka was sent away in disgrace.

And just a few days after that, the man from Balilubka returned to Nissan, head hanging low.

"I've been to see the holy R' Levi Yitzchak," he confessed in shame. "He ordered me to beg your pardon for all the pain I caused you."

Nissan was a good-hearted fellow. He forgave the man — and then generously gave him employment in his inn.

A WEDDING WITHOUT A GROOM

MUSIC AND VOICES FILLED THE WEDDING HALL IN THE French city of Strasbourg. The large crowd of guests had broken into small groups, all of which were carrying on animated discussions in every corner of the hall.

One late arrival, expecting to find the meal nearly over, was surprised to see that it had not even begun. Sensing the tension in the room, he crossed the hall and joined one of the groups.

"*Baruch haba!* Welcome!" they greeted him, laughing.

"What's going on?" he asked, casting a curious eye over the room. "It looks like the *chuppah* hasn't even taken place yet!"

"Of course not. Is it possible to have a *chuppah* without a *chasan*?"

"*What?*"

One of the other guests was kind enough to explain. "The *chasan* hasn't arrived yet. We're all waiting for him, but he hasn't come!"

Gradually, the whole story emerged. The groom was supposed to arrive from Sternowitz, capital city of Bokovina, after a two-day trip by train. But when the *kallah's* parents came to the station late at night to meet him, they were shocked to see every last passenger alight from the train without a sign of their future son-in-law!

They finally left the platform, hoping that the *chasan* would find his way to town himself, or perhaps go directly to the wedding hall on the appointed day. Naturally, no one had the least desire to call off the wedding because the *chasan* was late. But when the distraught parents checked their watches, the time stood at 10 p.m. The *chuppah* had been called for 8.

"Of course, we've heard about even longer delays," the guests whispered to one another. "But those usually happened because some honored guests were late. Not the groom!"

As the minutes ticked past, speculation about the young man began to fly. What could have happened to delay him so? The rumors sprouted like mushrooms after a rain.

And in the women's hall, the bride sat waiting, her face as white as the dress she wore. The whisperings had not escaped her. Her quick breaths said that she was near fainting. Someone with presence of mind fetched a glass of cold water to revive her.

"Excuse me!" A postal agent burst suddenly into the hall. In his hand was a telegram. "Excuse me, but I need to find the parents of the bride!

Three days earlier...

Approaching the Sternowitz station, the long shriek of the train's whistle sliced through the music of early-morning birdsong. A speeding train slowed down and came to a halt beside the platform. Passengers descended with alacrity, intent on arriving at their various destinations.

In the midst of the milling crowd stepped a young man with the beginnings of a beard and the garb of a *chassid*. He held a suitcase in one hand and a suit bag in the other. He was in a great hurry.

Yesterday had been his *aufruf,* when he had been called up to the Torah, and this morning he had left his hometown of Gura-Humar on the first train to Sternowitz, now puffing away again with gathering speed. He still had a great deal to do today. More than anything, he was anxious to get to his *chuppah* on time.

"The day is short and the work is great," he told himself, stopping for a moment in a quiet corner to take a notebook from his bag. He was a methodical young man, and the day's plans were written neatly under the date.

"*Sunday. Daven Shacharis at the Rebbe's shul, together with the Rebbe. Ask the Rebbe for a blessing for my marriage. Then go to the Polish Consulate to arrange a visa. Buy a train ticket for the Sternowitz-Strasbourg line. Parting and final blessing from the Rebbe. Then to the station to catch the midnight train.*"

With quick steps, he walked to the Jewish section of town, headed for the *beis midrash* of his Rebbe, R' Menachem Nachum of Boyan-Sternowitz, eldest of the four sons of R' Yitzchak, author of the *Pachad Yitzchak,* of Boyan.

"Michel, you're a lucky man!" he told himself happily. "In a few minutes you'll be seeing the Rebbe's face. And in just four days, a new Jewish home will begin as you stand beneath the *chuppah!*"

His heart beat strongly with the force of his emotions. He was the happiest man alive. He was about to be married! A joyous smile spread across his face.

A little while later, he was standing wrapped in his *tefillin* in the *beis midrash,* reciting the words of *Shacharis* with fervor. He followed the Rebbe's every movement. Every sigh, every tear, every gesture imprinted itself on the young *chassid's* heart.

When the *davening* was over, he was summoned to an inner room. With uplifted heart, he told the Rebbe where he was headed. He described his plans for the rest of the day and the rest of the happy week. The Rebbe blessed him warmly.

The first part of his day's schedule was over. It was time to set about the business of getting to his *chuppah.*

The guard at the Polish Consulate glared down at him through a small window in the iron gates. His eyes held open disdain. "What do you want?"

"I'm taking the train from Sternowitz to Strasbourg, France tonight. The train has to pass through Poland, so I need an entry visa."

"Come back tomorrow," snapped the guard. With a resounding clang, the window in the guard booth slammed shut.

For three frozen seconds, Michel stood stunned. Then, recovering his wits, he began to pound frantically on the window. "What do you mean, tomorrow?" he cried angrily. "I have to leave tonight, do you hear?" His throat was becoming hoarse. "Open the gate!"

The gate creaked on its hinges as it slowly opened wide. The uniformed guard walked through it, eyes shooting sparks of hatred. As he approached the young *chassid,* Michel could smell the alcohol on the man's breath. He took a startled step back.

"The consulate is never open on Sunday," the guard informed him, slurring his words. "Sunday is our day of rest. If you continue to disturb me, filthy Jew, I will break every bone in your body!"

Michel felt as though the earth had slipped from beneath his feet. His mind whirled like a wheel that went nowhere. If he got his visa tomorrow, he would only be able to take the Strasbourg train on Monday night. The journey, including brief stops at various stations along the way, took no less than two full days — 48 hours in all! He would arrive in Strasbourg at midnight on Wednesday night.

In other words, forget about the wedding!

He returned to the iron gate and pounded on it with both fists. "I'm getting married. If you don't give me the visa now I won't arrive in time for my wedding!"

Drunken laughter was his reply. "All the better ..." The gate did not open.

When his first panic had subsided, Michel assessed his options. It was useless to try to arouse the compassion of the drunken, Jew-hating guard. Even if he could be induced to open the gates, it was highly doubtful whether His Excellency, the Ambassador, was inside today. That illustrious figure would no doubt be attending his own prayer services on a Sunday morning; and if he did happen to have stayed at home, he would be furious at being woken just to provide a Jewish bridegroom with a visa. What did it matter to His Excellency whether or not a sniveling Jew came to his wedding on time? Those anti-Semites would be glad if all Jewish weddings went up in smoke.

There was only one recourse: the Rebbe!

Michel hit the streets. His feet moved with difficulty because his spirits were dragging extremely low. He covered the walk from the consulate to the Rebbe's house in a gray fog. On his arrival, it did not occur to his benumbed mind to ask the Rebbe's *gabbaim* for permission to enter. Nor did he think to check whether this was the Rebbe's time for receiving callers. All thought was frozen. He merely walked up to the door of the Rebbe's room and, without knocking, opened it and walked in.

"Michel! What's the matter?" The Rebbe gazed into the *chasan's* pale, grim face. "Why are you so upset?"

"I've just come from the Polish Consulate." Michel's voice was lifeless, like the eyes he cast down in despair. In a few broken sentences, he explained his predicament.

"Imagine the embarrassment in the wedding hall in Strasbourg," he finished, in tears. "What will my in-laws say? What will the guests whisper amongst themselves? What will the *kallah* think of me?"

Perhaps, in his heart of hearts, Michel was hoping for a miracle. The Rebbe would stand up and shake the earth. Pulling every string he knew, the Rebbe would magically pull a visa out of the consul on his day of rest.

But all the Sternowitzer Rebbe did was smile. "I don't understand. It is forbidden to be ungrateful." He gazed hard at his distraught visitor. "Do you hear, Michel? It is forbidden to be ungrateful!"

Michel Wenger was a Ruzhiner *chassid*. Like his fellow *chassidim*, he knew that his Rebbes, stemming from the holy Alter of Rozhin, uttered words that were very deep. They never offered an explicit rebuke, but spoke rather in delicate hints. The truth was hidden somewhere beneath layers of concealment — but they spoke directly to the heart.

Michel toiled for hours to grasp the deeper meaning of the Rebbe's words: "It is forbidden to be ungrateful." And, as our Sages have assured us, if a person toils, he will find. Michel at last understood what he had been struggling to see. After all, hadn't he been taught this very thing all his life? "Everything that Hashem does is for the benefit of His servant."

If *HaKadosh Baruch Hu* had sent him the ordeal of postponing his wedding, He must have had a good reason for doing so. Why become so agitated and distressed? Michel must recognize his Creator's goodness in granting him this favor!

"It is forbidden to be ungrateful."

Hadn't the author of the *Ohr HaChaim* said that there is no uglier trait than ingratitude?

Now Michel understood why the Rebbe had smiled in acceptance. The Rebbe lived every day with a sense of gratitude. The Master of the Universe wanted things to turn out this way. So be it!

With a newfound peace of mind based on his heightened spiritual understanding, Michel embarked on the long and wearying trip from Sternowitz to Strasbourg.

The memory of the Rebbe's select few words imbued the young bridegroom with serenity and strength. Even the prospect of the embarrassment that awaited him did not detract from his calm. At one of the stations, he sent off a telegram to Strasbourg, and this is what it said:

"I will be delayed one day because of troubles getting a visa. Do not worry. Every delay is for the best. The chasan, Michel Wenger."

The wedding was postponed for one day.

"The *chasan* is arriving at the station now!" The word spread like a sibilant wave among the large crowd. It surged forward and offered the surprised *chasan* an extraordinary welcome. Michel stepped off the train. To the bombardment of questions, he returned only a few terse sentences. The Rebbe's remark won the people's hearts at once, and enveloped them in a sense of deep peace and acceptance.

The wedding, held by force of circumstances one day later than originally planned, served as a sterling lesson to all of Strasbourg Jewry regarding just how far faith in our teachers can — and must — reach.

THEY CHANGED HIS NAME

"CHAIM YISRAEL! CHAIM YISRAEL!" A VOICE SHOUTED from behind. The young yeshivah man spun around to see who was calling him. His small son stopped, too, and waited impatiently at his father's side.

Nearby, a stranger stood and watched with a grin.

"And what is making you so happy today?" another man asked, walking up to the smiling watcher.

"I am enjoying the name 'Chaim Yisrael.'"

"And what is so funny about the name 'Chaim Yisrael'? demanded the other. "Do the names 'Yitzchak Isaac' or 'Shlomo Zalman' also make you laugh?"

"Can't you tell the difference between idle laughter and laughter that comes from deep satisfaction? I don't find the name Chaim Yisrael funny. Heaven forbid!"

"Then what's this all about?"

The man smiled once more. "I took tremendous pleasure in seeing that young man — the one whom someone just called 'Chaim Yisrael.' You see, at his *bris*, he was named 'Chaim Yaakov,' and then, one sunny day some years later, it changed to 'Chaim Yisrael.' Five years have passed since his name was changed, but no one has made a mistake with his name — not even once. Everyone calls him 'Chaim Yisrael,' as though he had had that name from birth."

His companion stared. "What kind of riddles are you talking?" he asked, poking a finger into his ear and twirled it pointedly, as though he suspected that organ of misleading him. "Who is that young man, and why did they change his name from 'Chaim Yaakov' to 'Chaim Yisrael' — and just who, exactly, was the one who changed it?"

"Ah, that's a long story!"

"Well, tell me."

"You want to hear the whole thing?"

"Everything — from the beginning!"

A light summer breeze ruffled the leaves on the trees in the garden of the small house. Beneath the warm, early-morning sun, droplets of dew glistened on those leaves. As they stirred in prayer to their Creator, thanking Him for the life-giving dew He bestowed on them each morning, several tiny drops joined to form one large one. The weight of the drop propelled it down the length of the leaf and onto the pane of a nearby window. From there it rolled into the room itself, to mingle with the burning tears on the cheeks of Sara Bluma, young wife of R' Chaim Yaakov.

"Hashem, why have You forsaken me?" she wailed over her book of *Tehillim*. She was seated at the bedside of her husband, an extraordinary *talmid chacham*, who was lying gravely ill. "Have You decreed that my husband die at such a young age, without leaving behind any offspring?" The bitter tears intensified. R' Chaim Yaakov had suddenly fallen ill several days before, and the progress of his illness had been swift and frightening. He lay now in bed, unmoving as a stone, despite every effort to get him back on his feet.

The first to be summoned to his bedside had been Feivish Kramer, the local Jewish medic. He prescribed various powders and potions, which had helped not a whit. Then a doctor was brought from a nearby town. He brought leeches and bled the patient copiously, until R' Chaim Yaakov nearly died of loss of blood. Another doctor came, wrinkled his nose and shouted, "Leeches for such a sick man? What kind of insanity is this? Quickly, bring *bankes* (vacuum cups)!"

The cupping process took place at once. The cups were placed on the patient's back, with pieces of paper burning inside to consume all the oxygen until the cups were vacuum sealed. They remained in place until R' Chaim Yaakov's back resembled a large cookie sheet peppered with round cookie-molds, all ready to pop into the oven. As a remedy for various ailments, vacuum cups had been found effective to a degree. But they could do nothing against the kind of serious illness which R' Chaim Yaakov was battling.

When both the local medic and the two other "doctors" had done nothing to help her husband, Sara Bluma went to the hospital and brought back an expert.

"Fools!" the physician thundered. "You have neglected this patient. Your husband, madam, is suffering from an advanced liver infection. How in the world anyone thought that leeches or *bankes* were going to help is beyond me!" A bark of scornful laughter punctuated his remarks. "If I didn't think moving him would cost him his life, I would order the patient admitted to the hospital at once!"

He sent an assistant to fetch a rare and costly medicine. Every hour on the hour, Sara Bluma poured a large spoonful into her husband's mouth.

But instead of improving, the patient's condition grew steadily worse.

His breathing became shallow and took on a strange, whistling quality. As R' Chaim Yaakov's chest rose and fell like a bellows, his fever mounted. A hoarse rasping came from his throat with every breath. When the big doctor was brought again from the hospital, he shook his head and said soberly, "I think we're too late."

The room slowly filled. Members of the *Chevrah Kaddisha* (the Jewish Burial Society) murmured prayers at the ill man's bedside. Two candles stood burning at the head of the bed. Heartbroken wails flew into the air like wounded birds.

"Where is Sara Bluma?" one of the *Chevrah Kaddisha* men asked suddenly. "It is time to start saying the *Krias Shema*."

But Sara Bluma had vanished. The whole house was searched, but R' Chaim Yaakov's young wife was nowhere to be found.

At first, the watchers were certain that R' Chaim Yaakov's soul would depart this world without his wife being present. Then it began to seem as though he had promised not to abandon this life without her permission. Despite all the signs of impending death, the patient lingered on.

"Her husband is dying, and she's running around!" the people complained. At last, Sara Bluma returned home, out of breath.

"Where were you?" they demanded. "The situation is extremely serious. At a time like this, you should not leave your husband's side. You must prepare yourself for the worst."

"I went to the post office," she said calmly, taking off her coat.

"To the *post office*? *Now*?"

"I sent a telegram to Shinova — to my father-in-law, R' Mattisyahu, who is a devoted *gabbai* of the Shinova Rebbe, R' Yechezkel Shraga. I asked R' Mattisyahu to beg the Rebbe to pray for his only son." She looked around at the sea of faces. "Well, isn't that what we've always been taught? 'Even with a sharp sword poised on his neck, a person should not stop praying for mercy.' And that is exactly what I did!"

At that very moment, in the *beis midrash* of the Shinova Rebbe, the *chassidim* had already gathered for *Shacharis*. The several scores of men who had come early that morning found themselves spectators to a moving scene.

The telegram, which the post office had brought to the *beis midrash*, struck the *chassidim* with shock and grief. Who did not know the outstanding scholar, R' Chaim Yaakov, who was the faithful *gabbai* R' Mattisyahu's only son and light of his life? The young patient's many friends and acquaintances were wracked with pain at the news of his illness, as well as with pity for the father's great distress.

R' Mattisyahu stood waiting in his accustomed spot; he did not wish to disturb the Rebbe in his preparations for prayer. Had he known the true measure of danger in which his son stood at that moment, it is doubtful whether he would have waited at all. Again and again, he perused the telegram in his hand: "Your son Chaim Yaakov is very sick. Please mention his name to the Rebbe for a speedy recovery."

When the Rebbe entered the *shul,* the *gabbai* handed him the telegram. The paper rustled like a leaf in his trembling fingers.

R' Yechezkel of Shinova read the message. For a moment, his face darkened. He closed his eyes in fervent concentration, then said, "Please send a return telegram immediately. I guarantee that the sick man will recover quickly."

As a messenger was sent hurriedly to the post office, the Rebbe gathered together ten men. On the spot, they conducted a name-changing ceremony.

"Not [Chaim] Yaakov will your name be called," the Rebbe announced, "but rather [Chaim] Yisrael ... because you struggled with the Angel [of Death] and conquered" (see *Bereishis* 32:29).

The second telegram reached the *beis midrash* at the conclusion of *Shacharis.* It told of the patient's sudden turn for the better. The *chassidim* were amazed.

Only later did the facts emerge. As the members of the *Chevrah Kaddisha* gathered in the dying man's room and prepared for his departure from this world, R' Chaim Yaakov suddenly opened his eyes. In a weak voice, he asked for a drink of water. He drank a little, then closed his eyes again.

A few minutes later, he looked up once more and whispered, "It will be all right. *'Lo amus, ki echyeh* — I will not die, but I will live!'" And from that point, hour by hour, his condition improved.

The Rebbe took the news calmly. "It is understandable," he commented.

"Understandable?" R' Avraham Yehoshua Freund, the Rav of Nasoid and one of the Shinova Rebbe's foremost *chassidim* — and one of the ten men who had participated in the name-changing ceremony — repeated incredulously. "Doesn't the *Gemara* say (*Gittin* 28), 'Most dying men die'?"

R' Avraham Yehoshua's faith in the Rebbe was unshakable; it was not disbelief that impelled his question, but a longing to understand. The Rebbe, however, did not explain.

Two days later, R' Avraham Yehoshua Freund took R' Mattisyahu, the *gabbai*, into a quiet corner. He was consumed with curiosity. "Tell me your son's secret, and why he merited such an open miracle. And tell me the meaning behind the Rebbe's surprising remark that the matter is 'understandable.'"

"To explain that, I would have to go back twenty-two years," R' Mattisyahu sighed.

"Fine!" The Rav fixed the *gabbai* with an expectant gaze.

"All right, then. Listen."

"Twenty-two years ago, a terrible epidemic raged through the city of Shinova. Many succumbed and died. It was a very contagious disease that passed rapidly from person to person. Because of this, people refrained from visiting the homes of the sick. They lay in their beds groaning, and no one cared.

"Perhaps I am erring by saying that no one cared," R' Mattisyahu amended quickly. "The truth is that no one wished to become infected with the sickness that had already filled rows and rows in the cemetery. Our Rebbe, R' Yechezkel of Shinova, was very upset. He knew that it was the fear of losing their very lives that prevented the people from extending a helping hand to their fellows — and no other reason.

"But the suffering of the sick people who had no one to visit them twisted like a knife in the Rebbe's merciful heart. It should not come as a surprise, then, to hear that when I volunteered to visit those unfortunate people and help nurse them, the Rebbe was beside himself with emotion. He was powerfully grateful to the faithful *gabbai* who was prepared to risk his life and scoff at danger. As for me, I entered the lions' den and emerged safely.

"Later, however, when the epidemic was already over, I became so ill that I had to take to my bed, too weak to stand. I had been lying there for several days when the Rebbe came to see me at home.

"'Do not worry, R' Mattisyahu,' R' Yechezkel told me. '*HaKadosh Baruch Hu* will give you your reward: You shall recover.' The Rebbe smiled. 'This is your hour. Ask what you will.'

"'The Rebbe knows that I desire no riches or glory,' I murmured weakly. 'I would have asked for life, but if good health is already assured for me and I may make another request, it would be this: Please let the Rebbe pray that I may father a living son.'

"The Rebbe blessed me with these words: 'A male child, *zera shel kayama* (enduring offspring).'

"The following year, my son Chaim Yaakov was born — the son whose name was now changed to Chaim Yisrael," R' Mattisyahu concluded his tale.

R' Avraham Yehoshua sat quietly, digesting what he had just heard. Suddenly, he exclaimed, "Of course! Now I understand what the Rebbe meant when he said that it was 'understandable.' Your son, Chaim Yisrael, has not yet fathered a child. Had he died, Heaven forbid, the Rebbe's blessing to you would not have been fulfilled!"

Smiling, the Rav tendered the *gabbai* his warmest wishes for the son who had just escaped by his fingernails from the Angel of Death's clutch. "May he merit a male child — *zera shel kayama*!" Hearing this blessing, R' Mattisyahu's face lit up like the sun.

Indeed, the Rav of Nasoid's blessing came true as well. A year later, the fully recovered R' Chaim Yisrael fathered a son.

"Now do you understand why I laughed?" the man finished his story. "It was a joyous laughter. Should I not take pleasure in the sight of Yaakov, who became Yisrael, walking with his little boy?"

THE HEROIC RABBI

I T WAS VERY LATE AT NIGHT. NOT A SOUL STIRRED IN THE streets. The lights had been extinguished hours before, and every window in Kushta was dark — except for one. In the home of the elderly *gaon*, R' Moshe HaLevi, Chief Rabbi of Turkey, known to all as *Chacham Bashi*, the library light was on and the Rabbi was poring over his *Gemara*.

A brilliant man, R' Moshe was well versed in all four sections of the *Shulchan Aruch*, as well as the "fifth part" — the common sense and understanding of human nature so vital for Rabbis and *Poskim*. From every corner of the land Jewish scholars came to him with their questions, which R' Moshe would resolve with a logic and a breadth of wisdom that did away with all doubts. Right now, he was absorbed in learning a very difficult *sugya*. Though the hour was late and he had spent a long, arduous day dealing with all manner of communal responsibilities, he did not desist.

Suddenly, a soft knock at the door startled him out of his concentration.

Who could be coming at such a late hour, he wondered, as he hurried to the door. "Who is it?" he called.

"I have been sent here by His Majesty, the Sultan. I bear an important message!"

The door creaked lightly on its hinges as R' Moshe opened it for the messenger. The man was dressed in a Turkish royal uniform, a wide sash at his waist. Leading him courteously to a seat, R' Moshe asked, "What is the urgent matter that has brought you here to my home so late at night?"

The messenger fixed his features into a mask of importance. "The Sultan requests the document containing the pledge of good faith."

"The pledge of good faith?"

"Yes, the special pledge that the rulers of Turkey signed in previous generations, in which they obligate themselves not to harm the

Jews in the practice of their religion. The document, I believe, is here in the *Chacham Bashi's* home, is it not?"

"Yes, it is," R' Moshe HaLevi answered slowly. He looked at the messenger. "Do you know what the document is? I will tell you. After their expulsion from Spain, the Jews settled in any country that would take them in — including Turkey. My father's fathers arrived here, and found immediate favor in the eyes of the Turkish rulers, who recognized the Jews' talents and the treasures they could bring to the country.

"The Jews of Spain were intelligent and educated in every field, and the rulers of Turkey wished to harness their knowledge for the good of their own people. To this end, they sought to curtail the Jews' religious freedom. The Spanish exiles, well used to suffering and persecution, agreed to help the government in any way it wished — but asked the authorities to sign a 'pledge of good faith' not to harm the Jews in matters of their faith.

"This document was placed into the possession of the *Chacham Bashi* of that generation, and has since passed from one *Chacham* to the next down the years. It is now in my own possession, more carefully guarded than anything else in my home." R' Moshe HaLevi paused, then asked, "And why does the new Sultan want the document? Does he not believe in its existence and therefore wishes to see it with his own eyes?"

The messenger glanced around, as though to make certain that he was not overheard. "His Majesty has decided to institute a military draft of all young men — including the Jews. This runs counter to what was written into the 'pledge of good faith.' Therefore, the Sultan wishes to take possession of that document — so that he may nullify it!"

R' Moshe paled. Without any warning, he had been thrust into a dilemma of monumental proportions. He was, as the saying goes, between a rock and a very hard place. To hand over the document was to condemn Jewish youth in Turkey to a spiritual holocaust. In the Turkish army, they would not be able to observe the Shabbos and would be forced to eat non-kosher meat — not to mention the utter impossibility of learning the holy Torah. But to refuse to give the Sultan what he had explicitly requested would constitute outright rebellion.

The *Chacham* wrinkled his high, scholarly brow and considered the matter deeply. After a long period of thought, he told the messenger, "I must beg the Sultan's pardon, but the situation is a complex one. While it is true that the document was given to me to hold, in actuality it belongs to the entire Jewish community. Without the consent of our community leaders I am unable to give up the document — even to the Sultan.

"Let me have a few days. I will call a meeting of all the Jewish community leaders in Turkey to consider the matter. When a decision is reached, it will be sent directly to His Majesty."

This was not the answer the messenger wanted. Furious, he stood up and stalked out of the Rabbi's house.

The next morning, Rabbis and other community leaders throughout the land were summoned to an urgent meeting, to decide how to avert the evil poised above their heads. One Rabbi alone was not summoned: the outstanding *gaon*, R' Shlomo Eliezer Alfandri, the flower and pride of Turkish Jewry. Simply put, R' Moshe HaLevi was afraid of R' Shlomo Eliezer's reaction. The venerable Rabbi was known as a zealot whose life was completely given over to Torah and piety. In his passion, he might speak out in a way that would arouse the Sultan's fury.

But R' Shlomo Eliezer learned of the emergency conference through means of his own. On the spot, he decided that, "where there is [a possibility of] the desecration of G-d's Name, one need not attend to a Rabbi's honor." He arrived at R' Moshe HaLevi's house at the height of the meeting. Every person there leaped to his feet in reverence for the extraordinary *gaon*.

R' Shlomo Eliezer did not waste a second. He asked for permission to speak, then screamed out from the depths of his heart, "My brothers, they are preparing to injure the bird of our souls, the students of our holy yeshivos! It is forbidden for us to yield to the Sultan's demands. Today they will draft our yeshivah boys; tomorrow they will begin to curtail all our religious observances — and the next day, they will decree that we must all convert to Islam!"

An awed silence filled the room. Who dared take issue with such a man? Even their host and chairman of the meeting, the *Chacham Bashi,* R' Moshe HaLevi, knew that truth was on the side of this uninvited guest. With great humility, he stood up and called out, "Heaven has declared the ruling in accordance with R' Shlomo Eliezer Alfandri — as the *halachah* is with him everywhere. Nobody will contradict his holy words!"

All too soon, however, it became apparent that R' Moshe's was the minority opinion. The Rabbis were deathly afraid of the powerful Sultan, who was capable of inflicting grievous punishment on those who thwarted his will. On the other hand, it was impossible for them to come out openly against R' Shlomo Eliezer.

Caught on the sharp horns of this dilemma, they decided — not to decide.

Word quickly reached the royal court that R' Shlomo Eliezer's forceful stance had prevented the conference from falling in with the Sultan's wishes. "I will have my vengeance!" the Sultan screamed in a fury. He sent his servants to summon R' Shlomo Eliezer to him at once.

R' Shlomo Eliezer was heroic. Fear of a fellow human did not enter his heart; he feared only Hashem.

Dressed in his finest clothing, he set off for the Sultan's palace.

Scores of uniformed royal guards surrounded the palace. The mere sight of them was calculated to turn any visitor's bones to jelly. Tall and muscular, they wore their swords dangling from their sashes, within instant grip of their ready fingers. There was menace in their very gaze. But R' Shlomo Eliezer was not afraid of soldiers. He stood still and erect until he was summoned to enter through the palace gates.

Within minutes, the venerable Rabbi was standing face to face with the Turkish Sultan.

The ruler stared at him ferociously, then barked, "Who are you?"

"My name is Shlomo Eliezer Alfandri, and I serve as Rabbi in this city," he replied with quiet confidence.

"I heard that you have been inciting citizens of this city against me and my government," the Sultan said with a menacing look. "Is this true?"

R' Shlomo Eliezer met the ruler's gaze directly. "Heaven forbid. It has never crossed my mind to rebel against His Majesty's rule. At the conference of Rabbis, I declared that it is not possible for the pledge of good faith, granted to the Jewish community hundreds of years ago by Turkey's venerable rulers, to be abolished. Such a thing would heap shame upon the government. Therefore, it is in the interest of the royal house to let us preserve this vital document and not to allow it out of our hands."

He spoke without fear. The Rabbi's face seemed to the Sultan like that of an angel. All at once, the Turkish king was afraid. Not only did he not punish R' Shlomo Eliezer, but he actually granted him a reward: the title of *Chacham Bashi*, which afforded him a broad authority. The Sultan appointed him the new *Chacham Bashi* in the city of Damascus, then under Turkish rule.

Despite this small triumph for the Jews, however, the Sultan's goal remained unchanged. He planned to draft Jewish youth into his army. His imagination painted a vivid picture of thousands of heroic Jewish soldiers joining his other troops, to the Sultan's greater glory. The draft threat continued to hang like a sword over the heads of the Jews.

To their shame, there were some Jews who had a hand in stirring up the cauldron. Members of the so-called "Higher Spiritual Committee," desirous of demonstrating their loyalty to the new Sultan, called on all Turkish Jews to do their share for the government that did so much for them.

Once again, the Rabbis were called to an urgent meeting at the home of R' Moshe HaLevi. And, again, it was R' Shlomo Eliezer who stood valiantly — and nearly alone — against the tide of opinion. "Do not be afraid of any man!" he cried. Fearlessly, he denounced the "Higher Spiritual Committee." Only two Jewish leaders emerged on his side: R' Chaim Winutra, and R' Yehoshua ben Menachem Tzuntzin.

R' Shlomo Eliezer Alfandri's courageous voice rang out: "Know this, my brothers: Military service involves desecration of the Shabbos, eating non-kosher meat, and many other prohibitions. If we allow this to go forward, what will be said? 'The zealous ones allowed it!' Is there a greater *chillul Hashem* than this?

"And what will we answer on the day of reckoning, when we will stand in judgment before the Creator of the world? Will we have any answer? After all, it is not as though we have no choice. We have in our possession a pledge of good faith signed by previous rulers. The law is on our side. It is the new Sultan who seeks to nullify that pledge, which guarantees our right not to be injured or subjected to any decree that will harm us in the practice of our faith. The Sultan has no power to force us in this matter!"

The tears streamed from his eyes and flowed down his beard as he finished his impassioned speech. When he was finished speaking, the weeping intensified until it was a veritable storm.

Every member of that rabbinical conference knew in his heart of hearts that R' Shlomo Eliezer was right. But most of them did not dare support him publicly, out of fear of the harsh Sultan. Before R' Shlomo Eliezer's speech, they had already resolved to inform the ruler of their preparedness to support the draft. Now, after hearing R' Shlomo Eliezer, they found such an action difficult if not impossible.

The meeting ended — again — without any firm resolution.

That same day, R' Shlomo Eliezer learned that a certain community leader — a wealthy man from Kushta — was working energetically behind the scenes in support of the draft. As a result he was enjoying a meteoric rise in the royal court. R' Shlomo Eliezer put on his rabbinic robes and went to see the man.

But all the pleasant, coaxing words in the world did not deter the man from his course. He answered disdainfully and closed his ears to the Rabbi's rebuke.

R' Shlomo Eliezer's face betrayed his disappointment. Abandoning cajolery, he thundered, "If you continue along this path, your end will be a bitter one. Salvation will come to the Jews from another source — and you will be lost!"

The man waved a dismissive hand. "Today is not Purim. Don't quote to me from *Megillas Esther*."

Just four hours later, as the wealthy Jew sat in the royal palace along with the Sultan's other advisers working on the military draft campaign, he was beset by sudden strong pains in his chest. He toppled to the ground. Within seconds, his face had darkened alarmingly. Only a few moments passed before his soul departed his body right there on the marble floor of the Sultan's palace.

Kushta was abuzz. The people took the tragic incident as a clear sign that Heaven was on R' Shlomo Eliezer's side. His enemies were overcome with terror ... all except the rich man's sons. These were brazen young fellows who cared nothing for the venerable Rabbi or anyone else. They made preparations to bury their father with pomp and ceremony.

Only one problem stood in their way. The custom in that place was for the greatest of the Rabbis to deliver the first eulogy — and there was none greater than R' Shlomo Eliezer Alfandri. Reluctantly, they were forced to ask him to open the proceedings.

The sons sent messengers to seek the Rabbi. The messengers' instructions were to ask R' Shlomo Eliezer to either deliver a eulogy for their father, or to waive the honor of speaking first. They sought him out in all the places where he was usually to be found — in the *beis din* and the *beis midrash* — to no avail. At last, they tracked him down to his own home, where he was sitting alone in his room absorbed in volumes of *halachah*. When they presented their request, R' Shlomo Eliezer responded angrily, "Those scoundrels! Was it not enough that their father raised his hand against the Torah? Must I now eulogize him as well?"

The dead man lay in humiliation, his funeral delayed. No one dared eulogize him without R' Shlomo Eliezer's permission. Finally, the dead man's sons, together with several people high up in the government, came to R' Alfandri's home with a purse full of gold dinars. In every way they knew, they asked him to forego his right to make the first eulogy, so that the deceased might be granted his final honor. In that merit, they were prepared to donate all the money they had brought with them to charity, as the Rabbi saw fit. The government officials added their plea that no further shame be heaped on the "notable deceased."

With tears coursing down his cheeks, R' Shlomo Eliezer stood up. He cried out, "You have seen Heaven itself smite down your father in justice. Yesterday, I went to the deceased man's house and begged him from the depths of my heart not to follow the suggestions of the wicked. But he did not want to listen to me, and even went so far as to speak brazenly in my face. It was the hand of G-d that has struck him down, not I. I do not want your money."

Still weeping, he set down the purse of gold.

In that moment, all knew that the heroic Rabbi could not be bought for any price. The sons and government officials left his home, disappointed. The wicked Jew was carried to his final resting place in shame.

And, a few days later, the Sultan yielded to the pleas of the righteous R' Shlomo Eliezer Alfandri, and abandoned his plans for the draft.

A SIMPLE MARBLE PLAQUE

"THIS *BEIS MIDRASH* WAS BUILT THROUGH THE GENEROSITY of one man — whose name shall remain anonymous — who donated the sum of 110 gold napoleons."

The plaque appeared on the northern wall of the Beis Yaakov *shul*, located in Jerusalem's Beis Yisrael neighborhood. It had been there for more years than the number of gold napoleons it mentioned.

During all those years, the text had often aroused people's curiosity. Who was the mysterious donor whose name remained so firmly cloaked in anonymity?

Theories abounded. Many contended that he was probably someone who had settled outside of *Eretz Yisrael* and wanted to keep his donation secret. It is the nature of man, when a mystery exists, to set his imagination working overtime trying to solve it. Rumors strange and varied flew, and complete legends were woven about the man behind the modest marble plaque hanging in the *shul*.

The stories had one common denominator: One and all, they belonged to the realm of fantasy. There was nothing to link any of the wild speculations to the true tale behind the anonymous donor. Nothing at all.

Thirty or forty years ago, Jerusalem's important community activists were the *gabbaim* who ran the charity funds and *kollelim*. These men worked strictly on a volunteer basis, with no salary or recompense. In their hands they held a powerful communal authority; a single word from a *gabbai* could make things happen. This authority derived not from any particular material or economic advantage — money was very tight in those days — but simply from the high level of integrity and dedication these men consistently demonstrated.

R' Shlomo Zalman Porush, founder of the well-known Porush family in Jerusalem, was one such man. All his life he devotedly served the public needs. He founded the *Shaarei Chesed* charitable organization and managed it for more than half a century. He was also responsible for building the community that bore the same name, and without which it would be impossible to imagine life in Jerusalem at that time. Not only did his free-loan fund provide loans for the city's poor — and all without charging a cent in interest or "banking fees" — but, as we have said, it also provided a powerful economic base from which the neighborhood was built that later boasted the famous grandson who was named after him: the *gaon* R' Shlomo Zalman Auerbach.

Among his other public duties, R' Shlomo Zalman Porush was in charge of Jerusalem's Minsker *Kollel*. This *kollel* provided support for hundreds of families who had emigrated to *Eretz Yisrael* from White Russia, and who struggled daily with the difficulties of survival as they became absorbed into their new home. It was a hard life, a life characterized by chronic poverty under the cruel and corrupt Turkish rule.

No *kollel* was able to guarantee comfortable living conditions or real financial support to the families who depended on them. The help extended was minimal, along the meager lines of bread and water. But Jerusalem's Jewry had learned to be content with little.

Before each Jewish holiday, the *kollelim* made a mighty effort to recruit additional funds from philanthropists abroad, to lighten the immigrants' lot. The main thrust of these efforts centered on the month of Nissan. Pesach, with its demand for *matzos,* wine, and other holiday needs, was the festival that critically stretched the budget each year.

Winter, 5647 (1887)

The month of Shevat had come and gone. Purim, too, was a thing of the past — and still, the envelopes had not arrived: the crucial envelopes that brought the annual Pesach supplement. Twice, R' Shlomo Zalman traveled by camel to the port city of Yaffo to visit the "National Russian Bank" — and both times, he came away disappointed. Though the clerks checked carefully, they could find no evidence that the money had been sent.

R' Shlomo Zalman was filled with anxiety. Who, better than he, knew how fully Jerusalem's destitute depended on this help before Pesach? Where would these unfortunates find the money for *shemurah matzos,* for wine, for holiday food? And what about new shoes for the children in honor of the holiday, with their old ones ruined by the winter rains?

His heart weighed down with worry, R' Shlomo Zalman returned to Jerusalem. As he went, he considered the problem and came up with a temporary solution. There was an elderly Jew in Jerusalem by the name of Feivel Stoller ("the carpenter"). Feivel was not a rich man, but because he had no children and few guests, he had managed over the years to amass a considerable amount of money from his carpentry work. He planned to use these savings for his own and his wife's old age.

Nobody else knew about the carpenter's little nest egg. Only to R' Shlomo Zalman had Feivel whispered his secret. "If you ever need a short-term, interest-free loan for community needs, you can get it from me," Feivel had said.

Now, as R' Shlomo Zalman traveled homeward, he knew that this was the moment.

Immediately upon his return to Jerusalem, he made for Feivel's house. He was concerned that the carpenter would consider the amount he needed too high. Feivel was known to be a suspicious sort of man; the only one he really trusted was R' Shlomo Zalman. But it was an open question whether the large amount of money he was about to request exceeded even the old carpenter's trust in him.

R' Shlomo Zalman made his impassioned plea to Feivel — and saw, to his relief, a spark of compassion in the older man's eyes. The carpenter asked him to wait a moment, and disappeared into another room. When he returned, he was carrying a bundle of 200 gold napoleons — the full amount that R' Shlomo Zalman had requested.

The *gabbai* lifted his head with relief and happiness. "R' Feivel, you have purchased your World to Come in a single hour," he announced in a ringing voice. "Jerusalem's poor will be able to prepare for Pesach, thanks to your generosity!"

A small smile played on Feivel the carpenter's lips.

R' Shlomo Zalman put the money to work at once. Hundreds of *kollel* families received the extra support in honor of Pesach, without ever suspecting the pressure under which the *gabbai* was laboring. Each day that passed without word from Yaffo increased his anxiety.

Finally, a few days after Pesach, when R' Shlomo Zalman was at his wits' end, the Russian Bank sent word that the sum of 110 gold napoleons had been transferred to the Minsker *Kollel's* account.

R' Shlomo Zalman wasted no time in starting off for Yaffo. On his return to Jerusalem, he made directly for Feivel the carpenter's house.

He was still missing 90 napoleons with which to fully repay the loan, but Feivel was happy to take a partial repayment. "Don't worry," he told the *gabbai*. "When you get the rest from Russia, you can pay me then."

Two months passed before R' Shlomo Zalman received word that the additional 90 napoleons had arrived at the bank. He shot out of Jerusalem like an arrow from its bow.

With the gleaming gold coins wrapped in a red kerchief, R' Shlomo Zalman rapped on Feivel's door. Feivel opened it a crack, then exclaimed respectfully, "There was no need to trouble yourself to come to me! We could have met in *shul*."

The *gabbai* unwrapped the kerchief. "This is not something I'd want to show off in public," he said with a smile.

"Ah, you've brought the money." The old carpenter's face lit up. He led R' Shlomo Zalman to a table, where they sat down side by side. Feivel counted the money.

"I don't understand," he exclaimed. "I see only 90 napoleons here. But I loaned you 200!"

Now it was the *gabbai's* turn to be surprised. "Don't you remember, Feivel? I already paid back 110 napoleons two months ago."

"No, no!" Feivel said forcefully. "You did not return even a penny until now. Your debt is still 200 napoleons!"

R' Shlomo Zalman tried to prod the old man's memory. "We were sitting here, the two of us. The table was spread with an embroidered blue cloth, and the bundle of money was wrapped in a white handkerchief." But his efforts were to no avail. Feivel, though an honest working man, was elderly now and suffered from a weakened memory. He was positive of his position, and nothing that R' Shlomo Zalman said was able to shake him. While he did not believe that the *gabbai* was a thief, he was equally certain that the money had not been repaid.

Unable to come to terms, they decided to bring their disagreement to the *beis din*. A few days later, the two entered the R' Yehudah *HaChassid shul* in Jerusalem's Old City. There sat the *beis din,* headed by the elderly *gaon*, R' Shmuel Salant, the city's Rabbi.

The court investigated the facts of the matter. Both sides agreed that R' Shlomo Zalman Porush had borrowed 200 gold napoleons from Feivel Stoller. The *gabbai* claimed to have repaid 110 napoleons of that sum, but he had no witnesses and no written receipt; the men had conducted their transaction on their word as honorable Jews, without putting anything in writing or summoning witnesses to the deal. Now Feivel was sure that he never received the money. With no other proof to rely on, R' Shlomo Zalman was required to swear an oath that he had returned it. Only then could he be freed of his obligation to pay the disputed 110 napoleons.

The *gabbai* was overwhelmed with terror. Swear a Torah oath? G-d-fearing men shrank from oaths the way they would from a blazing fire — even when called upon to swear about the honest truth. After a little thought, he asked the court to give him a few days in which to consider the matter. The *beis din* acceded to his request, and granted him a week.

It was a difficult seven days for R' Shlomo Zalman. He debated hotly with himself until he came at last to a conclusion that was not easy for him. At the end of the week's adjournment, he presented his decision to the court.

"I have never sworn even a true oath," he said emotionally. "Therefore, I beg of your honors to release me from the obligation to swear this time. Because I cannot and will not swear an oath, I will take it upon myself to pay Feivel back, for the second time, the 110 napoleons that I already gave him in Nissan. But because I do not have such a large sum, I will not pay it back all at once. I will give him 50 napoleons in the next few days, and pay out the rest in small monthly payments."

R' Shmuel Salant smiled his famous, shrewd smile, and turned to Feivel the carpenter. "What do you say?"

Feivel hesitated. "I agree. Very reluctantly… but I agree."

"And I do *not* agree!" R' Shmuel said with the same smile. He stood to his full height, turned a penetrating gaze on R' Shlomo Zalman, and declared with the power of the authority vested in him, "I hereby order you to accept the court's decree and swear an oath that you returned the 110 napoleons!"

R' Shlomo Zalman's face turned white as snow. "Doesn't the Rebbe believe me?" he asked in a low voice.

"I believe you completely," R' Shmuel said, sitting down again. "I know you to be a man of complete integrity, a man whose hands are clean of the slightest taint of thievery. And yet, I require of you to swear."

"Why?" The question burst from everybody's lips.

R' Shmuel Salant explained. "Are you familiar with human nature? Do you have any idea what people will be saying from now on? 'Look at that "honest" man whose home is bare and who supports himself so meagerly. Where did he come up with 50 napoleons to pay to Fcivel all at once? What the carpenter claimed must be the truth, and R' Shlomo Zalman tried to fool him. When he saw that his plot had been foiled, he decided to play the *tzaddik* who refuses to swear.'"

R' Shmuel turned to speak directly to R' Shlomo Zalman, the defendant. "As a public servant, you must beware of anything that might lead people to gossip in such a manner. Therefore, so that no one will be able to speak badly of those who toil on behalf of the community, I order you to swear. If your accuser is wrong, the sin will fall on his head, and you and your family will go along in peace."

R' Shlomo Zalman burst into bitter tears as he accepted the court's ruling. Once again, he asked for an adjournment of three days in order to prepare himself for the ordeal. This was Monday; the *beis din* agreed to put off the swearing of the oath until Thursday.

The next three days passed like a nightmare for the honest *gabbai*. He fasted during all of them. At midnight on Wednesday, he rose in the dark and conducted a *Tikkun Chatzos* amid copious tears. At dawn, he immersed himself in the *mikveh* that was situated in the courtyard of the Tiferes Yisrael *shul* of R' Nissan Bak. He *davened Shacharis vasikin*, then returned home. That day was like a mixture of Yom Kippur and Tishah B'Av in R' Shlomo Zalman's home. As he got up to walk to the *beis din*, his entire family accompanied him with heartbreaking cries.

Before entering the *shul*, R' Shlomo Zalman put on a white *kittel*, as on Yom Kippur. In fear and trembling he stood before the court, prepared to fulfill R' Shmuel's decree.

A few days after he swore the oath, real-estate agents began knocking at his door in the Zichron Tuviah neighborhood. Apparently, R' Shlomo Zalman had spread the word that he was interested in selling his apartment as soon as possible.

His family was astounded and dismayed. The *gabbai* turned to them and explained, "What did you think? How can I come up with 50 napoleons? On the day that I decided not to swear the oath, I resolved to sell the house, which is worth about that sum. I planned to earn the rest by taking on another job on the side."

His son, R' Naftali Tzvi, a wise young man, protested, "But, father, now that you have already sworn — even though it was against your will — you do not owe the money anymore. What's the point of selling the house now?"

His father's face grew long and sober. "I am not prepared, under any circumstances, to benefit from money that I saved by swearing a Torah oath," he declared firmly. "I've decided to sell the house, move to a rented apartment, and to dedicate the entire sum of 110 napoleons to the shul in the Beis Yisrael neighborhood. The *shul* is in the process of being built, but a large sum with which to finish it is lacking. I will donate the money anonymously, and it will serve a holy purpose that will stand forever."

The following year, at the height of preparations for Pesach, while R' Shlomo Zalman's wife toiled to clean the house and the *gabbai* himself was absorbed as usual in his constant work on behalf of the city's poor, a woman came running up to their house. She was Tovah Zelda, housemaid of Feivel and Perel Stoller.

As she burst breathlessly through the door, it was clear to all that she was almost beside herself with excitement.

"What happened?" R' Shlomo Zalman's wife asked quickly.

The maid caught her breath and managed to blurt out a few words. "They found it! The money!"

"Who found what money?"

Gradually, Tovah Zelda calmed down enough to speak coherently. "Feivel Stoller and his wife, Perel. Perel and I were cleaning the house just now, when we found, on the highest kitchen shelf up near the ceiling, the money wrapped in a bundle inside a white handkerchief — exactly the way R' Shlomo Zalman described it to Feivel back then, 110 gold napoleons! They sent me right over to beg your forgiveness in their name."

R' Shlomo Zalman forgave them. However, the Stollers found it more difficult to forgive themselves for the distress and agony they had caused him. Their anguish was overwhelming — so much so that, when summer came, Feivel the carpenter fell ill and passed away. Several weeks later, his wife, Perel, followed.

And only a small marble plaque on the northern wall of the Beis Yaakov *shul* remains as testimony to a life lived in purity and innocence, both inside and out.

IN THE TOWN SQUARE

L IFE PROCEEDED PEACEFULLY IN THE TOWN OF VILKOMIR, near Kovno. The Jews of Vilkomir got along exceptionally well with their gentile neighbors. Polish noblemen were frequent visitors at the elegant inn run by R' Shlomo Chanhas, which stood on the town's main street. Pleasing both to Heaven and to his fellow men, R' Shlomo was a wealthy individual and a pious one. He was learned in Torah and performed many acts of kindness for others. His money flowed liberally to support the poor, and for the sake of maintaining harmonious relations he even supported several of Vilkomir's non-Jewish destitute as well.

Almost every Jewish man in Vilkomir attended the daily Torah *shi-urim* that took place in the *shul* before *Minchah* and after *Maariv*. They soaked up a page of *Gemara*, a class in *Mishnah* or *halachah*, with a thirst that knew no quenching. "My Jews in Vilkomir," the Rabbi once remarked at an important rabbinical conference, "do not learn Torah out of fear of being asked 'Did you set aside time for Torah?' in the Heavenly Court after 120 years!"

"Why, then?" the other Rabbis asked in surprise.

"They learn Torah for its own sake, because their Creator wishes them to — and because in every line they learn they sense a spiritual sweetness that has no parallel in the pleasures of this world. They speak to me of Torah with purity, and without the slightest falseness or desire to curry favor," the Rabbi said with visible contentment.

Only one Jew in Vilkomir shunned the Torah classes. He had not been seen in *shul* for years, and his hand never bestowed charity anywhere. This was Dov Ber Hershenson, whom everyone called "Berka": the only assimilated Jew in all of Vilkomir. He had long since moved away from the Jewish section of town to live among his gentile cronies. Whenever he encountered a fellow Jew, his face would fill with hatred. He was ashamed of his Jewish antecedents and more than ready to go to the local church to convert to Christianity. However, there was no burning need for this, as he was accepted gladly by the gentiles despite his Jewishness.

Conversion or no conversion, Vilkomir's Jews did not view him as a brother. The nickname "Berka" was a pejorative one. Whenever anyone mentioned the name, the Jews would spit on the ground to show their disdain.

That year, 5591 (1831), was not an easy one for Polish Jewry. Political upheavals were constant. While Czarist Russia was engaged in a war against its Turkish enemy, Poland — under Russian dominion for years — seized this chance to throw off the Czar's rule. The Polish nobility revolted against the Russian government and tried to take the reins of power into their own hands. But mighty Russia was made of stern stuff. The Poles were unsuccessful in their attempt to usurp power, but they did manage to rile up the Russian government. With a battle to fight on two fronts, the Czar chose to concentrate on Turkey. Only a few divisions of troops were sent to subdue the rebellion in Poland. Total chaos reigned in the land.

The first scapegoats, naturally, were the Jews. The Russian Cossacks accused them of aiding the rebels, while the Polish nobility accused them of betraying the Poles by spying for Russia. The masses, incited by this rhetoric, began to attack Jews everywhere. This suited the Polish noblemen's purposes, and they began a series of public executions.

A gallows was erected in each city. Every day, scores of men were taken out — genuine rebels and spies, and imagined ones — to be hanged in the town squares. The lion's share of these victims were Jews. They were slaughtered *en masse*, without pity. The accusations leveled against these men were varied: spying, inciting rebellion against Poland, and even the ludicrous charge of buying from the Russian soldiers goods stolen from Polish citizens.

One day, it was Vilkomir's turn to fall into the hands of the Polish army.

The conquering troops — mostly farmers burning with a lust for Jewish blood — sought, and found, some easy prey. Just days after marching into Vilkomir, the so-called "traitors" were arrested: the town Rabbi and eight other respected Jews. Among these was the wealthy R' Shlomo Chanhas. He was treated by his captors with particular humiliation. Hands tied above his head and his long coat tucked up around his waist, R' Shlomo and the others were led barefoot through the streets toward the town jail, to the accompaniment of raucous laughter from Vilkomir's gentile population. The Jews' hearts contracted, both with the pain of mortification and from a belated realization of their neighbors' true nature.

A military court was hastily assembled. The nine Jews were accused of spying for Russia and sentenced to death by hanging — all in the space of five minutes.

Gloom fell over Vilkomir. The Rabbi, other Jewish community leaders, and R' Shlomo Chanhas were slated for execution for crimes they did not commit. To everyone's amazement, Berka was also arrested, making for a total of ten altogether. On the day of judgment, not even his friendliness with the local gentiles was able to save him.

A frenzied meeting took place in Vilkomir's *shul.*

"*Rabbosai*!" shouted Gronom the Blacksmith, "we cannot wait a moment longer! We must do something!"

"True," the other Jews assented. "We must not be silent. We must do whatever we can!"

"But what can we do?" someone asked.

The question effectively silenced the group. From their earliest youth, it had been the Rabbi who guided the community and told them how to behave in situations such as the one in which they now found themselves. With the Rabbi himself among the victims languishing in prison, the Jews were like a flock of sheep that has lost its shepherd.

Putting their heads together, they struggled to come up with a plan. At last, they resolved to follow the example of their fathers before them: They would fast and pray, and at the same time send messengers to the rebel leaders begging them to spare the lives of their unfortunate brothers.

But even after all the fasting and praying and sending of messengers, the decree was not lifted. Even worse, the conquerors decided to move the executions up by a few days, lest the Russian army return to retake control of Poland before they could carry out their evil designs.

Vilkomir's church bells began to toll at daybreak. The public streamed into the town square to witness the executions. "Jewish blood will pour like water," the gentiles chuckled, rubbing their hands with glee. They had never before seen a public hanging, and today they were to be treated to no less than ten!

The square was crowded with people, held back by tall wooden partitions from the center, which was empty. Only the accused and the executioners could approach the center of the square, where ten gallows had been erected. The nooses swung gently in the breeze.

Several noblemen stood as close as they could, in order to witness the spectacle from the best vantage point. The accused were led into the center of the square. Drunk with bloodlust, the mob screamed insanely. On their side of the partition, the Jews stood silent and helpless. There was nothing left to do.

R' Shlomo Chanhas did not agree. Suddenly, he lunged away from his place in line and approached the leaders of the local rebels — three noblemen whom he knew well.

"What is this, Jew?" roared the head rebel in a fury. "How dare you leave your place?"

"Wadislaw, have you forgotten me?" R' Shlomo asked in a voice that was soft but forceful. "What have we done? What is our crime? You are about to shed innocent blood!"

Wadislaw was taken aback. His acquaintanceship with R' Shlomo went back a long way, too long to pretend it did not exist. After an awkward pause, he said, "You are spies. You helped the Russians."

R' Shlomo fixed the Pole with a penetrating stare. "Wadislaw, are you not ashamed to level such a false accusation? You have known me for years. I have always treated you with friendship and respect. Pyotor and Branislaw can testify to that, can't they?"

Now the other two noblemen were thrown into confusion. R' Shlomo took advantage of the weak moment to continue quickly, "I've heard you whispering secrets many times, but I never revealed them to a soul. And I am the one whom you are accusing of revealing secrets to the Russians?"

The three Poles were silent. Every word R' Shlomo had spoken was true. "You are right, Shlomo," Wadislaw said at last. "You are acquitted. We will hang your friends."

Fresh strength flowed through R' Shlomo's veins. "No!" he cried. "My fate is that of my friends! We are innocent of any wrongdoing. We have never spied for the Russians. Do not let innocent blood be spilled!"

The crowd was watching with growing impatience. "What's going on? Why are they chattering with that Jew? Let them hang him already!"

From moment to moment, however, it became clearer to the mob that the long-anticipated spectacle was not going to take place. The three rebel leaders had already signaled to set the Rabbi free, along with R' Shlomo Chanhas and seven other respected community leaders. R' Shlomo had linked his fate to theirs. If they would be hanged, so would he. He was not prepared to stand apart from his brothers in their time of trouble.

The three noblemen held a hasty conference. They could not let all their prey slip through their fingers. Someone had to pay the price.

The honor fell to Berka, the assimilated Jew. He, of all the group of accused Jews, was the one who would hang. He, who had made merry with the gentiles and felt as much at home with them as a fish in water.

Branislaw went over to R' Shlomo and explained the position. "We thought that Berka was one of us. It turns out that he was the worst of all of you, a genuine spy. A dark cloud of suspicion hangs over his head. We cannot acquit him. He will hang."

R' Shlomo refused to accept this. With tears in his eyes, he pleaded with the rebels to release Berka as well. "He did not do anything. I will take responsibility for him. If you do not wish to free him — hang me in his place!"

His emotional words softened the rebels' resistance. They were on the point of releasing Berka as well, when the crowd roared with anger and disappointment. Their fury at losing their promised treat threatened to turn the mob ugly enough to overrun the square and carry out their own "judgment" on the ten Jewish defendants.

"Shlomo, we have no choice. The crowd wants to see a Jew die." Pyotor pointed at the surging mob. "If we don't hang at least one of you, a great deal of innocent blood will indeed be spilled on this spot."

A storm was raging in Berka's heart. All his life, he had denied his own Jewishness. He had looked upon his heritage as an unwelcome burden and sought out the company of non-Jews. Now, the truth stared him in the face, and it wasn't pretty.

At this moment, in this supreme test, he saw at last who stood by him and who was prepared to stab him in the back. The Jews he had always despised were prepared to hang in his place, while the gentiles he had so admired wanted nothing more than to see his neck in a noose.

Reflections of genuine repentance pulsated in his heart. Hot tears spurted from his eyes as he begged the executioner to give him one brief moment.

In a high, penetrating voice that pierced the listeners' ears like a speeding arrow, he cried, "*Shema Yisrael, Hashem Elokeinu, Hashem echad!*"

The hangman placed the noose around Berka's neck. He kicked aside the support beneath the victim's legs. Berka began to sway back and forth.

Suddenly, the noose broke. Berka fell to the ground with a thud. A few seconds later, he rose shakily to his feet, breathing heavily but quite alive.

The hangman was at a loss. An unwritten but universally acknowledged law stated that a man sentenced to death who fell living from the gallows was to be awarded his life.

The mob was not ready to concede defeat. "Kill him!" they screamed like inflamed beasts on the scent of blood.

The noblemen conferred briefly. Then Wadislaw walked over to Berka and announced out loud: "Berka can win the right to life — if he will state, here and now, that he wishes to convert!"

"Bravo!" thundered the crowd. Though a conversion was not as much fun as an execution, it was nevertheless a diverting spectacle.

Berka the Assimilated, who had lived most of his life as a complete gentile and had only been waiting for the right moment to have himself baptized a Christian, did not hesitate for an instant. Without so much as a glance at his judges and executioners, Berka stood tall and proud before the crowd and let loose a mighty cry: "*Shema Yisrael, Hashem Elokeinu, Hashem echad!*"

At once, the noose was replaced around his neck. The word "*echad!*" was still echoing through the packed square when Berka's soul flew from his body, directly to a higher world.

The anniversary of Berka's death was scrupulously observed by the Jews of Vilkomir for many years. During all that time, *Kaddish* was faithfully recited for him. Father to son, the story of Berka the Assimilated was passed down. The tale of his life and of his death *al kiddush Hashem*, for the sanctification of G-d's Name, was told and re-told: the tale of "Berka the Penitent."

THE REBBE AND THE YARMULKE

T HE LINE INCHED FORWARD SLOWLY. PEOPLE HAD BEEN waiting months for the opportunity to meet face to face with R' Yisrael of Ruzhin. When they finally merited the privilege of entering his room, they found their cares slipping off their shoulders, in tears or even in silence.

One of those waiting outside the door was a Jew from Galicia. He had come to ask the Rebbe for a blessing that he and his wife might be granted the off-spring that had been denied them so far. For three weeks, the man waited patiently in line. Each morning brought fresh hope, and each evening ended with the prospect of a further wait the next day. Then, one evening, the *gabbai* announced, "The Rebbe is very weak. He will not be receiving any more people in the next days!"

Pandemonium broke out. Those who had waited in line were upset, and they expressed their distress quite vocally. Loudest of all was the childless Galician Jew. "I've waited three weeks — for nothing?"

He pushed his way to the Rebbe's door, seized the handle, and burst inside.

The *gabbai* dashed after him, red-faced with rage at the man's effrontery. "Is this how you invade the Holy of Holies?" he shouted. He reached out to take hold of the Galician's coat, then dragged him outside, fuming, "A little *derech eretz*, brazen one!" The act made the Galician break into wails and tears. The other *chassidim* joined in the confusion, making a terrific tumult. At last the Ruzhiner inquired as to the cause of the commotion.

The two men — the *gabbai* and the insulted Galicianer — stood before the Rebbe, stating their complaints.

"Why did I come to see the Rebbe?" the Galicianer wailed. "To ask for riches? For honor? The only thing I wanted to beg for was children. And look how the *gabbai* treated me!"

The Rebbe wished the man well.

"Near the end of that Galicianer's life, he moved to the holy city of Tzefas. By that time, he had the children he had always longed for. He had merited seeing his children and grandchildren involved in lives of Torah and *mitzvos*."

Thus concluded R' Mordechai Chaim of Slonim, when telling the tale. He had known the old Galicianer personally.

The holy courtyard of Ruzhin was like a magnet, drawing thousands of *chassidim* and enthusiastic admirers who came to bask in the Rebbe's presence and to hang upon his words. One day, the word spread like wildfire: The Ruzhiner Rebbe's uncle, the holy R' Mordechai of Chernobyl, was coming to town. It was well known that the Chernobler Rebbe esteemed his nephew greatly, and would visit from time to time.

Uncle and nephew sat together at the table, surrounded by a huge sea of *chassidim*, every one of them listening with rapt absorption to the Rebbes' holy words. Suddenly, R' Mordechai lifted his eyes — which were generally cast down — and gazed around him. On the table stood a *menorah* made of pure gold. The flames in its eight branches illuminated the *beis midrash* with a thousand dancing lights. The Ruzhiner's *chassidim* had bestowed the *menorah* on their beloved Rebbe that very evening, in honor of Chanukah.

"What is the nature of this *menorah*?" asked the Chernobler. It was unclear whether or not he meant anything specific by the question. But the Ruzhiner Rebbe took his uncle's words as bearing the deepest significance. (So greatly did the nephew revere the uncle, that when the Ruzhiner Rebbe's son [the future Rebbe of Hosiatin] was born, he named the child Mordechai Shraga. The "Mordechai" was after his uncle, the Rebbe of Chernobyl, who was still among the living.

"You do not understand," the Ruzhiner had said, in the face of his *chassidim*'s astonishment. "Why are you surprised that I named my son after my uncle? Isn't it already fifteen years since he's been completely detached from the slightest thread of the material world?")

In such awe did the nephew hold his uncle's every utterance, that he negated himself completely before him. At the Chernobler's question, the Ruzhiner said at once, "It is a golden *menorah* that the *chassidim* have bought — and it belongs to my uncle!"

"Very good," the Chernobler said. "I thank the *chassidim* for such a fine gift."

When the older Rebbe stood up to take his leave, the *gabbaim* began to carry the shining *menorah* out with him. The crowd of *chassidim* stood and watched. Out of reverence, they were silent; they knew that they had no part in and no grasp of the secrets of these holy beings. Still, their hearts pained them over all the money they had wrenched from their pockets to bring pleasure to their Rebbe — in vain.

No one said a word, except for one hot-headed young man, who lost his equilibrium at the sight of the departing *menorah*. Before anyone could stop him, he burst into impulsive speech. "But we bought the *menorah* for our Rebbe, may he live!"

To his ill fortune, the Chernobler heard him. He stopped walking, once again lifted his eyes, and fixed the young *chassid* with a penetrating gaze.

"I am certain that this young man will not live out the year," he said in measured tones.

An electrified silence filled the *shul*. The crowd was stunned at these incredibly sharp words. But not a soul dared open his mouth.

No sooner had the Chernobler's retinue disappeared from view than the young *chassid* flung himself at his Rebbe's feet. "What I did was not for my own honor, or for that of my family. A jealous spirit seized me on behalf of my Rebbe's honor. Why have I been made to pay such a terrible penalty?" He wept and wailed on the ground, oblivious to anything but his own anguish.

The Ruzhiner looked down at the young *chassid* with compassion. "Please get up," he said. "All hope is not lost. You still have a chance. I see one thing you can do."

The *tzaddik* ordered a certain *yarmulke* to be brought to him. It was a woolen *yarmulke* that he himself had worn long before. The Rebbe bent down and filled the *yarmulke* with dust.

"Wear this *yarmulke* for a full year, beginning today," he instructed the young *chassid*. "Do not let it leave your head day or night. When you go out, when you sleep, and when you rise, make sure it is stuck firmly on your head!"

With grave emphasis, the Rebbe repeated the warning a second time. Then he continued, "When a full year has gone by, return to me, and we will see how to placate my holy uncle."

The young man's heart nearly burst with joy. He had just received an explicit assurance that he would live out the year. He carried out his Rebbe's instructions to the letter — and even more. In order to make sure that the *yarmulke* never left his head, his wife sewed straps of yarn at its edges to hold it in place. In this way, for a full year, the *yarmulke* did not budge.

When the year was up, the *chassid* returned to Ruzhin, healthy and whole. The Rebbe received him warmly, and blessed him.

"How can it be?" whispered the other *chassidim*, seeing the young man return in good health. "Why, with our own ears we heard something very different from the Chernobler — something that was stated very explicitly."

It was not long before they learned the answer to their question.

The Chernobler Rebbe had returned to pay his nephew another visit. Shortly before his arrival, the Ruzhiner sent the young *chassid* to the marketplace to buy nuts ("*nisselach*" in Yiddish).

When the *tzaddikim* were seated together at the table, the Ruzhiner signaled the *chassid* to approach. Trembling, the young man came to within an arm's length of the Chernobler Rebbe, who turned to see who was standing so close.

"Is this one still in the world?" R' Mordechai of Chernobyl asked in surprise. "I thought that he would be covered in dust for some time now!"

"As my uncle can see for himself," said the Ruzhiner with a smile, "I have indeed covered him with dust."

And he went on to relate to his uncle what the *chassid* had done all year, and how he had worn dust on his head for a full twelve months.

"He now wishes to beg my uncle's forgiveness," the Rebbe finished. "And to that end, he has brought you a present — *nisselach* — so that the verse '*v'nislach*' ('and he shall be forgiven') shall be fulfilled."

At the Ruzhiner's command, the young *chassid,* knees knocking in awe and fear, came close and placed a saucer filled with nuts on the table. The Chernobler looked at him with a radiant smile. And everyone knew that the verse had indeed come to pass: "*V'nislach lechol adas bnei Yisrael … ki lechol ha'am bish'gagah,* And the entire congregation of Israel was forgiven … for it happened to all the people unintentionally."

A MODZHITZER MELODY

T WAS JUST AFTER NOON WHEN MAJOR PETEROV WALKED OUT
of the garrison.

The sentries stood at attention as he passed. The conductor of the
military orchestra was held in high esteem, and not only among the
ranks of the soldiers. Major Peterov's reputation had spread far and
wide, to the highest echelons of both the military and civilian popu-
laces in Russia.

Right now, he sought a short respite from the nonstop pressures
of his job by taking a stroll through the streets of Modzhitz, the city in
which the barracks were situated. Dusk was falling over the houses as
he reached the *chassidishe shul.*

At that hour, the *chassidim* were seated at the third Shabbos meal,
together with their Rebbe, the great R' Yisrael of Modzhitz. They were
singing *zemiros* in an emotion-laden tune. The sweet melody burst
from their full hearts, made its way through the *beis midrash* walls,
and went on to carve a path among whatever other hearts it might
encounter outside.

Major Peterov, of course, had a musical ear. Hearing the song, he
stopped walking and listened, as one mesmerized. For a long time he
stood rooted to the spot, listening to the *chassidim* sing. His heart
melted completely. Without quite realizing what he was doing, he
walked into the *shul.*

Inside, in the near-dark, the *chassidim* sat and sang. The air held
a faint redolence of fish sauce, in which they had dipped *challah* at the
meal. Peterov peered into the gloom, trying to see.

Gradually, he began to make out the scene. He took in the *chassidim,* seated with their "Rabbin," whom he knew they invested with
superior spiritual authority and by whose word all matters of importance were decided in their lives. The Major bent forward to whisper
something into the ears of one of the *chassidim* at the table. As though

bitten by a snake, the *chassid* leaped out of his seat and flew to the head of the table, where the Rebbe sat.

"The conductor of the military band wishes to speak with me?" the author of the *Divrei Yisrael* repeated calmly. "Please ask him to wait until after *Havdalah.*"

Some time later, *Havdalah* over, the officer entered the Rebbe's room. Profound emotion had nearly stolen the power of speech from him. The Rebbe was astonished to see the tall army man, bedecked in the symbols of an outstanding military record, standing before him tongue-tied.

"What is it you wish to say to me?" the Rebbe asked gently.

To his surprise, the officer began by stating simply, "I am a Jew." After an emotional pause, he went on, "I was born in Russia, to a religious Jewish family, but while still a young boy I was forced to leave my parents' home and was raised in a gentile environment. When I came of age, I was drafted into the army as a simple soldier. I climbed higher and higher, until my superior officers discovered my musical abilities and directed me to the military orchestra. There, too, I rose rapidly from a plain musician to the top man. Now I live here with my comrades; I am in a high-ranking position and have been appointed head conductor of the orchestra."

"In that case, what is it you wish from me?" asked the Rebbe. "You sound as though you have everything you need."

The officer replied emotionally, "I don't know what Judiasm is. For many years, it did not interest me at all. But today, as I passed in the street and heard your songs, the Jewish spark ignited inside me. I felt that I have a soul, and that it is thirsting for spirituality — not just a military existence of drills and uniforms, an orchestra and choir and musical notes. Rebbe, I am a Jew and I want to do something as a Jew!"

The Rebbe sat and thought. Presently, he asked the major, "What do you remember from your parents' home — of your Jewish life?"

The officer creased his brow in thought. He sighed at last, and said, "Nothing. It is an absolute blank."

"Maybe just a word or two?" the Rebbe urged.

Humbly, the major said, "All I remember is '*Shema Yisrael*.'"

"Excellent! In that case, continue to live as you have been doing. Do not change any of your habits, lest the army look with disfavor upon your moving closer to your Jewish roots and remove you from your position. However, from time to time, say those two words: '*Shema Yisrael*.'"

"Nothing more?" the officer asked, clearly disappointed.

"It is enough," said the Rebbe.

Without a word, the major left the Rebbe's room.

Several days passed. Major Peterov returned to the Rebbe's house with another question. His wife, too, was Jewish. When he had taken her into his confidence about his experience outside the Modzhitz *shul* and his encounter with the Rebbe, she had sensed the same spiritual yearning in her own soul. What, she wanted to know, was she to do?

The Rebbe was renowned for his wisdom. He gazed deep into the officer's eyes and saw that the man was telling the truth. "Tell your wife not to change her usual habits in any way — except for this: Several times a day, she, like yourself, should say the words '*Shema Yisrael*.'"

A few weeks later, the major paid yet another clandestine visit to the Rebbe's home. Should any of his enemies reveal to his superiors that Peterov was spending time with the Jewish "*Rabbin*," his military career would crumble into ruin.

"I don't know how to explain it," the major said, clearly in the grip of some powerful emotion. "Ever since my wife and I began to say '*Shema Yisrael*' several times a day, a transformation has taken place in our souls. We feel as though we are dry as an earthenware pot, desperate with a spiritual thirst. Rebbe, we cannot be satisfied any longer with merely saying '*Shema Yisrael*.'"

The Rebbe began to instruct the Russian army officer in the basic practices that every Jewish child knows. *Netilas yadayim*, a little information about *kashrus* — and the essential brick in the edifice of

Judaism: Shabbos. With every new teaching, the Rebbe warned repeatedly, "Take care that this remains absolutely secret. No one must find out what you are doing!"

Peterov nodded his head, and for a long time no one sensed any difference in him or his wife. The radical transformation that had taken place in his home was hidden under a thick cloud of concealment, as in the times of the Inquisition. A great many Russian soldiers dined at the major's home, and not one of them noticed the way Peterov and his wife refrained from eating non-kosher meat. His visits to the Rebbe became more frequent and more regular. From time to time, the Rebbe added fresh brick and mortar to the edifice of Jewishness that the Peterovs were slowly building.

The couple celebrated the Pesach holiday in the manner of Torah-observant Jews the world over. Their home underwent a thorough cleaning. The *chametz* was burned and new dishes purchased. They tried to dispense with all guests for that week. Only one soldier, a member of the military choir, clung tenaciously to the major and was not prepared to budge from his side for even a week. He refused to understand Peterov's hints and disregarded even the major's blunt statements. Major Peterov managed to persuade the soldier to eat in the army mess on the night of the *Seder*, but the next day at noon he was back at the house, beaming and merry.

The Peterovs' patience was at an end. Angrily, they told the stunned soldier that they were eating only *matzos* that day, so he must eat his bread out of doors!

Obligingly, the soldier stepped outside and began to eat. The base commander happened to be passing at that moment. Seeing one of his troops feasting on the street, he became enraged. He waved an imperious hand, summoning the soldier to him.

"Where did you get your military manners from?" the commander asked sternly. "A Red Army soldier, eating in the street?"

In his panic and confusion, the soldier nearly choked on the food. He swallowed his mouthful painfully, then stammered, "They — they chased me out of the house!"

"Who did?"

"Major Peterov and his wife."

The blood rushed back into the general's head. Red-faced, he wheeled around and started for the major's door. The soldier was relieved; the general's fury was directed elsewhere now.

Without knocking, the commanding officer threw open the door and walked into the house.

"Why did you send that soldier out of your house, Major Peterov?" barked the general.

Then, all at once, he absorbed what he was seeing. "Aha, what is that flat bread you're eating? Are those the *matzos* that the Jews eat on their Passover holiday? *Matzos* that have been baked with Christian blood!"

The Peterovs had been found out. The major tried to exonerate himself, but the rabidly anti-Semitic general wasn't listening.

For Peterov and his wife, the next few days were tense ones. However, the suspense did not last long. The major was summoned to the military command center in the big city for a talk with the supreme commander of the army.

Late at night, Peterov slipped into the Modzhitzer Rebbe's house. With tears pouring down his cheeks, he related all that had happened to him. "The commander-in-chief is known for his cruelty and ruthlessness. In the eyes of people like him, soldiers are worth less than garlic peels. He is liable to shoot me on the spot, like a mad dog!"

R' Yisrael considered the matter long and hard, then advised, "As you enter the supreme commander's office, do not wait even an instant. Tell him at once that you have something extremely important to reveal to him. His curiosity will force him to desist from killing you until he hears what you have to say."

Encouraged by the Rebbe's suggestion — and, even more, by his warm blessing — the major traveled to the city for the dreaded meeting.

His fears were not unfounded. The commanding general was waiting for him in his office with a cocked and loaded pistol in his hand. He intended to shoot, no questions asked. All of the musical conductor's glowing achievements and sterling reputation had been erased in an instant.

"I have something extremely important to reveal to the commander!" Peterov blurted through bloodless lips, as he stared into the barrel of the pistol aimed at his heart.

"What is that?" asked the general, curious despite himself. His expression remained cold and forbidding as he added, "As long as you know that your secret activities have made you a dead man."

Slowly, with deep feeling, Peterov began to describe his childhood to the general. How he had been born, pure and innocent, to a Jewish mother and father who observed the Torah and *mitzvos*. But his innocent childhood was not to last long. He had been cruelly wrested from his parents at a tender age, and shortly afterwards inducted into the army, where he had forgotten his heritage entirely. Now, after so many years, something astounding had happened. As he had strolled through the streets of Modzhitz one Shabbos, his ears had caught the sound of *chassidim* singing. At that moment, a buried spark of Jewishness had ignited, and from that day onward his Jewish soul had demanded its due.

As the commanding officer listened, the severity of his expression softened slightly. Still, the words he spoke were hard as stones.

"It is hard for me to believe this. In my opinion, it's a lie! It is impossible that a grown man of sense can pass down any old street, and because of some song he happened to overhear, his world turns upside down!" He leaned back in his large chair, arms folded cynically across his chest. "Play me one tune that you heard that day. The melody that induced in you this radical change of heart."

Peterov heaved a sigh of relief. A small ray of hope had begun to shine. The general wished to hear a tune? By all means! "I'll need a violin," he said. Such pure melody required expression through the proper medium.

A violin was brought to the supreme commander's office. Presently, the room was filled with the sweet, soft notes of the Modzhitzer *niggun*. Peterov had deliberately chosen a melody that was calculated to melt the hardest heart, a jewel from the treasure-house of the Rebbe, R' Yisrael. It was the song of the soul as it raps on the heart's gates with a plea: Do not turn me away! Please, I beg of you, let me come in.

Toward the end, the song changed. It acquired a rhythm that was filled with joy and hope and a passion for life. With eyes closed, the general listened to the entire song, humming the last bit along with the violin. When the final note had faded away on the air, he sighed with regret.

"Another tune," he ordered, opening his eyes.

Peterov lifted his bow and launched into a second song from R' Yisrael of Modzhitz's wellspring of melody.

"Another!" said the general with pleasure, when that song was done. The violin was working its magic on him. After the third melody came a fourth, and then a fifth.

For an entire hour, Modzhitzer melodies filled the Russian general's office. The violin performed flawlessly under Major Peterov's nimble fingers. To his good fortune, he had learned many of the Rebbe's tunes by heart. When the last song was finished, the major stood before the supreme army commander, the violin hanging limply from his hand. The general gave him a penetrating stare. Peterov's heart thumped painfully in his chest as he waited. Had his sentence been softened?

"Peterov, listen well," the general said at last. "I am a gentile. I have no spiritual connection with Jewish songs. And yet, I felt now as though my heart were melting with their sweetness. In that case, I can only imagine what you, who were born a Jew, might have felt!"

By this time, the commander's expression was anything but severe. "I permit you to continue living as a Jew, as the composer of those wonderful melodies has been instructing you. But there is one condition." He wagged a threatening finger in Peterov's face. "This must not affect your performance as a soldier in any way."

Peterov promised fervently that it would not.

From that day forward, the Peterovs continued to grow in their observance of the *mitzvos,* until they were complete Jews in the fullest sense of the word.

A year later, Major Peterov came to the Modzhitzer Rebbe's home to invite him to act as *sandak* at the *bris* of his newborn son. And when R' Yisrael married off his youngest child, the military orchestra arrived in full regalia. Conducted by Major Peterov, the soldiers played a beautiful accompaniment for the entire course of the wedding.

✦✦✦

The "Pension Reich" in Jerusalem's Beit Hakerem neighborhood was bustling with guests and visitors. Among the guests was one striking figure: R' Shmuel Eliyahu, the Modzhitzer Rebbe and author of the *Imrei Eish*. He had come from his home in Tel Aviv to spend some time in cooler Jerusalem during the hot summer months. With him was his son and eventual successor, R' Yisrael Dan Taub, *shlita*.

The Rebbe and another guest struck up a warm conversation. The guest, a top Russian scientist, wore a long beard and a hat and comported himself in every way as a G-d-fearing Jew. "What is your honor's name?" the scientist asked.

"They call me Taub," replied the Rebbe, in an attempt to conceal his identity.

The scientist would not be satisfied with that. He persisted in his questions until he discovered at last that his conversational partner was none other than the Modzhitzer Rebbe.

Overcome with emotion, the scientist rose to his feet and extended a hand to the Rebbe. "I am very glad to meet you," he exclaimed, eyes alight with happiness. "My name is Peterov. My father was conductor of the Russian army orchestra in the big garrison in Modzhitz — and your grandfather was *sandak* at my *bris*!"

Two things emerge with stark clarity from this chain of events: the power of a Modzhitzer *niggun* to melt hearts... and the power of two words, "*Shema Yisrael*," to ignite a flame in a Jewish soul and restore it — even after long, dark years of exile — to its rightful place.

THE REBBE INCURS A DEBT

FTER THE PUPA REBBE, R' YOSEF GREENWALD (AUTHOR OF *Vayechi Yosef*) emerged from the Valley of Death that was the Nazi Holocaust — in which he lost his wife and ten children — he wandered from place to place until he finally arrived in America. There, he settled in the Williamsburg neighborhood of Brooklyn and opened his Pupa Yeshivah, offshoot of the large European yeshivah that had been destroyed by the Germans, and began at once to teach Torah.

He began with only tens of students at first, but their numbers quickly grew. As the institution blossomed, Pupa began to send off shoots outside of Williamsburg. Schools for boys and for girls, yeshivos and *kollelim* for young men, sprouted in cities all across the United States, Europe, and in the holy city of Jerusalem.

For all his burning desire to spread the Torah's honor and to multiply Torah institutions in the world, the Pupa Rebbe was a tremendously humble man. He did not lead his many institutions with a strong hand at the helm, but rather quietly, from behind the scenes. It was not his way to issue orders and commands to his *chassidim* and his students; when there was a need to ask someone to do something, he did so in a mild tone, as though compelled to speak against his will. He was content to leave most matters in other people's hands.

At the end of his life, however, the Rebbe went counter to his own nature and mustered all his remaining strength on behalf of his precious Torah institutions. He personally attended fund-raising meetings and dinners for his schools and yeshivos. The number of people invited was small, and the Rebbe would approach each one with a personal plea for support.

One night near the beginning of Cheshvan, a "tea party" was conducted in the home of one of the Pupa Yeshivah's students. The purpose of the evening was to raise funds for the purchase of a new building to house a *cheder* for boys in Boro Park, the sons of Pupa *chassidim* living there. There were already many branches of the Pupa *cheder* for boys — known as *Kehillas Yaakov* — as well as girls' schools called *Bnos Yaakov*, but the Pupa community in Boro Park felt the urgent need for a *cheder* of its own.

A small group of wealthy individuals was invited to the tea party, men who had committed themselves ahead of time to generous donations.

The Pupa Rebbe was nearing his 80th birthday. His pale face reflected the hard times he had lived through and the burdens he had borne, yet he led the campaign with vigor. In his hand was a small notepad in which were written the contributors' names. He went around the tables, asking each in turn, "How much are you donating?" The answers were marked down in the notepad, after which the Rebbe showered blessings on each man's head. The donations began at $1,000.

The Pupa Rebbe reached the table where one of his foremost students was seated. This was R' Chaim Schwartz [the name has been changed to protect the individual's identity], a *chassid* in his 40's and a very successful businessman. R' Chaim knew no lack of money, yet he was not fully satisfied with his lot. He had five daughters, but not a single male child.

"And how much are you donating?" the Rebbe asked.

"Two hundred dollars."

"That's all?" the Rebbe said in surprise. "People were not invited here for small donations."

The *chassid,* who was an honest man, stood up respectfully before the Rebbe and said calmly, "I will tell the Rebbe the truth. What good is a boys' *cheder* to me, when I have only daughters? Let my friends contribute. They have sons; they can take care of themselves!"

The Rebbe's answer was swift and sure. "If you give, you will also benefit from the boys' *cheder*."

R' Chaim nearly fainted with joy. "The Rebbe is blessing me with a son?"

"Yes." The Rebbe's face shone like the sun at noon. "Give now, and this time next year you will be granted a living son."

"Ten thousand dollars!" cried the *chassid.*

The Rebbe did not become overly excited. He asked with a smile, "When will we see the money?"

R' Chaim's response was to dash out of the house as though on fire. He returned a short while later with $10,000 in cash, which he joyfully handed to the Rebbe. As he did, however, he said explicitly, "I would like the Rebbe to promise me a son."

"Promise? How can I promise? Am I in G-d's place? I can only give you my blessing. Hashem will help you to father a male child."

Ten months later, during the summer month of Av, as the Rebbe relaxed in the Catskill Mountains together with his yeshivah boys, all the chassidim were stunned to hear that R' Chaim Schwartz intended to pay a visit — together with his newborn son. He wished to honor the Rebbe with the role of *sandak* at the *bris*.

Taking mother and newborn on a two-and-a-half hour journey so soon after birth was considered an unusual action. R' Chaim was no impetuous youth of 20, but a settled man who had already arrived at the age of wisdom. But his heart was merry, for after five daughters, he had fathered a son!

R' Chaim had a younger brother, R' Yaakov Schwartz [name changed]. If R' Chaim had lacked but a son to complete his happiness, his brother had no children at all. It was already ten years since he had married, and still no sign of the longed-for offspring.

When R' Yankel Schwartz belatedly learned the story behind his nephew's birth, his heart began to sing a wordless tune. Until now, he had seen only his Rebbe's humble side, a man who always down-played his own worth and declined to offer blessings. Who am I, he seemed to be saying, to bless my people? Now, in his old age, a new side had appeared. The Rebbe was emerging as a man who could dis-pense salvation, a man who could promise and Hashem would fulfill.

R' Yankel did not hesitate a moment. He jumped into his car and drove directly up to the Catskills. When he reached the Pupa camp, he made a beeline for the wooden cabin that housed the Rebbe.

The *gabbaim* were surprised to see R' Yankel, the Williamsburg entrepreneur, among the campers. He had been up at camp just the day before, at his nephew's *bris*. "R' Yankel, you were just here yesterday. Why have you returned? Are your business concerns doing so well that you can afford to leave them?"

R' Yankel smiled. "My business is doing well, *baruch Hashem*. I wish to see the Rebbe, and it is urgent."

The *gabbaim* did as he asked, and brought him to the Rebbe's room.

R' Yankel pulled a wad of money from his pocket. Ten thousand dollars!

"What is this?" the Rebbe asked in astonishment.

"I've come to donate money toward the Pupa Talmud Torah being built in Boro Park."

"May Heaven's blessings shower on your head," R' Yosef laughed. "But what prompted you to hand over such a sum on an ordinary day like this? We're not having a 'dinner' now, or even a 'tea party.' What happened to bring you here with so much money so suddenly?"

R' Yankel admitted, "I heard that my brother donated this same amount and received a blessing for a son. He already had five daughters — but I, sadly, have been married ten years and have not yet merited any children at all."

"Aha! You wish to follow in your brother's footsteps. But the two situations are different. I asked your brother for a donation at my time of need, while you are bursting in on your own initiative just to imitate him. It is impossible to replicate the propitious hour."

R' Yankel tried to explain that his pain was no imitation, and was indeed many times greater than that of his brother. But the expression on the Rebbe's face told him that the time was not propitious. His stubbornness would avail him nothing. Sadly, he took leave of the Rebbe.

But before he left the camp, R' Yankel asked the *gabbaim* to do him a favor. "My whole life is bound up in this. If you see, one day, that the Rebbe is feeling exceptionally happy and that the hour is propitious, call me. Wherever I happen to be, I will come running."

Months passed. R' Yankel's request had been all but forgotten.

One day, the *gabbaim* went out to take a walk with R' Yosef in the fresh air, as they did every day on doctor's orders. The Rebbe fulfilled the medical injunction by walking with his *gabbaim* along a narrow stretch of pavement where there were few passersby.

R' Yosef's expression was happy and satisfied. As they walked, he and the *gabbaim* launched into a discussion of a marvelous new plan: a scheme to build a town, to be called *Kiryas Pupa*, outside of the city. It was a good plan from every angle, especially the educational one. It would allow youngsters to grow up away from the often sordid sights of New York City. The *chassidic* group would be able to flourish there, undisturbed.

"And the money?" the Rebbe asked. "How much would it cost to establish such a community outside the city?"

"A lot," the *gabbaim* answered. "A fortune."

"Where will we get it from?"

"We shall have to ask our wealthy men to carry the burden."

"It's not that simple," the Rebbe said. "We can't keep asking them for more and more."

One *gabbai* wrinkled his brow as something prodded his memory. Suddenly, he remembered. "Rebbe!" he said enthusiastically. "There are still men who have not made donations, but who wish to contribute with all their hearts."

"Who, for example?" asked the Rebbe.

"R' Yankel Schwartz. A while ago, he wanted to give a very generous donation, but it never came to actuality. Shall I call him?"

"Certainly!" the Rebbe said happily. "A Jew who wishes to contribute for a *mitzvah*!"

The young *gabbai* ran like a deer to R' Yankel's place of business. Bursting into the store, he gasped, "You were waiting for the propitious moment? It has come! The Rebbe is waiting for you, and he is very happy. There is no better time than right now."

R' Yankel did not hesitate an instant. Hastily, he hung a "CLOSED" sign on his shop door, then ran with the *gabbai* toward the place where the Rebbe was taking his walk.

When they arrived, the talk was still centered on the planned suburban community. "It will cost a great fortune to build," the Rebbe said aloud in a thoughtful tone. He had not yet noticed that R' Yankel had joined them. "Where do we find such a large sum of money?"

R' Yankel decided it was time for him to take part in the discussion. "Rebbe, I can donate a significant amount — a very large amount — to help us over the first hurdle."

The Rebbe leveled a gaze at him. "You? R' Yankel?"

"Yes."

The Rebbe was silent — but his eyes kept on smiling.

R' Yankel moved closer. "Rebbe, I am prepared to donate any amount the Rebbe says, on the condition that the Rebbe will guarantee me living offspring. I want children!"

The words burst from him in an anguished cry. Eleven years of pain spurted in a mighty torrent from his heart.

The Rebbe was quick to put the *chassid* in his place. "Guarantee? No! One does not make conditions with the Master of the Universe!"

"All right." R' Yankel breathed deeply. "I will make my contribution without conditions."

"Meanwhile," said R' Yosef, "do not contribute anything. Thousands, tens of thousands — do you think it is possible to 'buy off' Hashem with a bribe? He, of Whom it said, 'Who does not show favor and does not take bribes'!"

A tense silence fell over the entire group. It seemed to them that even the birds had stopped chirping, and that the trees were bending lower to hear what the Rebbe said.

"Give *tzedakah*," the Rebbe said gently. "A simple thing, to give *tzedakah*. Let us hope that, in the merit of that *mitzvah*, you will find the salvation you seek."

R' Yankel had waited only for this moment. In a twinkling, he pulled out his checkbook and signed a blank check. Then he handed the pen to the Rebbe. By this time, they had reached the Rebbe's house. The Rebbe went into his room and sat down.

"The Rebbe can fill in any amount that seems reasonable to him," R' Yankel offered generously.

The Rebbe reflected a moment, while the *gabbaim* stood by in suspense. How much would the Rebbe write? A five-figure amount? Six? Seven? R' Yankel had said, "any amount." Perhaps he was prepared to mortgage his house and all his belongings for the sake of his most ardent desire.

The Rebbe put the pen to the check and wrote: "$180."

"This is ten times *chai* (18)," the Rebbe explained to Yankel. "I bless you with finding salvation in the merit of this *tzedakah*."

R' Yankel's eyes glowed. Their vision dimmed momentarily as his eyes filled with tears. With a shaking hand, he wrote out a second check for an enormous amount. "Still," he said, with a quaver in his voice, as he handed over the check, "I'd like to contribute for the sake of the new *chassidic* community. I had the good intention of donating money, and I do not want to take that back."

꧁꧂

Purim, 5744 (1984)

It was several months later. R' Yankel approached the Pupa Rebbe, carrying a huge basket of *shalach manos* in his arms. He whispered that there was not yet even the shadow of a sign of salvation.

The Rebbe sighed. "Then I am a debtor. What can I do?"

A half year later, on the thirteenth of Av, 5744 (1984), *Shabbos Nachamu*, R' Yosef Greenwald, the Pupa Rebbe, departed this world. His son, R' Yaakov Yechizkiyahu, was appointed to take his place.

Ten months after the Rebbe's passing, word spread through the Pupa community: "R' Yankel Schwartz has had his salvation. A baby girl has been born to him!" And the chassidim added a footnote: "The Rebbe paid his debt after his passing." They took this as an example of the famous saying of *Chazal,* "*Tzaddikim* are greater in their deaths than in their lives" (*Chullin 7*).

What they learned a week later, however, was the most startling of all.

The current Pupa Rebbe summoned a meeting of the men responsible for erecting the Pupa village being built in Westchester, New York. He handed them an envelope containing a very large sum of money.

On the envelope, in his father's handwriting, were the words: "I received this money from R' Yankel Schwartz, for the building of the *chassidic* village. Do not use the money until R' Yankel has his salvation."

"The time has come," the new Pupa Rebbe announced with satisfaction. "My father was not a debtor for even a moment! On the contrary — only now that R' Yankel has been granted his salvation did my father permit us to use the money!"

THE MILLION-DOLLAR HORSE

WITH PLODDING PERSISTENCE, THE BROWN HORSE dragged the huge stone around and around in a circle. Five solid hours of walking in a circle was capable of driving any horse — even this one, considered one of the best at the flour mill — out of its equine mind.

A friendly tap on the shoulder startled the horse and made it temporarily increase its pace. "You're tired, my friend?" Shmulik asked with a compassionate glance. "Okay, let's free you from that harness and return you to the stables."

Shmulik, manager of the flour mill, knew his horses as well as he knew the palms of his own hands. There were those who claimed he knew them better than his own hands. After all, when did he have time to study his palms, thickened and calloused from years of hard work?

They called it "Frankel's Mill." Located in the Old City, where most of Jerusalem's Jews lived at that time, the mill was owned by R' Yehoshua Heshel Frankel-Teomim, who had earned the esteem and respect of his fellow Jews in great measure. The respect came mainly through his own efforts: He was a Torah scholar and a pious man whose fear of sin preceded his wisdom. Another important factor was his family *yichus*. R' Yehoshua Heshel was descended from a long chain of prestigious families. His grandfather was a brother to the renowned *gaon*, R' Baruch Frankel-Teomim from Leipnik, father-in-law the holy *Divrei Chaim* of Sanz. The mere fact that he was first cousin of the great Sanzer Rebbe would have been sufficient to garner him a king's honor in old Jerusalem.

All day long, R' Yehoshua Heshel involved himself with Torah and Divine service. From daybreak until midnight, his routine was one long, continuous chain of Torah and prayer. Though he owned the famous flour mill, he was able to leave the work in others' hands. From time to time, he would check on the situation at the mill. His sharp eyes were quick to spot any deviation from proper procedure. He would take the necessary measures to ensure that the workers were doing their job, make a quick tour of the stables and the grinding stones, then return to his Talmud.

Shmulik, the mill manager, was R' Yehoshua Heshel's right-hand man. Thanks to him, the owner was able to sit and learn in peace, knowing that his business was in capable hands.

The mill drew the children of Old Jerusalem like a magnet. On their way home from *cheder*, the little boys found a thousand excuses to get underfoot and bother the workers at their jobs. What could be more interesting than the mill, forever coated in a dusting of flour that crept onto your clothes and into your shoes?

On the outside, the mill looked like any other building in Jerusalem, built entirely of stone. Inside, however, all was different. In the center stood a giant grindstone, with another great rock riding just above it. The flour was ground between the two heavy stones, then poured directly into a large sack. When the sack was full, a new one was inserted in its place. The flour in the full sack was then distributed among a number of small bags, to be sold to grocery stores in larger or smaller quantities, as needed.

But even more fascinating than the mill itself were the nearby stables. The horses roused the children's imagination like nothing else. How long, they wondered, could a horse walk in a circle? True, the horses' eyes were covered so that they did not realize they were walking the same endless circle, yet even a horse has its limits.

In the stable stood two or three other, fresh horses, ready and waiting to take the first one's place when it tired. The children found the stables to be a source of endless interest. They would poke their heads through the opening in the stable door, calling to the horses and feeding them the crusts of their lunchtime sandwiches. There was also a special game — tickling the horses' nostrils with a long straw. The children would collapse in laughter at the long, shrill whinnies of protest. The Arab mill workers, alerted by the sound of their laughter, would come charging furiously at the intruders — but the children always managed to run away just in time.

Shmulik the miller had been devotedly managing the flour mill for many years. The mill worked twenty-four hours a day, and its schedule ran as regularly as clockwork. Shmulik was responsible for negotiating with the wheat merchants and for seeing to it that the flour reached Jerusalem's Jews. Shmulik seemed to be everywhere at once. He knew every crack and cranny of the old mill and had complete access to the money till. Occasionally, when taking his salary, he would grant himself a generous loan from the mill funds, with the full knowledge of the owner, who trusted his integrity implicitly. R' Yehoshua Heshel knew that he could count on his devoted manager always.

Then the day came when Shmulik did not rise from his bed. That very day, his fellow citizens carried him to his final resting place on the heights of *Har HaZeisim*, the Mount of Olives. They eulogized the miller, praising his honesty and dedication to his job. Nearly-forgotten snippets from his life were resurrected and remembered — memories long covered with a dusting of flour and time. Children who had since grown up and married came to beg the deceased man's forgiveness for their childish pranks.

R' Yehoshua Heshel returned from the funeral teary eyed. Parting from the man who had been so close to him was very difficult. But there was no time for prolonged grieving. The exigencies of life would wait for no man. Jerusalem needed its flour.

On the day after Shmulik's burial, R' Yehoshua Heshel ran around the city seeking a new manager to run the mill. He was looking for a capable and responsible man, a man whom he could trust to manage his business so that he himself could learn Torah with an untroubled spirit, just as he had succeeded in doing during Shmulik's lifetime.

He found the man he wanted. That very evening, he started a dialogue with Itzik, an energetic young fellow with glowing eyes. R' Yehoshua Heshel led Itzik through the mill, teaching him the secrets of the trade. The young man absorbed everything at once, and was able to step into the departed Shmulik's shoes the very next morning. The mill had not stood idle for more than two days before the horses were once again plodding their endless circles around the grinding stones and filling the sacks with fresh white flour.

Itzik brimmed with enthusiasm for his new job. He spent several weeks learning every aspect of the business, working almost around the clock in his zeal. When he was familiar with every stone and every crack in the old mill, he was ready to turn his mind to streamlining its routine, grown rusty with age and repetition. One day, he inspected the horses in the stables, then asked R' Yehoshua Heshel for permission to inject fresh blood into their ranks. His employer agreed.

The next day, Itzik went to *Shaar Shechem,* the Damascus Gate, where young, strong horses were for sale. He bargained with the Arab sellers in their own tongue, felt each horse, and tested its muscles. Finally, he chose two horses that seemed strong enough to drag the heavy grindstones. His return to the stables, leading two fine, proud horses, drew a long string of children and other curiosity-seekers in his train.

Itzik had not erred in his choice. Both of the horses he had chosen revealed a capacity for hard work. However, there was a definite difference between them. While one horse worked "by the book," no more or less than any other reasonably energetic workhorse, the second behaved in a truly astonishing fashion. The usual five-hour stint of labor passed like minutes for this second horse. While others, by the end of the shift, were nearly ready to collapse, this horse was still as fresh and strong as though it had not done a stitch of labor. It rebelled firmly against being led back to the stables, and indicated in every way it knew that it loved its job and was not prepared to give up even a moment of it.

As Itzik watched and marveled, the horse worked double and even triple the usual shift. It rested briefly and worked at length. In the morning, when the stable doors were opened to let it out, the horse would neigh happily, and always tried to be the first one at the grindstones. While dragging the heavy stones, it would move practically at a gallop, turning them with wondrous speed that left everyone slack-jawed with amazement.

In short, the new horse was a gold mine. Even its physical appearance gave the impression of supernatural strength. The horse worked as hard as five horses together.

In tiny Old Jerusalem, there were no secrets. The children were quick to spread tales of the wonder horse throughout the city. Likewise, the mill's Arab workers told of the *jinn* (spirit) that looked like a horse but was apparently much more. Everyone was talking about the amazing horse, and some rapid calculators figured out that, should the horse continue at its present rate of work for ten years, it would be worth a million napoleons.

It was not long before the news reached the Turkish Pasha.

"A magic horse," he murmured. "That horse is worth millions. I will confiscate it from that Jew. Such a capacity for work should be placed in the service of the Ottoman Empire! I will house the horse in my best stable and feed it the best food. The *jinn* horse will serve me day and night."

His resolution fixed, it remained only for the Pasha to decide how to get his hands on the horse. He was undecided whether to simply take it by force, or — to avoid angering the Jewish community — to hire a couple of capable horse thieves to do the job for him. One thing he did know: Before another few days had passed, that horse was going to be his!

After a long internal debate, the Pasha decided on a third course. To avoid arousing anger, he would buy the amazing horse from the miller. He was prepared to pay 25 napoleons for it. "What are 25 napoleons compared to millions?" he laughed to himself.

Two days passed. R' Yehoshua Heshel woke up in the middle of the night in a panic. For a moment, he lay rigid in his bed, heart in a turmoil and nerves still jangling with terror. Then he washed his hands, leaped out of bed, and hastily dressed. Seizing a lantern, he went out into the narrow streets and began walking toward the mill.

The mill workers were astonished to see their employer at such an hour. His visits were infrequent, and had never taken place so late at night. Was he trying to catch them being lazy on the night shift? They watched closely to see what he would do next.

R' Yehoshua Heshel cut a path through the startled workers and made straight for the stables. "He's going to the *jinn*," the Arab laborers whispered to one another.

At the sight of R' Yeshoshua Heshel, the horse whinnied with delight, almost as though it had been expecting him. It gazed intently at R' Yehoshua Heshel, who gazed just as intently back. R' Yehoshua Heshel was silent for a long moment, eyes closed. Then, in a trembling voice, he said three times: "Shmulik, I forgive you completely!"

When he had finished saying the sentence for the third time, the workers crowded behind gasped aloud, and started back in confusion.

The *jinn* horse had fallen down, dead on the spot!

The staggering news spread throughout Jerusalem the next day. People stood in small groups all over the city, discussing nothing but the wonder-horse's strange and sudden death just an instant after R' Yehoshua Heshel Frankel finished saying for the third time that he forgave it.

In *shul,* after *davening,* R' Yehoshua Heshel found himself surrounded. Nobody was prepared to let him go until he had revealed the story behind his mysterious night visit to the mill. And why had he called the horse "Shmulik"?

At last, R' Yehoshua Heshel gave in to the pleading. This is the story he told:

"Last night, Shmulik came to me in a dream. In the dream, I remembered very well that he had passed on, and I asked him what his judgment had been in the Heavenly Court. Shmulik told me, in a sorrowful voice, that the Court had weighed all his deeds very carefully.

"'I won't go into details,' Shmulik said, 'but I will tell you this much. Because of my many expenses and the cost of marrying off my children, from time to time I helped myself to a loan from the mill's cash box — with your knowledge, and also sometimes without it. Heaven forbid, I was no thief; I intended to pay it all back. But, in the end, I left the world while still owing you a large sum. The Heavenly Court decreed that I return to this world in the guise of a horse, and repay my debt in the form of hard work. My soul passed into the form of a young, strong horse.

"'Itzik bought the horse that contained my soul. The moment I arrived at the mill, I began to work with a special power that was granted me by Heaven, so that I might be able to repay my debt to you down to the last penny. I worked with amazing diligence. The hours I put in were extraordinary in both quality and quantity — all in order to be able to repay what I owed as quickly as possible, and to repair my defect in the world of souls.

"'Now, however, it has been revealed to me that the Turkish Pasha is getting ready to buy me from you for 25 gold napoleons. This caused me bitter anguish. Were I to fall into the Pasha's hands, I would not be in a position to repay my debt! That is why I beg of you, R' Yehoshua Heshel, to go to the stable and to tell the *jinn* horse — in other words, me — three times that you forgive my debt completely.'

"And that," concluded R' Yehoshua Heshel, "is exactly what I did. The horse died, and Shmulik the miller can now go to his rest in *Gan Eden*."

HIS REWARD IS GREAT

H E WALKED AMONG THE SKELETONS OF UNFINISHED buildings, and his heart was uplifted and joyous. As a gentle breeze carried on its back the fragrance of oranges from a nearby orchard, everything in the man's soul sang praises to his Creator. His happiness knew no bounds.

The building was progressing at a satisfactory rate. The workers were arriving on time each day and the houses were inexorably rising, story by story. The last load of cement had arrived by boat ahead of schedule. All was moving along nicely.

Yechiel Wachs [the actual name has been changed] was a successful building contractor during a period when *Eretz Yisrael* hardly recognized such a concept. These were the years between 5680 and 5690 (1920-1930). The section of the country known today as Gush Dan boasted far more orchards than dwellings. Yechiel Wachs was a man of action. He was also blessed with a fine financial sense, which helped him to know when and where to invest his capital. The construction business was booming at that time, and he dedicated his energies to erecting building after building. On his payroll were scores of diligent laborers — every one of them a Jew. Yechiel was in hot competition with the giant Solel Boneh conglomerate which had been responsible for building most of the homes in Gush Dan.

In the Ramat Gan area (called in those days "Ir Ganim"), the people knew the name Yechiel Wachs as well as they knew Solel Boneh. The large company had constructed twenty-five buildings in Ramat Gan; Yechiel had single-handedly put up twenty. And he was only one person, as opposed to a bloated corporation that never lacked for funds.

It was a Friday morning in May. Yechiel walked from house to house, inspecting each one's progress. He was putting up ten three-story buildings at once. Construction was at its height. The foundation pillars were being poured in some homes, while in others the work had moved on to the second stories. The project called for impressive quantities of cement.

Cement. That was the key word in those days. Without it, not even half a room could be built. Because *Eretz Yisrael* still had no factories for its manufacture, the precious commodity was brought in from Britain — at a steep price. Transporting the cement by boat added substantially to the cost, as did the barrels in which they were brought. (The concept of bagging the cement in sacks had yet to be born.)

The factories would fill their ovens with a mixture consisting of one part special sand and three parts limestone, mined on the Isle of Portland off the coast of England. When the mixture had cooled, it formed small pebbles, which were then ground into the powder known as "cement." The cement was poured into wooden barrels bearing the legend "Portland Cement" in black letters.

The day before this story opens, dock workers at Yaffo harbor had unloaded over 150 barrels of cement from a British merchant ship. Not all the barrels were designated for Yechiel Wachs; more than half belonged to the Solel Boneh construction company.

This was a goodly number of barrels. Yechiel's men were waiting to meet the shipment at the port, where they signed customs documents prepared by the British Mandate and patiently underwent the long and complex procedure of receiving authorization for the cement. When all the paperwork had been completed, the barrels were carried out of the port. Yechiel's industrious crew loaded them onto horse-drawn wagons, which carried the cement to the construction site.

At the same time, a team of Solel Boneh workers loaded their quota of cement onto their own carts, and drove them to their own building site, located at the end of the same street.

Yechiel personally supervised the unloading. He inspected the green-gray material, sniffed its aroma, and nodded in satisfaction at its quality. Portland cement was always top-quality — and he had paid a small fortune for it. In fact, he had sunk every available penny he had into this shipment. If something should happen before the cement was poured, he stood to lose everything. But why were such morbid thoughts flitting through his mind? Everything always turned out all right. Why should things be any different this time?

At noon, Yechiel left the construction site. He made sure that all the workers left before him. He was a pious Jew who was careful to observe the Shabbos faithfully. Work always stopped at noon on Friday, and no one would return to the site until Sunday morning. This was the weekly routine, and today was no different.

Yechiel climbed onto his wagon. The horse walked slowly through the streets of small Tel Aviv, crossed the city, and brought Yechiel Wachs to his home in Yaffo.

As he stepped off the wagon and entered his house, a cool wind gusted suddenly. He noticed a gray mass on the horizon, but Yechiel paid these things no mind. It was May. The rainy winter season was over.

❧

Yechiel was just placing a pot of chicken soup on the stove when he heard a stir outside, in the street. Several men had approached his house and were discussing something in excited tones. Presently, a shower of knocks fell on the door.

Yechiel opened it. His workers burst into the house, their expressions agitated. "Yechiel! We must do something!"

Yechiel understood their agitation. He was not blind; he had seen the buildup of heavy gray cloud all across the sky. Quietly and calmly, he asked, "What happened?"

They pointed at the sky, which was rapidly darkening. "Look. It's about to start pouring. The rain will ruin our cement!"

It is important to note that the barrels had arrived uncovered. The precious cement was completely exposed to the elements. Despite the fact that it was spring, the dry season in *Eretz Yisrael*, the clouds that were swiftly overspreading the sky had a wintry look about them. Cement, when combined with water, hardened and turned to concrete. Until the cement was ready for use, water was its greatest enemy.

The workers had no uncertainty about the right course to pursue.

"We have to get over to the site right away, take some lumber, and cover the barrels. If the rain falls on them, all the cement will be ruined. There goes the whole investment!"

Yechiel glanced at his watch. There were still three hours remaining until Shabbos. A great many things needed to be done in that time: traveling to the site by horse and wagon, covering the barrels with lumber or any other available material in order to save the cement from the threat of approaching rain, and then traveling back home again to his home in Yaffo — all before Shabbos began.

"Will you manage to finish everything before Shabbos?" he asked skeptically.

The workers did not deny that the task would require desecrating the Shabbos. In any case, they themselves were not Shabbos-observant. Yechiel drew himself up to his full height, and said in a voice filled with strength and determination, "No! I do not permit you to go. I will not sell the Shabbos for all the treasure in the world!"

The workers could not believe their ears. "What's happened to you, Yechiel? Are you prepared to lose so much money because of Shabbos? And who said that *you* have to go? We will go ourselves. All the work will be done by others. You can sit home and benefit from our labor."

But Yechiel was adamant. "Not under any circumstances will I allow this! I do not want any man to desecrate the Shabbos because of me. Anyone who dares go to 'Ir Ganim' now will be fired!"

"But all the cement will go down the drain. It's worth a fortune! You might have to declare bankruptcy because of such a loss," the workers protested vehemently.

Yechiel lifted his head proudly. "It would be worthwhile losing my entire holdings rather than injure the holy Shabbos by even a hair."

His iron determination awed the workers, who quickly retreated. Apart from the practical considerations — no one wished to find himself without a job on Sunday — they had very real respect for a man who displayed such firm values as their employer. Clearly, his piety preceded his wisdom.

After the workers left, the wind began to howl in earnest. Yechiel ignored the change in the weather and the cloud cover that was strengthening by the minute. He refused to think about the vulnerable barrels of cement lying exposed on the building site.

It had not yet begun to rain when he walked to his usual *shul* for Friday night services, but the cold had intensified and the wind was blowing even more strongly. It felt like the dead of winter instead of the height of spring. The men came to *shul* wrapped in thick coats, marveling endlessly over the sudden wintry turn of the weather in May.

It was while Yechiel was holding his *Kiddush* cup and swaying fervently that the first flash of lightning lit the black sky. This was followed by a tremendous crash of thunder. A volley of lightning and thunder followed — and then the skies opened up. In a twinkling, the streets of Yaffo and nearby Tel Aviv became deserted, as heavy rain lashed the streets.

Yechiel went on with his Shabbos meal, locking his heart against the slightest depressing thought.

"Such a heavy rain … The barrels will become a mixture of cement and water. By Sunday morning, they will be filled with concrete, and not cement." This brief reflection might have wreaked havoc with Yechiel's spirits, had he allowed it entrance. But he was strong. He did not permit a single thought of this kind to sneak into his consciousness. He had erected a "Great Wall of China" in his mind that Shabbos, and it boasted not a single crack. "On Shabbos, all your work has been done."

All that Friday night, lightning and thunder continued to play across the skies, while a furious downpour washed the city. Yechiel the builder's home was snug and dry. The oven gave out a pleasant warmth, and the hot-water urn on the stovetop provided refreshing cups of tea for the whole family. But the illumination in the house did not come from brilliant flashes of lightning or even from the powerful "Blitz lamp." It came from Yechiel's glowing countenance, which shone with the special radiance that the Shabbos lends to those who have withstood a difficult test.

Yechiel sat and took pleasure in his Shabbos table. He sang hearty *zemiros* with his sons and told *divrei Torah* on the weekly Torah portion. When the meal was over, he sat and reviewed the *parashah* with *Targum* and *Rashi*. Then he went to bed, content as a baby secure in its mother's arms. He rose at dawn, recited the entire book of *Tehillim* as he had been accustomed to doing for years, then went off to *shul* for *Shacharis*.

Yaffo's sidewalks greeted him with clean-washed smiles as he walked. The heavy rain had left not a scrap of dirt or litter in its wake.

Yechiel was not troubled in the least. His *davening* and his meals took place to the accompaniment of a spiritual pleasure such as he had not known in years.

As he stood up to recite *Havdalah* on *motza'ei Shabbos,* the clouds began to disperse. The gray curtains parted here and there to let out a gleam. A moon, one-third full, revealed itself in the skies, awaiting those who would come out to bless her. Yechiel said *Havdalah* with such fervor that his wife wondered which was glowing brighter: the *Havdalah* flame or her husband, purified in the furnace of testing fire.

But the moment Yechiel set down his goblet and sensed the departure of the Shabbos, a bitter depression fell over him. His heart was consumed with sorrow. "Woe is me! I have lost my fortune in a single moment. The rain ruined my cement, and I had sunk everything into it!"

His knees buckled. He leaned limply against a wall for a long moment. Then, slowly, he went to the stable and harnessed his trusty horse to the wagon. Flicking his whip lightly, he called, "Hurry, run with all your might, and take me to view my great loss with my own eyes!"

As though he understood his master's anguish, the horse picked up its feet and galloped swiftly the whole way there.

This was in the days before streetlights had been put up to illuminate the area. All was covered in thick darkness. Yechiel arrived at the construction site armed with a storm lantern. Raising his arm to let the lantern cast a broader light, he walked over to his lot, heart fluttering like a butterfly as he prepared to witness the devastation.

A gasp of astonishment escaped the builder's lips. His eyes nearly bulged out of their sockets. All the barrels — more than 70 of them — were completely covered! They were covered with slats of wood, with sheets of tin, and even with large stones that sealed the barrel-tops as securely as carpenter's glue.

"Am I going insane?" Yechiel wondered. "Or maybe I'm dreaming?"

He moved closer to the barrels. Trembling, he removed one cover. He felt a need to touch the miracle with his own hands.

A fine powder met his seeking fingers. He brought a bit to his nose and sniffed and then began coughing and sputtering as grains of cement flew up his nose.

An intoxication, finer than any induced by liquor, filled Yechiel's heart. An image from his childhood rose up in his mind — a sweet and magical image. He pictured the same angels that had accompanied him last night, on Shabbos, flying from his home and making straight for "Ir Ganim" to cover his barrels — so that he might not lose his fortune for the sake of observing the Shabbos.

The sweet dream remained with him all that night.

The next morning, Yechiel returned to the building site with a merry heart. From afar, he made out the hoarse cries of Avrum Hachigazi, construction foreman of the Solel Boneh firm on the adjoining site.

"Fools! Imbeciles! You are as senseless as camels! I sent you to cover the barrels of cement. How is it that they remained uncovered? All the cement has been ruined. There is no work today!"

"B-but we were here. We covered up everything," stammered his workers.

"Liars!"

Yechiel approached the red-faced Hachigazi. "Why are you so angry, Avrum, my friend?" he asked.

The foreman whipped his head around. "Don't *you* come around at a time like this, rubbing salt into my wounds. On Friday night, I sent twenty of my workers to cover the cement barrels. I don't know what they did here. They claim to have covered every last barrel. But see what happened — the barrels are all open and filled with rock-hard concrete. They are a gang of tricksters. I'll fire every one of them!"

Yechiel took a step closer and said quietly, "Your crew is not lying, Avrum. They did cover the barrels."

"Not true," snapped the foreman.

Yechiel pointed at the other end of the street, where his own barrels stood. Softly, he said, "They covered the barrels — only not yours.

In the dark, they made a mistake. Someone up there gave them different orders."

TWO NIGHTS IN R' AVRAHAM'S LIFE

THE FIRST NIGHT

THE HOLY CITY OF JERUSALEM HAS ALWAYS BEEN BLESSED with numerous Torah scholars. These precious individuals sequester themselves day and night in the tent of Torah, sleeping little and eating less. Poverty is as familiar to them as their own names.

One such man was R' Avraham Wilhelm, an outstanding *talmid chacham* known to his contemporaries as a veritable lion of piety and religious zeal. He was knowledgeable in the entire *Shas* as well as all portions of the *Shulchan Aruch*. His father, the *chassid* R' Nachman Yosef Wilhelm, had been born in Poland, where he lived until the outbreak of World War I, which sent him, his wife, and their young family fleeing to Egypt. There Avremel spent his first years, until the family moved to *Eretz Yisrael*.

When they lived in Egypt, his mother, Brachah Feiga, toiled from morning to night for a few paltry pennies. Avremel, the oldest son, felt his heart constrict with pain at the sight, and he set his young mind to work devising ways to ease her suffering. He thought and thought — until he hit on a plan.

One morning, Avremel went down to the river. There, on the banks of the Nile, sat a number of Arab fishermen. At their feet were buckets of small fish, to be used as bait with which to catch larger fish. Avremel carefully inspected the little fish until he found a few that bore the fins and scales that testified to their *kashrus*. Then, bashfully, he asked the fishermen if he might take them. "We are hungry. There's nothing to eat at our house," he explained.

The boy's sweet manner charmed the fishermen. Generously, they offered, "Take the whole bucket!"

Avremel ran home, the bucket banging against his knees with every step. He filled the pail with fresh water. When his mother came home, tired after a long day's work, she was sure to shower him with her grateful kisses.

But it did not turn out that way at all.

When Brachah Feiga returned that evening, her body aching from backbreaking labor, she was happy at first to see the fish to feed her hungry children. But when Avremel innocently explained to her how he had obtained them — by going down to the river and skipping three hours of learning in *cheder* — her mood changed in an instant. Brachah Feiga burst into tears and hurled the fish into the rubbish. "I do not want to benefit from *bitul Torah*!" she cried. "No, Avremel. Three hours stolen from your Torah learning? The price you paid is too steep!"

His mother's tears seemed to soak into the child's very bones, leaving an impression that remained throughout the rest of his life. He grew up to become one of Jerusalem's foremost Torah scholars. On his *shtender* at the yeshivah, he always kept a small cardboard sign to discourage the other youths who tended to waste precious time in idle chatter. The sign said, *"Please do not disturb me in the middle of learning!"*

That night, Avremel awoke two hours after midnight. This was nothing new; he rose at that time every night. He would make his way through the dark streets to Yeshivas Meah Shearim, where he pored over his *Gemara* in sweet solitude until it was time for *Shacharis*.

That night, the *yetzer hara* had apparently decided to launch a full-scale attack on the young scholar. It was the height of a cold, hard winter, but tonight the cold seemed to have reached a new level. The moment Avremel stuck one foot out of his bed, he was assaulted by waves of icy air. But he was a staunch soldier who did not know the meaning of self-indulgence. Gathering his strength, he got out of bed, dressed hurriedly, and went out into the street.

So strong was the buffeting wind that Avremel hardly knew whether he was coming or going. Every step forward was immediately countered by a powerful gust pushing him back. A drenching rain, carried by the wind, soaked him to the skin within minutes. His old shoes turned into streaming sponges, while his torn coat let in generous quantities of freezing rain. An inner voice insisted plaintively, "Why do you bother with all this? You are endangering your health! You'll catch pneumonia. *Pikuach nefesh* takes precedence over all else!"

With iron will, Avremel pushed these thoughts aside and plowed on through the wind and the mud puddles. He had walked only a few more steps when he was blinded by a sudden burst of lightning, followed by an ear-splitting boom of thunder. His heart nearly leaped out of his chest. The rain rapidly turned to hail, which covered everything with a white, snow-like blanket. The treetops bent low beneath their burden of icy pellets, and many branches snapped and fell beneath the weight. So impenetrable was the darkness that Avremel could scarcely distinguish his right hand from his left. Only the lightning flashes illuminated his way from time to time through the deserted Meah Shearim streets.

He reached the yeshivah at last. The building was empty and dark, which was not surprising. Who would have chosen to come out at such an hour, on such a night?

Avremel Wilhelm had chosen to come!

The key rested in his pocket. With frozen fingers he pulled it out and unlocked the *beis midrash* door. An instant later, a muffled shriek escaped his lips.

Ghosts!

Dead men were strolling through the *beis midrash*!

He stood frozen, eyes staring out of their sockets and the blood slowly turning to ice in his veins from sheer terror. Gradually, reality reasserted itself. No, there were no corpses in the room. The tiny flame of the *ner tamid* had formed shadows that scurried up and down the dark walls. And that fluttering *tallis* ... did it conceal a swaying dead man within its folds? No — wrong again. It was just an empty *tallis* on a *shtender* which the wind was blowing to and fro in silent billows.

Slowly, a resolution formed itself in Avremel's mind: It's either them or me! "Them" were his fears, which he resolutely banished. Lighting a kerosene lamp made the shadows disappear. Avremel began to sway gently over his *shtender*. In a moment, his sweet *Gemara* chant filled the *beis midrash*.

No sooner had he sunk into the depths of his learning than the Satan leveled its next attack. Up in the storm-tossed sky, two clouds met and clashed, producing a violent burst of lightning and thunder even stronger than before. The Satan appeared determined to chase Avremel from the *beis midrash*, come what may.

The room was periodically lit with an eerie, brilliant light. Crashing thunder demolished the peace and silence of the *beis midrash*. Through the cracked window whistled a furious storm wind. With one powerful gust, it snuffed out both the *ner tamid* and the kerosene lamp. The *beis midrash* was plunged into total blackness.

All of Avremel's fears, lulled into quiescence during his interval with his *Gemara*, sprang to life anew. He was alone in the dark. Outside, the lightning and thunder played their eerie games. With each breath of wind, the *tallis* billowed and swayed like a dead man about to approach.

Avremel quailed. His teeth chattered uncontrollably and he shivered from head to toe. In the grip of an unreasoning terror, he burst into panic-stricken tears. He was scarcely past boyhood. This situation was beyond his power to handle.

HaKadosh Baruch Hu saw the fears besetting this youth who had dedicated his nights to learning His holy Torah, and took pity on him. At that moment, the door to the *beis midrash* opened suddenly. On the threshold stood the stooped figure of the *gaon* and *tzaddik*, R' Zelig Braverman, one of Jerusalem's Torah giants.

R' Zelig walked into the *beis midrash* and relit the kerosene lamp. In its golden glow, he spotted the lad at his *shtender*. The huddled appearance, the tear-stricken face, told their own story. R' Zelig walked over and began to comfort him.

"Do you want to learn with me?" R' Zelig asked presently. Avremel accepted the offer with alacrity.

Then, as the wind and rain continued to rage outside — unheeded now — the two sat and learned together… And there was light!

THE SECOND NIGHT

If the previous story gave us a glimpse of R' Avraham Wilhelm's diligence in Torah, the following will describe another night — a difficult night that was destined to remained etched in his memory his entire life — a night in whose merit the Jewish People were to be enriched by one of its great Rebbes.

R' Avraham had a sister. Rebbetzin Esther was married to the *tzaddik*, R' Yochanan Twersky, who was later to be named the Rachmastrivker Rebbe. One of the couple's children was Itzik'l, a youngster filled to the brim with Jewish *chein* that radiated from his innocent face.

Every morning, Itzik'l would wake up early and hurry to his *cheder*, where he soaked up Torah knowledge with a tremendous thirst. One day, he returned home at noon complaining of severe stomach pains. After he had lain in bed for several hours with no improvement, his mother sent for the doctor.

As the doctor examined the boy, his expression grew very grave. He directed Rebbetzin Esther to take the boy quickly to nearby Hadassah Hospital (the early building was situated in the heart of Jerusalem). There, the medical staff diagnosed a serious kidney infection.

In those days — some fifty years ago — the discovery of antibiotics still lay in the future. As a result, many died of infections which are easily treatable today with our cornucopia of medicines and sterile hospital conditions.

Shortly after Itzik'l was hospitalized, his condition worsened. His kidneys ceased functioning and he lay at death's door. Family members and groups of *chassidim* poured out their hearts in prayer for the boy, pleading for Heavenly compassion and added years of life. But Heaven, it seemed, had turned a deaf ear to all the prayers. Not only did the patient's condition not improve, but it steadily deteriorated until nearly all hope was lost.

Because his illness was considered highly contagious, Itzik'l lay in a room of his own in quarantine. His parents, who sat at his bedside day and night, wore special sterile clothing to protect them from the disease. They kept a constant watch at their son's side, until their energies waned and they themselves were perilously close to collapse. Their spirits, too, were terribly low as they saw their beloved child slipping away from them.

The patient's uncle, R' Avraham Wilhelm — by this time a married man with young children of his own — took up his share of the burden. Despite his own numerous responsibilities, he spent long hours at his nephew's bedside, encouraging the child in every way he knew. More than once, he succeeded in lifting Itzik'l's spirits and even managed to elicit a weak smile.

"What are you doing lying in bed?" he would "scold" the boy with mock severity. "Do you think you're getting ready to die? Let me warn you — dying is not such a simple matter. Pretty soon, we'll be celebrating your bar mitzvah! Lots of people will come to join in the celebration — among them important Rebbes and Rabbis, as befits your prestigious family. *Nu*, it's time to get better and prepare your bar mitzvah *derashah* — a little *pilpul* to make those scholars wrinkle their brows!"

In this way, he kept Itzik'l's mind focused on positive things. When it was his Uncle Avremel's turn to keep vigil at his bedside, the child's lips would curve upward in a feeble smile. "Mother and father stand here and cry. You, though, come here and cheer me up," he said happily.

A few days later, however, he was no longer talking this way. Itzik'l's condition became so bad that the doctors threw up their hands. "We have done everything we can. The boy will need the miracle of *techiyas hameisim* (resurrecting the dead) to recover now."

From that moment, R' Avraham scarcely ever left the sickroom. Hour after hour, he remained glued to his nephew's side, trying with all his might to find the words to cheer Itzik'l and to put off the dreaded end. The doctors encouraged this, claiming that the patient's mental state had a definite effect on his physical condition.

The more the illness strengthened its grip on the boy, the more steadfast his uncle became. When Itzik'l's condition was deemed beyond hope, R' Avraham remained in the sickroom for nearly two solid days and nights. As dusk approached on the second day, he felt his strength failing completely. Only then did he permit himself to go home.

A short time after R' Avraham left, Itzik'l lost consciousness. It was only with the greatest difficulty that the medical staff succeeded in arousing him.

"Tonight is the critical point," the doctors told the family soberly, "what we call the crisis. The illness will either go one way — or the other. If the boy gets through the crisis, there is a shred of hope that his life will be spared. If not …"

It was not necessary for them to end the sentence.

A relative ran from the hospital, making directly for R' Avraham's house. He woke R' Avraham from a deep sleep.

"*Pikuach nefesh!*" the relative cried emotionally. "Itzik'l is on his deathbed. Only you can save him! You have managed to lift his spirits and make him happy through even the most difficult moments. Maybe you can do it now, and give him the strength he needs to ward off the Angel of Death!"

R' Avraham was a soft-hearted man who did not know how to say "no." This time, however, he shook his head. "I can't," he whispered. "I'm at the end of my strength. I sat with Itzik'l for two solid days and nights, hardly eating or sleeping at all. I mustered all my energy to talk with him nearly all the time. Another night like that will finish me, Heaven forbid."

Even as he spoke, his head fell back onto his pillow and his eyes closed as slumber claimed him once again. Two nights without sleep!

But his relative was insistent. "Wake up, Avremel! Wake up, and take pity on poor Itzik'l!"

For the second time, R' Avraham was shaken out of a bottomless sleep.

"What do you want from me?" he mumbled. "Am I in G-d's place? Can I provide a cure? If Hashem wishes it, salvation will come from wherever it comes. But if I don't get a little sleep right now … Do you want me to die?"

In desperation, the family turned to the boy's grandfather, R' Dud'l of Rachmastrivka. R' Avraham was always reverently attentive to the Rebbe's teachings. Perhaps R' Dud'l could influence him to return to the hospital.

"Tell him that I ask it of him," the Rebbe instructed. "I take upon myself full responsibility to see that nothing bad happens to Avremel!"

As fast as their legs could carry them, the relatives ran back to R' Avraham's house, where they once again dragged him mercilessly from a deep slumber.

Still immersed in the mists of sleep, R' Avraham listened to the Rebbe's promise. The words took a few moments to work their way into his drowsy brain.

"The Rebbe guarantees that I will not be harmed? Then I'm getting up this instant!"

His eyes felt heavy as lead, and his entire body ached and groaned. And yet, even in this difficult hour, R' Avraham's ability to think clearly did not desert him. He decided to prepare himself for this critical night in every way he could. He made his consent contingent on two conditions. First: that teams of people would pray for the boy throughout the night, pleading for a speedy recovery for the patient — *Chai Yitzchak ben Esther*.

The second condition was that he be provided with three things: good cognac, strong smelling-salts, and 96 percent-pure alcohol. With all his heart, he hoped that these three things would keep him awake during this, his third sleepless night in a row.

The doctors were waiting for him outside the sickroom.

"If you see any change in the boy's condition — whether for good or ill — call us at once," they warned. "Correct treatment at the critical moment can radically alter the patient's prospects!"

Trembling, R' Avraham entered the room. He bent over to look at his beloved nephew's face. It was yellow-gray, and the boy's breathing was labored. R' Avraham feared that Itzik'l was very close to dying. With a heavy heart, he sat down by the bed. He felt a powerful urge to cry, but a stronger will prevailed. "This is not what they summoned me here for," he reminded himself sternly.

Watching his nephew, he was heartened to see signs of life. Itzik'l's eyelashes fluttered slightly.

"Uncle Avremel, is that you?" he whispered weakly. "How happy I am that you've come! I can't bear to see my mother and father's pain. They are sure that I'm going..."

"Nonsense!" R' Avraham declared robustly. His forced laugh rang hollow in his own ears. "Where do you get such foolish notions?"

The sick boy was silent. Without losing a minute, his uncle showed him the bottle of cognac. "In case you want to share a toast with me, like the *chassidim* do!" he suggested with a smile. He went on to relate riveting stories and heartwarming tales. Speaking thus took every ounce of his strength. He imagined he could already hear the Angel of Death's wings beating in the quiet room. But he would not desist. He spared no energy in distracting Itzik'l's mind from his illness. From time to time, the boy responded to his uncle's efforts with a weak smile. R' Avraham talked on.

Suddenly, he noticed with alarm that Itzik'l was no longer responding. "Itzik'l, what's the matter?" he called fearfully. "Answer me!"

With thudding heart, he shook his nephew. But Itzik'l did not react at all. As R' Avraham hesitated, debating whether he dared leave the patient and run for the doctors, he heard the dread sound of the death-rattle coming from Itzik'l's throat.

There was no time to fetch the doctor or anyone else. "Perhaps I can do something before he slips away entirely!" R' Avraham thought. Being not only a wise man but also a learned one, he rapidly reviewed the laws to determine whether he was permitted to continue treating the patient. Was this a case of *pikuach nefesh*, which supersedes all else — or was the boy already beyond hope, making it forbidden to touch him in any way lest it hasten his death?

In R' Avraham's considered opinion, this was not yet a case of actual dying. His hands began to move of their own accord. He seized the bottles of cognac, alcohol, and smelling-salts, poured some of each into a bowl standing near the bed, and stirred them vigorously together. With a lightning motion, he ripped the sheet off Itzik'l and began to rub the pungent mixture onto the boy's stomach.

For ten full minutes, he applied the strong mixture to Itzik'l's skin, listening anxiously all the while for the sounds of breathing.

After a while, it seemed to him that the boy's breathing sounded a little less labored than before. Encouraged, R' Avraham continued to rub his mixture into Itzik'l's forehead, stomach, and entire body.

Thirty minutes went by while R' Avraham continued his desperate massage. His own body was bathed in perspiration, but he had no time to feel his own exhaustion. Harder and harder he worked, rubbing and massaging. Suddenly, he heard a weak voice. It was speaking his name.

Lifting his head, R' Avraham found himself staring into his nephew's pale face. Itzik'l's eyes were wide open, and they held an expression of curiosity and surprise.

"Uncle Avremel, is that you? Where am I? Am — am I still in this world?"

A surge of joy threatened to lift R' Avraham off his feet. "Itzik'l! *Baruch Hashem!*" he cried. "Not only are you alive, but you are healthy and whole. Come, get up and eat something!"

Itzik'l smiled. "You know, I was already in the Next World," he confided softly. "I don't know how I came to wake up like this. And you're right. I do feel better."

R' Avraham stood looking down at his cherished nephew. When he saw that the boy's condition had stabilized, he allowed himself to dash out and call for the doctors.

"What happened?" they asked urgently, as they came at a run. "Has the crisis come?" They were certain that the worst of all had happened.

"Come and see," R' Avraham said with a mysterious smile.

Shock and wonder swept the doctors when they saw Itzik'l. His eyes were open and his cheeks had regained a bit of color. R' Avraham was chased from the room while they conducted a full examination of the patient.

"His condition has improved immeasurably," the doctors confirmed at last. "R' Avraham must have had a hand in this somehow. Such a miracle could not have occurred by itself!" They went out into the corridor in search of him.

"What did you do?" the physicians demanded. "How did you bring about this miracle? You've managed to bring the dead back to life!" In an emotional undertone, they added, "Not only has the boy come through the crisis, but his kidneys have begun to function again. What secret medicine did you give him?"

R' Avraham showed them the bowl, and the pungent mixture he had rubbed into the patient's body. "This is the 'medicine' I used," he replied humbly. In his own modest fashion, he related what had happened in the sickroom that night.

The doctors weighed this information in light of their own medical knowledge, and accepted its validity. "There is something in what you say," they conceded. "The strong mixture, combined with vigorous massage, warmed the kidneys and caused them to evict the toxins. In that way, you got them to begin functioning again, after they had shut down completely."

But despite their technical understanding, the doctors were still unanimous in declaring, "It is a medical miracle! There is no precedent for this kind of treatment — and certainly not with a patient who had already crossed the threshold between life and death."

So moved were the hospital staff by this miraculous cure, that they held a big party in the patient's honor once he had recovered sufficiently to participate. They invited the greatest physicians of the day, including some from abroad, to witness the miracle with their own eyes.

Well into his old age, R' Avraham Wilhelm would retell the story from time to time — always with deep emotion.

"*Baruch Hashem*, I had a great merit," he would say happily. "Hashem gave me the privilege of saving a Jewish life. And not just any life — the life of a great Jew and a great Rebbe: R' Chai Yitzchak Twersky, the Rachmastrivka Rebbe in the United States!"

THE OLD MAN IN THE CAVE

THE MEYEROWITZ FAMILY LIVED IN THE MARMARUSH region, on the Romanian-Czechoslovakian border. They were a warm family, with roots that extended deep into Jewish community life for generations. Life flowed peacefully in their home town. The men left for *shul* in the morning and then set out to work to support their families; the women kept house and raised the children.

Then the peace was shattered, suddenly and irrevocably, by the cruel Nazi invaders. All of Europe was eventually sucked into the maelstrom of war, but the Jews of Poland and Lithuania felt the enemy's snakebite first. While cattle cars were transporting their hordes to the Auschwitz and Treblinka death camps, Hungarian and Romanian Jewry still enjoyed relative quiet. During the first years of the war, the danger seemed remote.

But no immunity lasts forever. In the month of Sivan, 5704 (1944), the Nazis began their mass deportation of Hungarian Jews. The Meyerowitz family, like all the Jews in the region, made its final journey to the gas chamber and the smoking crematoria.

Gedaliah Meyerowitz was a lad of 17 then, strong and tall. The terror and anguish he felt on entering the gates of Auschwitz were feelings he would carry with him forever. The Jews were immediately ordered to line up for the infamous "selection." With a flick of his wrist, Dr. Mengele, the "Angel of Death," sent the entire Meyerowitz family to the gas chambers. Then his cold eye fell upon the strapping Gedaliah — and he motioned the youth over to the other line.

Gedaliah was separated from his whole family, but he was alive. A single, lone branch had survived out of the large, flowering tree that had been the Meyerowitz clan, and that had now gone up in tragic, horrifying smoke — may Hashem avenge their blood!

He did not remain in Auschwitz for long. The Nazis, taking note of Gedaliah's physical strength, had different plans for him. Together with a large group of similarly endowed young men, Gedaliah was sent into enemy territory. They were put to work in a German munitions factory, where they labored twenty-four hours a day turning out artillery shells for the German war machine.

They worked in groups of twenty. In Gedaliah's group were twenty Jews, prisoners of war from every part of Europe. Their lot was miserable. They suffered from hunger, thirst, senseless violence, and frequent lashings. The only thing that lifted their flagging spirits was the fervent hope that the situation would not last much longer. It was not a baseless hope; the Third Reich was faring badly on the battlefront. But as the Germans floundered in their final death throes, their cruelty grew even more pronounced.

One day, as the team of forced laborers toiled beneath the S.S. whip, there came the sudden wail of the siren. Its ululating alarm sent the workers scurrying away from the highly flammable arms and explosives. But before they had managed to run more than a few steps, they heard the roar of Allied planes overhead — and right on its heels the terrible shriek of scores of bombs dropping to earth.

A series of powerful explosions rocked the munitions factory. The walls began to buckle inward as freshly-made artillery shells exploded right on the assembly lines. The entire building crumbled, burying hundreds of workers and soldiers in the rubble.

When the smoke had cleared, the revealed spectacle was horrifying. The decimated factory had turned into a giant slaughterhouse. Dead bodies were scattered everywhere, while the few wounded survivors groaned pitifully as they wallowed in their own blood.

Gestapo soldiers were sent to clear the ruins. They did not find a single uninjured laborer. It never entered their minds that the Jewish group had remained alive and, for the most part, unharmed — almost without a scratch! Under cover of the reigning chaos, the Jews escaped.

They hid by day and traveled by night. Within a short time, Germany was defeated. All of Europe was liberated from the grip of the Nazis. Poland was dotted with survivors, wandering about in search of a place to call home. Among them was Gedaliah Meyerowitz.

They sought sanctuary first in Poland, but discovered all too soon that anti-Semitism still flourished in that wicked land, which had betrayed good and honest citizens merely because they were Jews. Instead, the refugees decided to make their way to *Eretz Yisrael*.

Gedaliah had befriended another young man his own age. Both found themselves in an awkward position. Each had lost his entire family in the Holocaust and were the last remaining survivors of a once-vibrant clan. Neither had a penny to call his own. Neither owned any sort of passport or identifying document. The Nazis had not equipped their victims with documents.

But the two of them refused to despair. They walked through Europe until they managed to hook up with a group of Jewish survivors who were planning to smuggle a ship onto the shores of Palestine, right under the British Mandate's nose.

A few days later, Gedaliah was in Jerusalem.

He had parted from his friends, who had found shelter in the *kibbutzim* of the secular *Shomer HaTza'ir*.

"Did I survive, alone of all my family, just to become a complete gentile on some *kibbutz*?" he demanded when his friends tried to persuade him to stay. "It's Jerusalem for me, and a life of purity and holiness."

"You need a hospital, not Jerusalem," they scoffed. Gedaliah did not answer.

He looked terrible. Prolonged malnutrition under the Nazis, followed by his wandering across Europe and further deprivation aboard ship, had left their cruel marks. His body was dried and hard as a stick, and he weighed less than eighty pounds. But though his physical condition was low, his spirit was strong. He felt resolute and clear-headed as he traveled to Jerusalem.

Gedaliah acclimated himself to his new home in an amazingly short time. He made new friends, found a place to live and a part-time job. In the afternoons and evenings he made his way to the *beis midrash* in one of Jerusalem's older neighborhoods, and pored over a *Gemara*. He had years of Torah learning to make up. With all his might, he strove to make up the deficiency.

It was a stormy time for Palestine. The underground resistance groups battled in every way they could against the British, who controlled the land. Gedaliah heard his friends whispering about planned acts of terror. Much as he tried to resist, he found himself magnetically drawn to these secret conversations. They fired his imagination and ignited his senses. He had regained much of his health and had even put a little flesh on his frame. With each passing day, more of his old strength came flowing back.

Finally, he joined the *Etzel* (*Irgun Tzva'i Leumi*) and took part in several clandestine activities. Gedaliah advanced rapidly in the ranks of the underground group. His day was divided in two: During the day he learned Torah, and at night he involved himself in secret activities with his fellow *Etzel* members.

A few weeks later, when the *Etzel* attacked the "Augusta Victoria," Gedaliah was with them. Jordanian Legionnaires shelled Jerusalem from the high hilltops, causing heavy loss of life and property. Gedaliah was seriously wounded in the fight.

There were injuries all over his body, but the most critical was to his ankle bone, which a shell had shattered. He was evacuated to Hadassah Hospital in serious condition. Examining him, the doctors concluded that he would most likely recover from his other injuries. The ankle, however, was beyond hope. The entire foot, up to and including the ankle, was completely shattered. It was clear to even the most simple-minded that Gedaliah would never again walk the way he had walked before.

In an attempt to salvage what could be saved, the doctors planted a new bone in his smashed foot, to replace the shattered one. But the operation was ultimately unsuccessful. Gedaliah's foot rejected the foreign bone. Gangrene set in, and it was feared that the necrosis would spread to the rest of his body.

The moment the doctors entered his room with sober faces, Gedaliah knew they did not have good news for him. Still, he was unprepared for the terrible decree: "We must amputate the foot!"

Gedaliah faced them, defiant. "Pardon me," he said, mustering every reserve of calm he possessed, "but you'll have to cut off my head first!"

The chief medical man stared in amazement. "I've heard of people refusing to have their left arm amputated because of *tefillin*. But why refuse to take off a foot?"

"There's nothing to talk about," Gedaliah snapped stubbornly.

The surgeon moved closer. In a cajoling voice, he said, "You do not understand, Gedaliah. We want only what is good for you. If we do not remove the foot, the decay will spread to the rest of your body."

"I have only one thing to say," Gedaliah replied. "I am the last remaining survivor of my family — a family that numbered in the hundreds before the war. I must establish a faithful Jewish home in order to carry on my family heritage, so cruelly cut off. If you amputate my foot, who will agree to marry a cripple like me?"

The doctors saw that they were dealing with a supremely obstinate patient. They left him alone — for the time being.

Gedaliah wept soundlessly into his pillow. "Master of the Universe, what do I want? Only that You leave me my foot. I wish to marry and establish a good Jewish home, that's all!"

All at once, he sensed that he was not alone. Red-faced, he raised his eyes.

Two young Jerusalem yeshivah men with curly *peyos* stood beside his bed, regarding him benevolently.

"We won't tell anyone," one of the visitors assured him with a smile.

"We are visiting one ward each week, and we have not met you yet," the other added warmly. "Your tears move us enormously. Please, share your feelings with us."

Gedaliah did not need a second invitation. The two appeared to be good-hearted men and he felt free to include them in his world. In a broken voice, he related the events of his life, from childhood until his recent conversation with the surgeons.

The older of the two men, R' Hershel, spoke first. "In just a few days we will celebrate the *yahrtzeit* of R' Shimon bar Yochai. My brother, R' Mottel" — he pointed at his companion — "and I are planning to travel to Meiron. Come with us. Many Jews have found salvation at his grave site. Perhaps you will find yours as well!"

Gedaliah did not know whether to laugh or cry. "Don't you understand? I am wrapped in bandages from head to toe. My foot is shattered so that I can't take a single step. And you're talking about traveling to the Upper Galil?"

"You have nothing to lose," the brothers reminded him with a shrug and an affectionate smile. "After all, didn't you just suggest to the doctors that they cut off your head?"

The maneuver took place two days later, with all the secrecy and accuracy of a covert military operation.

At 2 a.m., the brothers came to the hospital carrying a stretcher bearing the *Chevrah Kaddisha* logo. There were many people injured in explosions and shelling at that time, and the *Chevrah Kaddisha* members would circulate among the wards to carry out their work as necessary. Without a word, R' Hershel and R' Mottel went directly to Gedaliah's bed, gingerly lifted him up, laid him on the stretcher, and covered him with a white sheet.

As a matter of fact, Gedaliah at that moment genuinely appeared more dead than alive. His entire body was swathed in bandages and was nearly paralyzed. He closed his eyes, hoping that the brothers knew what they were doing.

Minutes later, an old car chugged out of the hospital lot after passing several routine checkpoints. R' Hershel removed the sheet from Gedaliah's long-suffering face — and the three burst into hilarious laughter. Without any difficulty at all, they had succeeded in smuggling a patient from right under the hospital staff's noses.

Then, remembering what lay ahead, the laughter died. They still had to cover a long distance under terrible conditions, in a rickety old vehicle — and all this while transporting a critically ill patient.

Only one thing heartened them for the journey ahead. "R' Shimon is worth counting on in times of need!" (*Berachos* 9a).

Indeed, the journey proved every bit as difficult as they had envisioned. It took place at the height of battle, when both sides shot their bullets and grenades knowing that they were struggling for the very fate of the land. The so-called "neutrality" of the British Mandate only made matters worse.

The brothers placed Gedaliah onto a small, ancient bus that rattled and smoked and bumped its passengers unmercifully. The roads were not today's modern highways; they were narrow and winding, with cracks and craters in the asphalt that made the bus leap about like a mad thing. Worst of all, however, were the Arab ambushes that awaited Jewish vehicles in the dark, with snipers standing ready to shoot them at close range. The three men encountered this dangerous obstacle more than once on their long trip, but managed each time to escape miraculously unharmed.

After a day and a half, the bus pulled up at Meiron. It was Lag B'Omer eve. The two brothers, with the help of a few other young men, lifted Gedaliah's stretcher and carried him to R' Shimon bar Yochai's cave. There they laid him gently down, prayed briefly, and parted from him.

"We are going on to other grave sites of *tzaddikim* in the Galil," they told Gedaliah. "You, on the other hand, are in no hurry. Stay here today and tomorrow. *Daven*, eat, and then we shall return to take you back to Jerusalem."

"You are not afraid to travel further in the Galil?" Gedaliah exclaimed. "Think of the snipers!"

The brothers shook their heads decisively. "The Arabs grow stronger only when they perceive signs of weakness in the enemy. If we submit to their pressures, they will throw us all into the sea and be done with us! However, if they see that the Jews continue to travel as before, unafraid — then the land will be ours!"

With a last farewell, they cantered off.

In the cave, Gedaliah was alone.

He lay on a straw-filled mattress, a Book of Psalms in his hand. Turning to the first verse, he began to recite *Tehillim*.

He had plenty of time, and also plenty of tears to cry. They streamed from his eyes like an ever-strengthening spring. From time to time he paused in his recitation to utter a prayer from the depths of his broken heart: "My Father in Heaven, my dear Father! I do not ask You for honor or for wealth. Only two things I ask: to be healthy, and to establish a Jewish home, so that I may continue the chain of my family, of which I am the last remaining link."

Long hours passed before he completed the *Sefer Tehillim*. Seeing that his friends had not yet returned from their travels in the Galil, he began again at the beginning. There were not many people at the site in those days; many feared the trip in the sights of the enemy's guns, and the journey itself, even in better times, was not a pleasant one. Those who were present took note of Gedaliah's condition, and were careful not to tread on him by accident as he lay praying and weeping.

Suddenly, from the courtyard, came the sound of music. A clarinet and drums were approaching, keeping time with a singing, dancing crowd. Gedaliah, in this place for the first time, was bewildered. Inside the cave, weeping and wailing — outside, dancing and merriment. He expressed his confusion to some of the men praying near him. They explained that this was the long-standing tradition of Meiron: "Yom Kippur inside, Simchas Torah outside!"

Gedaliah lay back and watched the circle of dancers outside, his face reflecting his bemusement. Without warning, an old man detached himself from the crowd and approached Gedaliah. His face shone with a curious radiance as he placed a hand on the injured man's shoulder and said warmly, "Gedaliah, why do you lie here so sad and forlorn? Go out and dance with the others! It is a great *mitzvah* to dance with such joy!"

With that, the old man disappeared.

Gedaliah had never seen him before, but the man's words had been suffused with a particular sweetness that flew like an arrow, straight to Gedaliah's heart. Without thinking about what he was doing — and without wondering how the elderly stranger had known his name — he struggled to his feet and walked out into the courtyard. Leaning heavily on his cane, he joined the circle of dancers.

At first, it was difficult for him to move his aching body at all, and his shattered foot sent flashes of shooting pain that nearly made him cry aloud. He made a valiant attempt to forget everything — his own pain and the doctor's dire warnings.

At first, it was less a dance than the lurching of a crippled bear moving in circles around itself. From one moment to the next, however, Gedaliah's dancing improved. He grew lighter on his feet and his movements became more fluid. Hour after hour, he danced. Forgetting himself and everything around him, he kept pace with one group of dancers after another. Each time a new circle was formed, Gedaliah was part of it.

It was nearly dawn when the two brothers returned to Meiron. They rubbed their eyes in wonder at the sight of Gedaliah singing and dancing with enthusiasm.

"We left him nearly a dead man," they laughed happily. "Look at the power of R' Shimon bar Yochai!"

After an absence of a few days, Gedaliah returned to the Jerusalem hospital. He found the ward in an uproar. The doctors had no idea what had become of their patient. Had he died and was his body snatched away in the dead of the night? The possibility that the critically injured man had simply fled for four days was too remote to be considered.

When they learned the truth about Gedaliah's midnight escapade to Meiron, they were furious. The doctors' first impulse was to carry the patient off to the operating room at once, to try and repair the awful damage that his foolishness must surely have wrought.

Gedaliah refused to go. With a weary but contented smile, he pointed at his reddened eyes. "First let me sleep. I've hardly closed my eyes for four days."

The doctors yielded to his plea. However, to their chagrin, even after he woke from a deep sleep Gedaliah refused to undergo an operation. "I've been praying at the grave site of a holy *Tanna*. I'd like to wait a few days. Give R' Shimon a chance."

And when those few days had passed, the unbelievable occurred. The shattered foot — the foot that had threatened to spew poisonous gangrene throughout his entire body — recovered! The infection disappeared, leaving in its place the rosy glow of healthy flesh.

Gedaliah's foot was never completely healed. He would always walk with a slight limp. But, just months later, he merited the great joy of marrying. He and his wife had seven children, to whom he would relate the miracle that had occurred to him, and tell of the amazing old man who had revealed himself to Gedaliah on Lag B'Omer.

Every year on that day, to publicize the miracle, he would bring dozens of friends and acquaintances up to Meiron with him. Always, he searched the cave for a glimpse of the old man he had seen on that special day. But Gedaliah never saw him again.

THE PASSPORT PROBLEM

T HE TRAIN SPED ALONG THE TRACKS ON ITS WAY TO Alexandria, Egypt. The dusty windows to the right and left showed the same unending view: sand. In the crowded car, the heat was intense. To the right sat an Egyptian merchant in a red fez, his thick fingers endlessly rolling a set of orange Middle-Eastern beads that he wore around his neck. To the left was an Egyptian peasant on his way home to his village. Beneath his feet rested a wooden crate from which his newly-purchased chickens emitted a raucous clucking. From time to time, the peasant scattered grains of feed for them in an attempt to quiet their incessant racket.

The railroad car was packed with similar peasants, each with his woven basket filled with small brown eggs, or small melons, onions, cucumbers, potatoes, and other home-grown produce on their way to market in the big city.

In the entire car, there were only two Jewish passengers. One of them, R' Moshe Blau, was the leader of the Agudath Yisrael. The second, Mr. P., desired like R' Moshe to board a ship the next day for Europe from the port at Alexandria.

When the heat became unbearable, R' Moshe would take out a large handkerchief, with which he mopped his glistening forehead. How long, his manner seemed to ask, must this suffering go on? Then he would return his attention to the small *Mishnayos* in his hands, and forget everything else.

Long hours and numerous stations later, when the car seemed so full of passengers that they threatened to pour from the windows, the train finally pulled into Alexandria.

R' Moshe glanced at his watch, worried.

"There's time," his companion soothed him. "We still have several hours before Shabbos starts."

"There's no time!" R' Moshe returned anxiously. "We must reach the port with all possible speed. The ship leaves at noon tomorrow, or have you forgotten? We cannot embark on Shabbos."

"I don't understand you," Mr. P. protested. "Either way, we set sail on Shabbos. Let's use this opportunity to take a short stroll through the city and take in some of the sights of Alexandria."

"In traveling tomorrow, we do not transgress any prohibition," R' Moshe said. "Under our circumstances, it is permitted for us to sail on Shabbos on a ship manned by non-Jews, if it sails on a regular schedule. But if we reach the port after Shabbos begins, we will be transgressing several prohibitions — the first of them, carrying objects from one *reshus* [domain] to another!"

Mr. P. had no answer to this. They searched for, and presently found, a taxi to take them to the port at a reasonable price.

Even from the distance, they could make out the impressive lines of the ocean liner waiting at the pier. Dock laborers were busy loading wooden crates into the cargo hold. Apart from the two hurrying Jews, there were no other passengers in sight.

The boarding procedure proved straightforward enough. Two hours still remained before Shabbos as R' Moshe and Mr. P. boarded ship and found their cabins.

R' Moshe arranged his belongings, changed into his Shabbos clothes, and then sat down with a *Chumash* to review the weekly Torah portion. Being an organized man, he had planned his trip down to the last detail. That night, he made *Kiddush* over wine he had brought with him, and ate his meal in his cabin. The frugal repast consisted of two small *challos*, vegetables, and hard-boiled eggs. All the tasty delicacies he was accustomed to at home could not be taken along when he was traveling, but R' Moshe was not a self-indulgent man. A seasoned traveler, he did not need luxuries to be content.

On Shabbos morning, he awoke early, wrapped himself in his *tallis*, and prayed alone in his cabin. When he was done, he stood by the porthole to view the bustling port. Long lines snaked up to the ship as, one by one, passengers presented their tickets and were granted permission to board.

R' Moshe recited *Kiddush*, ate a little, and then walked out onto the deck. "When do our passports get stamped?" he asked a sailor.

The sailor threw a glance at the large clock fixed to the wooden wall. "Let's see, now. It's 10 o'clock, and we're set to sail at noon. In about another hour or so, officers of the Egyptian harbor police will come aboard to stamp the passports. Is yours ready? You know that without the stamp you are not permitted to sail with us."

R' Moshe felt in the pocket of his Shabbos coat. The passport lay snugly within, ready and waiting for the all-important stamp.

"I won't return to my cabin," he decided. "If the officers don't see me, I may be overlooked and lose my chance to sail. I'll wait out here, on the upper deck, where I'll catch sight of the officers the moment they come aboard."

He seated himself on a chair on the upper deck and began to peruse a *sefer* that he had brought with him. Every now and then, his glance raked the deck. Passengers ran to and fro in a great bustle. An elderly woman was shepherding ahead of her an Egyptian porter bent low under the weight of her three heavy suitcases. Youngsters in white sailor suits leaned over the deck rail, searching the harbor waters for fish. From time to time, one boy would nudge another with his elbow, then both would burst into merry laughter until an anxious mother came to drag away her child to safer territory.

R' Moshe looked worriedly at the clock. The time stood at 20 minutes to 12, and still no sight of the police to stamp his passport. He approached the sailor whom he had consulted earlier.

"I am still waiting for the officers. Where are they?"

The sailor stared. "What's the matter with you? The officers have come and gone. They stamped the passports and left a while ago!"

"Impossible!" R' Moshe cried. "I did not see a single Egyptian officer on the entire ship. Are you trying to fool me?"

"I promise you, I am not. You must have fallen asleep or been daydreaming if you didn't see them. The officers stamped all the passports."

Troubled, R' Moshe turned and quickly climbed the stairs to the captain's cabin. A practical and experienced statesman, he was not one to fall apart even in such difficult circumstances.

The captain was busy with his final preparations for setting sail. He had already inspected the navigation and steering equipment and had visited the engine room as well. Impatiently, his eyes fell on the religious Jew who had come to his cabin babbling about an unstamped passport.

"Do you know the rules?" he asked sternly. "Unless your passport has been stamped by the harbor police, you must leave the ship."

"When does the next ship sail?" R' Moshe asked.

The captain snorted with laughter. "Oh, in about a week."

"A week? That's impossible! There's nothing for me to do in Alexandria for a whole week. Besides, people are waiting for me in Europe. I must get there at the time we arranged."

"And what do you want me to do? The ship is set to sail in a quarter of an hour's time!"

A tense silence filled the cabin. Then the captain exclaimed, "I have the solution! Run down to the pier. On a nearby street you'll find the police station. They will sign your passport there. Hurry! Run!"

But R' Moshe did not run. There is a Torah from Heaven, and that Torah states what a Jew may and may not do.

"I can't do that," he explained to the stunned captain. "I am not permitted to carry my passport off the ship."

"Why not?" shrieked the captain.

Under other circumstances, R' Moshe would have laughed. Try to explain to a non-Jew the complex laws of carrying objects from *reshus* to *reshus* on Shabbos!

"Today is the Sabbath," he said patiently. "Carrying my passport off the ship into the harbor is forbidden according to the laws of the Jewish religion."

The moment he heard that the problem emanated from a Divine injunction, the captain's manner changed drastically. He gazed respectfully at R' Moshe, his entire demeanor expressing a desire to satisfy this pious passenger.

"No problem," the captain said. "I will send one of my sailors with you. If a non-Jewish sailor carries your passport, can you accompany him to the police station?"

"With great happiness!" R' Moshe replied radiantly. *HaKadosh Baruch Hu* does not abandon his servants who wish to observe His law.

Within a minute, the two were hurrying down the gangway. Grasping R' Moshe's passport, the sailor ran quickly toward a nearby taxi idling at the curb.

"Taxi!" he screamed at the startled driver. "Take us to the police station." He wheeled around to face R' Moshe. "We must travel by taxi. If we go on foot we'll be too late."

Gently, R' Moshe shook his head. "It is forbidden for me to ride in a taxi on the Sabbath. If you wish to have my passport stamped on my behalf, I will be very grateful."

The sailor gaped at him in amazement — a look that quickly disappeared as he happened to catch sight of the time. The noon hour was fast approaching. There was no time to argue with this obstinate Jew. The sailor seated himself in the taxi and sped on his way.

R' Moshe stayed behind, watching the taxi disappear around a corner and hoping fervently that all would go well. Turning, he made his way back up the gangway to the ship. As he went, he found himself reliving a very vivid memory. Something like this had happened to him once before.

He had been leaving Russia for *Eretz Yisrael*. This ship, too, was due to set sail on Shabbos. R' Moshe boarded on Friday afternoon and slept in his cabin that night. On Shabbos morning, he was informed that he must walk down to the harbor to have his passport stamped at the police station there. Otherwise, he would be barred from sailing. Officers would be boarding the ship before it set sail to check whether all passports had been duly signed.

This would mean taking his passport off the boat [*reshus hayachid* — the private domain] to the street [*reshus harabim* — the public domain]; from the street to the police station [*reshus hayachid*]; from the station to the street; and from the street back to the ship. Four cases of carrying things between different areas on Shabbos! And that didn't even begin to take into account carrying the passport to and from the ship in a public domain.

Distressed, R' Moshe had approached several non-Jewish passengers and attempted to explain to them with signs and gestures (he spoke no Russian) that he needed them to do him a favor and accompany him to the police station, carrying his passport. Most of the passengers merely shrugged, making no attempt to understand the meaning behind his gestures. At last he found one gentile who was about to go down to the station to get his own passport stamped. He agreed at once to take along the Jew's passport.

The two walked over to the station and took their places in line. R' Moshe's heart was filled with joy. *Baruch Hashem*, he had managed to surmount even this obstacle!

"Your passport, please." The clerk's voice roused R' Moshe from his thoughts.

The passport was stamped. R' Moshe looked up to find his gentile companion — but he was nowhere to be seen. The gentile had had his own passport stamped and then, without waiting, started back for the ship.

What could he do?

R' Moshe did not panic. Glancing around him, he noticed one of the police officers on the point of leaving the station. With hand gestures, R' Moshe asked the officer to take his passport outside for him. The policeman stared at him uncomprehendingly — but did as R'

Moshe requested. Outside, he returned the passport, demanding, "What are you, who are you, and what's all this about?"

R' Moshe evaded the questions. The important thing was that the passport was outside. Now it was time to face the next hurdle: getting the passport through the public domain.

"Less than four *amos*," the *halachah* states. Under duress, one can walk short distances.

R' Moshe took several small steps, then stopped. Another few steps, then another halt. Always, he stopped before he had walked four *amos*.

It was decidedly unpleasant, walking in this strange way through a street full of staring strangers. Then inspiration struck. R' Moshe began to feign a great interest in the shop windows, and in the posters pasted up in Russian on the walls he passed. This way, at least, he managed to avoid attracting unwanted attention.

Arriving at the ship at last, he breathed a deep sigh of relief. He waited until a gentile was preparing to climb the gangway, then asked him to carry the passport aboard for him. The gentile executed the transfer from public to private domain, for which R' Moshe thanked him gratefully.

Mission accomplished! He now had a stamped passport in his possession — and without having violated the holy Shabbos to get it. He could set sail along with the others.

In Alexandria, the clock chimed twelve times.

Passengers crowded at the deck rails, waiting impatiently for the ship's whistle to signal their departure. They waved down at friends and relatives who had come to see them off, calling out last words of farewell.

To general astonishment, the sailors delayed untying the ship from the harbor. The heavy anchor had not yet been lifted, though the hands of the clock stood at 5 minutes past 12. Then it was 12:10, but still the sailor had not returned. The captain glowered at R' Moshe and muttered through compressed lips, "This delay is because of you.

See what you've done to us. Something like this has never happened to me before!"

The story began to circulate among the hundreds of passengers waiting to sail. The blame for the delay lay at a Jew's door. A sailor had gone to have his passport stamped, and had not yet returned.

From minute to minute, the tension mounted. Hundreds of pairs of eyes were glued to the pier gates, but the sailor did not appear. The time was already 12:15, then 12:17. You could have sliced the tension with a knife.

But R' Moshe stood staunch, his hands resting calmly on the cool deck rail. "I wished to carry out the will of my L-rd," he murmured.

At 20 minutes past 12, a cry rose from the crowd. "There's the gatekeeper! I see him. I see the sailor! He's back, he's back!"

The taxi had pulled up at the curb and an extended arm waved from the window. Then the sailor jumped out, a broad smile of triumph spread over his face. He brandished the passport — stamped.

The crowd burst into spontaneous applause. Thunderously, they cheered the courageous sailor who had risked missing the voyage for the sake of one Jew. And they clapped even harder for the brave Jew himself, who had sanctified his G-d in full view of them all. He had shown them what it means to be a man.

The sailor hurried up the gangway and happily handed the stamped passport to his captain. The captain, in turn, passed it to R' Moshe with an expression that said, "You won." Then he hurried away to see to the lifting of the anchor. A group of passengers merrily lifted the sailor onto their shoulders in a victory dance.

Hundreds listened again for the shriek of the ship's whistle. But the drama had not yet played itself out.

The sailor approached R' Moshe. "Half a majida, please."

"What?" In the excitement of the moment, R' Moshe had forgotten trivial details such as paying for the taxi ride.

The sailor explained, "I paid the taxi driver half a majida. You owe me that sum. It seems to me that I'm not obligated to pay it myself."

"Of course not!" R' Moshe heartily concurred. "However, to my distress, I cannot give you the money today. You understand? Shabbos!"

"So what's to become of my money?" the sailor demanded.

"I will pay you tomorrow, don't worry."

The sailor's face grew very red. He was on the point of exploding in an angry tirade when Mr. P. appeared, approaching them at a run. In one hand he held a coin, glinting in the sun.

"Here is your half-majida!" he called to the furious sailor.

Then, turning to R' Moshe, he snapped, "Are you insane? At such a time, you want to teach a gentile sailor the laws of *muktzeh*? Pay me back on *motza'ei Shabbos*!"

R' Moshe did not answer. A small smile played about his lips. Indeed, it was "insanity" to cling to the Torah's law. A line from Yeshayahu came to mind: "*Vesar meira mishtolel.*" *Rashi* explains the words to mean that a man who is "*sar meira*" — that is, one who refrains from doing wrong — will be considered foolish in the eyes of men.

Well, then, thought R' Moshe as he made his way contentedly to his cabin — so be it. Far better to be considered a fool all his life in other men's eyes, than to be viewed as wicked for a single hour in the eyes of his Creator.